Walt Sherz

SANTOS-DUMONT

Also by Peter Wykeham
FIGHTER COMMAND

SANTOS-DUMONT

A STUDY IN OBSESSION

by

Peter Wykeham

HARCOURT, BRACE & WORLD, INC.

NEW YORK

For Ba

FOREWORD

Alberto Santos-Dumont, a great man by many standards, was over-estimated during the early part of his life, and has been under-estimated ever since. Many people like myself, fascinated by his character, achievements, and dual background, must have wanted to know more about him. There is surprisingly little to be read, and a short study of what there is shows many contradictions and confusions. Trying to straighten them out produced this book.

It is the first biography of him in English, and now that I have written it I think I know why. Beforehand it seemed incredible that so rich a subject could have escaped. But now it is apparent to me that his own countrymen, who rightly revere his name, are paradoxically responsible for his undeserved obscurity outside South America.

In Brazil they have taken his image and frozen it into a heroic statue. His accomplishments have been magnified, his faults eliminated; and his personality submerged in a sea of adulation. His native biographers (there are three main works) have addressed themselves to this public figure to such a degree that by the normal standards of serious historical writing their books are very unhelpful. I acknowledge and indeed quote them, but the Portuguese-speaking reader who may want to consult them is warned that they are divergent and unreliable.

I am sorry to say this, and it will bring me little credit in Brazil. Official and semi-official circles there tend to support the portrait which their biographers have produced, and oppose with a massive inertia any attempts to look beneath the surface of Santos-Dumont's public accomplishments. I hope they will understand that our own tradition is to tell the whole truth, so far as we can establish it, and to leave the judgement to posterity.

It has been said that no-one can write a good biography unless he is a little in love with his subject. Before beginning my research I was already an admirer of the warm, sympathetic character of the little Brazilian, with his courage, charm, and endearing oddnesses. Now that I know more of him (and not of course all to his credit), I am proud to endorse, in my different way, the fervent opinion of his countrymen; that he was a great pioneer, an imaginative prophet, and a man one would have dearly loved to know as a friend.

My respect and admiration for him have been increased tenfold by the writing of this book. I would want his own admirers to believe this, and to realise that because he was a great man, the truth cannot harm him. He was unique, and his place in history is assured, and that should be enough.

Hartley Wintney   P. W.
1961

ACKNOWLEDGEMENTS

The unusually complicated researches needed for this book would have been impossible without generous help from many quarters. I am grateful to the Government of Brazil, and particularly to Col. Alcídes M. Neiva, of the Brazilian Air Force, for their assistance.

I am indebted to Dr. Arnaldo Dumont-Villares for information and papers on his kinsman; to Charles W. Rule of São Paulo for help in Brazil, and to other Brazilian informants too numerous to mention.

I am most grateful to His Serene Highness Prince Rainier of Monaco for access to the Palace Archives of the Principality; and to M. Lisimachio of Monte Carlo.

My chief thanks for research in Paris are due to Lilian and Ralph Stuart-Smith, for tedious and complicated work, and for valuable advice. Also to Paul Winkler of Opera Mundi, for producing much material.

In Canada and U.S.A. my researches have been helped by Commander H. F. Bromwich of Ottawa, and R. Lee of Boston; and in Argentina by Oscar Fernandez Brital.

In England I have been allowed the run of Sir Robert Perkin's unique library of aviation history, and I owe my thanks to the libraries of the Royal Aeronautical Society and the Air Ministry, for co-operation and forbearance.

I am particularly grateful to Tom Bradley, of The Queen's Flight, for immense labours in translating from the Portuguese, and for reading the MSS. The task would have been impossible without his help. I also acknowledge with gratitude the loan of George and Sylvia West's valuable translations.

C. H. Gibbs-Smith and John Pudney have given me much help and encouragement. I am grateful also for assistance from Gp.-Capt. P. J. O'Connor, of the R.A.F. Neuro-Psychiatric Dept., Dr. A. Bevan-Jones, and J. B. Priestley, for advice on my subject's mental make-up, and to Flt.-Lt. Greenwood of the R.A.F. Medical Branch for information on his medical condition. G. H. Miles has been my consultant on aerodynamics. I have also had help from Lord Brabazon of Tara, Alvys Brunet, F. R. Drew, Henry Henghes, Harry Eeles, Stuart Tudor, John Kent, Floriano Sérgio Pacheco, B. J. Haimes, C. Hardie, and J. A. Crockett.

I hope they will all consider their various efforts well spent.

CONTENTS

LIST OF ILLUSTRATIONS

"Man I love not; I love that which devours him."

Hesiod.

Chapter 1

☆☆☆☆☆☆☆☆☆☆☆☆☆☆☆☆☆☆☆☆☆☆☆☆☆☆☆☆

The Southern Empire

On the afternoon of the 7th of March, 1808, with a fair breeze from the sea, the fleet of Dom João crossed the bar of the harbour of Rio de Janeiro, and anchored in calm water. After a long voyage the exiled Regent of Portugal found refuge in his greatest colony, the fourth largest territory in the world.

His transports had been escorted from Lisbon by a squadron of the British Royal Navy, frigates and ships of the line, whose taut pyramids of sail on the horizon to windward had reassured the royal party, day after day, as they held the weather gauge against the threat of the French fleet. In Europe the reigning houses fell one by one under the onslaughts of Napoleon. As the Revolutionary armies poured into Portugal the Royal Family had made their decision, and sailed for the New World.

Besides the British Navy Dom João had brought with him most of his own fleet, his family, many of his ministers, the larger part of his court, and a host of nobles and officials. The good people of Rio, not entirely unaffected by the collapse of the Spanish Empire in South America, watched the landing of this great array with mixed feelings. Napoleon, who seemed to be freeing most of their neighbours from the yoke of Spain, had pressed their own ruler more closely into their embrace. By the time the procession of long-boats had ferried the first few hundreds ashore, the loyal huzzas subsided into a wary hum of welcome, and Senhor Doutor Joaquim dos Santos, bringing up the rear, stepped ashore to a greeting which was losing a good deal of its early enthusiasm.

It had been much the same with the natives of the newly-discovered continent three hundred years before, watching with misgivings while the strange painted ships discharged their crowds of explorers, soldiers, and settlers. Haughty and implacable, they had brushed aside the Indians, disregarded the natural riches of the great continent, and pushed inland, past the coastal plain and the blue littoral, in their hungry search for gold. Behind them came the colonists, who cut the red timber, the tree called *pau Brasil*, which gave the country its name. After the treasure-seekers and the foresters came the administrators. They parcelled the country into large areas awarded to feudal holders, and on these lands first Indian and later African slaves cleared the ground for their masters. The great plantations grew from year to year, century to century, ripening under fertile sun, blessed with water and a fair climate, reaping sugar cane, and then tobacco, and then cotton, and sending it back to the markets of the Old World.

When the Captaincies and Viceroyalties of Spanish America began to crumble, Brazil stood firm; and before any unseemly ideas could take root it had received its lawful monarch, and provided a fit refuge for a Regent, soon to be a King.

In 1808 Rio de Janeiro, therefore, became capital of both Portugal and Brazil, and seven years later, since the exiled king stayed on, the former colony was elevated to the status of a kingdom, while the bitter wars and sufferings of her neighbours passed her by. When at last Dom João could sail for home, he left his son Pedro as Regent.

Brazil was now surrounded by republics, wreckage of the Spanish Empire, and these revolutionary examples, coupled with a sterner policy from a king once more setting his house in order in Lisbon, roused the plantation owners and merchants to revolt against the Motherland. The Regent sided with them, and the outraged father in Europe received the news of the crowning of Dom Pedro as Emperor of Brazil. Three years later, in 1825, Portugal helplessly recognised the final loss of her vast possession: Brazil became a nation.

The country flourished under the liberal reign of Dom Pedro. The ports opened once more to the commerce of the Old World, but now not Portugal alone, but Italy, England and France made contact with the fabulous Empire of the South. Immigration began on a larger scale, and soon the pale faces and sturdy bodies of Europe were seen once more, stepping on to the quay at Rio fresh from the hardships of a voyage under canvas across the South Atlantic, to stare wide-eyed at the many coloured splendours of the new land.

The latest wave included a Monsieur Dumont and his wife, their native France four weeks behind them, looking for opportunity and fortune. They came from a family which for generations had been jewellers in Paris, part of the clan of high-grade artisans that centred on the Palais-Royal. They brought their inbred skill for fine, exact work, to place it at the disposal of the new continent. They settled in the province of Minas Gerais, and there they found a modest prosperity, and sunshine and freedom.

Henriques Dumont was born at Diamantina, in the province of Minas Gerais, on the 20th July, 1832. It was the year after the abdication of Dom Pedro I, and the accession of his five-year-old son, Dom Pedro II. Monsieur Dumont died shortly after Henriques was born, but his mother had enough money to live comfortably, and to give her son a good education.

He was early taken under the wing of a godfather, who was much attached to him, and with his mother's consent he was taken back to France for the important part of his schooling. By his fifteenth birthday he was installed in the house of an aunt, Madame Coeuré, living at Sèvres, on the outskirts of Paris.

The young student showed an aptitude for mathematics, mechanics, and civil engineering, and also a stern and studious turn of mind. He had great determination, and was said to have climbed Mont Blanc alone. When it became time to crown his general education with specialisation he was entered at the engineering course at the *École Centrale des Arts et Métiers*, from which he graduated with distinction.

The new Empire of the South had limitless possibilities for this kind of young man. At the end of his studies Henriques said goodbye to his kind aunt, who thought not without some reason

that he was retreating into the jungle, and returned to Brazil.
There he began his career, in the Public Works Department of
the city of Ouro Prêto in the province of Minas Gerais.

He was already making his mark, as a civil engineer 24
years old, when he met Dona Francisca dos Santos, daughter of
Comendador* Paula dos Santos, a very highly-esteemed but
slightly sun-soaked resident of the neighbouring district of
Vila Rica. The Santos family were then established gentry, of
purely Portuguese descent, and the Comendador's father, the
Joaquim dos Santos of the Royal entourage, already mentioned,
had been a doctor and surgeon trained in Portugal, holding
letters patent issued by Dom João, to practise medicine in all
Portuguese possessions.

In later years Brazil absorbed her different nationalities and
races, and ironed out her class distinctions, with the bland and
effortless ease of a great new country. But at this time Portuguese
family pride ran high. In 1856, when young Henriques courted
Dona Francisca, there was more than a slight tendency to look
down on this penniless young State employee, with his obscure
French birth. But Henriques' obvious ability, drive, and
seriousness of mind won over the Santos family, no less than it
charmed his future wife. She was a woman of strict and fervent
religious beliefs, and when they were married it was more in
the approval of the church, the spirit of the pioneers, and the
call of duty, than in any sentimental or passionate spirit, that
they set out to build their future.

The Comendador was finally won over, and gave his consent.
In accordance with the normal custom of the country the names
of the two families were joined, with that of the husband last,
so that the young pair were henceforth known as Henriques
and Francisca Santos-Dumont. There is some hint of an attempt
by the bride's family to reverse this arrangement, but it came
to nothing, or possibly foundered on the rock-like character of
Henriques. At last there were no more complications, and the
nuptials were celebrated with universal goodwill.

The Santos family was not prepared, however, to let their
daughter become the wife of a minor civil servant, and Henriques'
new father-in-law suggested that they go into partnership to

---

* *Comendador*, by this time a minor title of honour, originally signified one
who enjoyed a benefice or revenue from an office held in trust.

acquire the Jaguará estate near Vila Rica. The theory was that it contained valuable mining prospects, and that Henriques would manage the mines while the Comendador put up the money. This project failed, due mainly to the complete absence within Jaguará of any mineable ores, and not unnaturally it caused some coolness between the Santos and the Santos-Dumont families.

But the dislocation of Henriques' career with the Public Works Department may in fact have made his future. He needed success, and what he really needed he could be relied on to obtain. His young family was on the way, first Henriques, then Luíz, then Maria Rosália, with others to come. There was no more time to spare for high-sounding schemes with his aristocratic in-laws.

Salvaging his share of the sale of Jaguará, he first used the money to start a service of small river steamboats on the Rio das Velhas, connecting Belo Horizonte with the interior of Minas Gerais. He imported the vessels with their machinery, and his engineering talents and business drive made the undertaking a success from the start.

Next he entered the timber trade, supplying and transporting the wooden props for the Morro Velho mines. In the meantime his family had increased to six, with the addition of Gabriela, Virgínia and Francisca. Henriques still kept pace, by contracting for various large engineering projects, such as the famous bridge at Sabará. In these works he was able to use his engineer's training to the full.

As a consequence of these successes he was able to obtain the contract for the building of a stretch of the Dom Pedro II railway, an important part of the enterprising (and now adult) Emperor's broad schemes of improvement. Henriques tendered for a particularly difficult section near Barbacena, and in order to supervise the work he moved with his family to a place called Cabangu, in the João Aires district. Cabangu was no more than the place name of the chief engineer's house.

The 20th of July, 1873, was Henriques' 41st birthday. He had come a long hard road, since he had borne away his bride from Vila Rica, and he was still working long hours on the railway. Such homely celebrations as might be expected of the occasion were hampered by the fact that Dona Francisca was

once more in labour. Henriques' chief birthday present was on
the way. Towards the evening a seventh child and third son was
born, Alberto. He was the last, and the family was complete.
Dona Francisca had done her duty to her husband and her country.

The railway contract came to an end: Henriques looked
around for the next undertaking. At this moment the Comendador, still languidly pursuing his declining dreams of wealth,
called with another proposition, and this time his son-in-law,
whose wits were sharpened by eighteen years' experience,
sensed that it was good. Paula dos Santos had bought a large
estate in the province of Rio de Janeiro, and suggested planting
coffee. Would Henriques run it for him?

Henriques would. For five years he managed the plantations
at Casal, learning the arts of agriculture and turning them into
science in his own hard head. The Brazilian plantations were still
extremely primitive, dependent on slave labour, and wasteful
of time and space. Henriques learned and noted, and decided
his future destiny. At the end of the five years' period he finally
parted with Dona Francisca's family, to set up as a planter by
himself.

He had to pool everything, all the savings of his strenuous
years. Gathering his entire resources, he bought a large estate in
the Riberão-Prêto area of São Paulo province, where the red
earth was proverbially fertile. At last he was set on his path,
and when Alberto was six years old the family moved to what
became known as the Fazenda Dumont.

In the ten years that followed, Henriques carried out all his
plans, just as he knew he would. He cleared the land and
constructed a plantation railway, put in five million coffee trees,
built machine-houses, store-rooms, drying grounds, yards,
colonies and management houses. He foresaw the end of slavery,
and arranged for Italian families to come from Europe at his
expense, so that European wage-earners gradually took over
from the Indian and Negro slaves.

While the Fazenda Dumont grew bigger and more efficient,
the demand for coffee grew with it. The estate prospered,
increased, flourished. Henriques Santos-Dumont began to be
known in Brazil as the Coffee King. And all the while his family
was growing up. His eldest sons could take their places by his side.

The girls were receiving a genteel education. His youngest son was finding his feet.

Little Alberto was a small, slight boy, just as in later years he was physically a small man. He was dark and wiry, with black hair and eyes, large prominent ears, and a face browned by the fierce plantation sun. He was eager and curious, yet also dreamy and reserved, and his tastes made him, from an early age, odd man out in the Santos-Dumont clan. In spite of his engineer's training Henriques was basically an out-door man. The red earth and the great spaces of the plantation made a deep appeal to him, and he loved to ride over the miles of his land, with his other sons beside him.

Alberto loved the country, but already his imagination and his mongoose-like curiosity were combining to take him out of the familiar world of his childhood. The sight of machinery fascinated him. When he was seven years old he watched the great steam traction-engines, imported from England, that pulled the trailers filled with coffee beans from the collection point overland to the plantation railway. He saw them used for felling trees and hauling logs over the ground. He soon persuaded the supervisor to let him drive one, a memorable treat even for a present-day boy, and a marvel in a land where machinery was so rare.

From the traction-engines he graduated, by the age of twelve, to driving the Baldwin steam locomotives of the plantation narrow-gauge railway; high, square, Puffing Billies with delicate cow-catchers stretched out in front, pulling trains of trucks loaded with coffee through the fields and the woods, to deliver them at the Works. Every overseer and foreman in charge of the plantation machinery was now his friend and conspirator, and when his father and brothers had ridden away on horseback to the boundaries of the estate to inspect the trees, or the drainage, or to supervise new clearing, Alberto would slip down to the Works, to look at the plant.

The handling of the crop was highly mechanised for, even outside the Fazenda Dumont, Brazil was already alive to the value of machine organisation. Had not Dom Pedro II been the first man in the world to speak on a public telephone service, when Mr. Bell had invited him to inaugurate his new apparatus, at the Philadelphia Exhibition of 1876? The great landowners followed this lead towards interests that enriched them; for Europe and the United States wanted coffee, coffee by the thousands of tons, and the customers paid good prices.

The plantation Works was designed to handle coffee on this scale. The trains brought in the rough red berries with their pods still covering the beans. They were shovelled into large washing-machines to remove the dirt, and carried by water streams to the *despolpador*, which cracked the pods and separated the two beans in each pod from the discarded husks. Conveyor belts carried the beans through driers to another building where the *descascador* accurately performed the delicate operation of breaking the skins and separating them from the naked beans. From another drier they went to a mechanical grader for separation into size, and so into bags for packing and shipment. Even at this time, in the 1880s, the beans were untouched by hand from the time when they arrived at the Works until they were packed and started their journey to the docks. It was by no means a primitive plant.

Young Alberto was completely intrigued by this train of processes. He watched for hours at a time, while the hopper lines and conveyor belts carried the gleaming heaps of beans in and out of the different machines. He played with the big steam engines that powered the plant. He learnt how everything worked.

He was particularly interested when something went wrong and he could help, or watch the repair. He noted that the most troublesome parts of the plant were the machines that produced a to-and-fro motion; shakers, drying trays, graders; for their reciprocating action shook everything, including the building which housed them. Their driving belts were always failing and having to be changed, and they needed a lot of power to run them.

Alberto reflected that this to-and-fro machinery was inherently bad. Machinery should rotate; or at any rate move smoothly. He distrusted all agitating devices in mechanics from that time forward, and so avoided the mistake, which so many inventors had made before him, of trying to design machinery as a mechanical copy of Nature. Vehicles which moved on legs, ships propelled by imitation fishes' tails, and lastly aircraft that reproduced the flapping flight of birds, had all led good minds astray. These byways were not for young Santos-Dumont.

By the time he was ten years old he had discovered and read many of the novels of Jules Verne, and his shy and rather lonely imagination went out to meet the visions of the great writer. He began to think about the mastery of the air, and in his boyish dreams he navigated the great new spaces with Hector Servadoc, Verne's captain of the "Clipper of the Clouds". Much later he recaptured this phase of his life in a fine nostalgic paragraph:

"In the long, sun-bathed Brazilian afternoons, when the hum of insects, punctuated by the far-off cry of some bird, lulled me, I would lie in the shade of the verandah and gaze into the fair sky of Brazil, where the birds fly so high and soar with such ease on their great outstretched wings, where the clouds mount so gaily in the pure light of day, and you have only to raise your eyes to fall in love with space and freedom. So, musing on the exploration of the vast aerial ocean, I, too, devised airships and flying machines in my imagination."*

He kept these musings to himself. His brothers would have mocked him mercilessly, and the younger people in his family's social circle were not over-receptive to new ideas. His father, though not unkind to him, did not fully understand his youngest son, and if Alberto had been an only child he would have caused Henriques much concern. Fortunately there were the others; and there was so much to think of and to do; and so Alberto's strangeness aroused no special alarm.

His playmates, therefore, were the sons of the chief functionaries on the plantation, and his shy incursions into the circle of those who were his social inferiors had an element of furtiveness. This familiarity might have been discouraged, if the big house had known too much about it. He would sit in the shade of a great tree, a little silent and retired in the noisy circle, while the other boys played a game which exists, with variations, among children all over the world. In Brazil it was called "Pigeon flies!"

The leader called "Pigeon flies!", "Crow flies!", "Eagle flies!", "Bee flies!", and so on, and at each true statement each boy raised a finger. But suddenly he would introduce a falsity such as "Tortoise flies!", or "Fox flies!", and anyone who was caught raising a finger had to pay a forfeit.

When first the leader introduced the words "Man flies!"

* *Dans l'Air*. A. Santos-Dumont.

little Alberto, fired with his half-understood reading of Jules
Verne and the deeds of the pioneer balloonists, raised his hand
high. The stubborn centre of the shrill arguments that followed,
he flatly refused to pay the forfeits, and his companions thereafter made a point, with many winks and nudges, of introducing
this gambit into the game whenever it was played. He always
refused to pay up.

To some extent he was honestly deceived. He had read, while
he was quite young and in no mood for analysis, of the exploits
of the Montgolfiers and Charles, of Pilatre de Rozier and Lilienthal
and Henri Giffard, and imagined the conquest of the air to be
a good deal more advanced than in fact it was. From the Brazilian
plantation Europe in general, and France in particular, seemed
fabulous places of dazzling splendour. Anything was possible
there.

Every St. John's day, on the 24th of June, when feasts and
fireworks were part of the Brazilian tradition, the older children
would make fire-balloons and send them up into the night sky.
Alberto learnt how to shape and glue the delicate tissue-paper
in panels, showing precocious deftness and skill. By the great
bonfires, which illuminated the house and the surrounding
trees like a soft floodlighting, he would gently light and inflate
whole fleets of these little Montgolfiers, and watch silently and
intently, deaf to the noise of the festa, while their small beacons
mounted into the darkness.

He also learnt to make and fly kites, as another pioneer
aeronaut, Samuel Cody, had done in Texas a few years before.
Cody was taught his kite design by the Chinese cook on his
father's ranch, and therefore had the benefit of several thousand
years' technical development behind him. Santos had no such
expert instructor, and there is no record of his kite-flying
achieving any special success.

He attempted to construct model aeroplanes of split bamboo
and paper, worked by small airscrews driven by twisted rubber
strands, on the principle used in children's toys to this day.
The plans on which these were built have not survived, nor do
they seem to have flown outstandingly well. This was scarcely
surprising, since Alberto had no data to work on that were much
more scientific than the artist's illustrations in his volumes of
Jules Verne.

In any case his vision of the future ship of the air was less as an aeroplane with wings, and more that of the true airship; lighter than air, forging through the sky on its passage or moving slowly and majestically in exploration; or even stopped and drifting at will. The air was an ocean, into which ships should sail to explore the new worlds, as the great Portuguese navigators of bygone days had sought for the earth's rim.

Dona Francisca was no great encourager of such childish fancies. She firmly, even rigorously, guided the moral education of her family, imbuing them with the strictest of religious teachings. This policy, as so often in such cases, did not produce a very successful or lasting effect, but it was enough to give her children what is usually called a sound Christian foundation.

Alberto's early education was in the family circle, where his first attempts at reading and writing were helped by his elder sisters. He was, as often happens with a youngest boy, something of a special pet to them, and his sister Virgínia was his particular friend and teacher. She remained his favourite member of the family long afterwards, when the other family ties weakened, and in later years her house became his true home whenever he returned to Brazil.

At the end of her day's instruction the lesson would sometimes be rounded off by an evening talk with his father. Like Dona Francisca, Henriques was a good and a kind parent, but neither of them could be called *sympathique*, and these interviews followed somewhat on the pattern of English Victorian domesticity, of the less attractive kind.

So it was something of a relief to go to a real school. He began in a local institute called the *Culto à Ciência*, followed by the *Instituto Kopke* and the *Colégio Morton*, in São Paulo. At the end of these rather scrappy preliminaries he enrolled in the *Escola de Minas* in Ouro Prêto (not a mining college, but the principal academy of the Province of Minas Gerais).

In his holidays he returned to his first love, the plantation; and to day-dreaming and Jules Verne. But he was showing enough practical application to still any fears, in Henriques' breast, that he might be harbouring an intellectual.

In 1891 the head of the family, now sixty years old, was as dynamic as ever, thinking and working for ever greater expansion, when misfortune struck him down. He was examining the installation of some mechanical coffee driers when he suffered a fall from his horse, and was carried home with a severe concussion. This was followed by a partial paralysis which showed no signs of mending. Henriques realised that his days as the active manager of his own estate were over.

More strangely, he showed no confidence in his elder sons' abilities to take his place, or it may be that as they grew up they brought themselves to admit that they had no urge to grow coffee. They were now in their early thirties, and it would have been natural to hand over to them. The Fazenda Dumont was more than thriving.

Whatever the reason, Henriques decided to sell up. His estate passed to the Brazilian Improvements Company, who shortly afterwards resold it to a British financial group. They kept it under the name of the "Dumont Coffee Company". Henriques received twelve thousand contos for his estate, a sum which cannot be adequately translated into present-day figures due to the alterations in money values and rates of exchange,* but at the time and place a very large fortune indeed.

The family Santos-Dumont were uprooted. Fortunately the four daughters had all married, Francisca to the engineer Ricardo Severo, and the other three, by a curious coincidence, to three brothers, Eduardo, Carlos, and Guilherme de Andrade Villares. The home of the Villares brothers, for some years, was in Portugal, and these three daughters were therefore already in Europe.

There was nothing to keep Henriques in Brazil, and in Lisbon and Paris there were specialists who might relieve his condition. In the same year of his accident, with nothing left to show for his life's work but a large fortune in the Bank of Brazil, Henriques Santos-Dumont sailed for Europe, taking his wife and youngest son with him.

* Approximately equal to $6,000,000 in 1895.

Chapter 2

☆☆☆☆☆☆☆☆☆☆☆☆☆☆☆☆☆☆☆☆☆☆☆☆☆☆☆☆☆☆

"Go to Paris"

During the leisurely steamship voyage to Lisbon, Henriques could give his first real attention to his youngest son. On the plantation he had seldom found much spare time, Alberto had been at school, and the older boys were the companions of his outdoor life. Now he could consider the small, thin, reserved youth beside him.

Henriques was old enough to be Alberto's grandfather. In the quiet after the shock of his illness, with the knowledge that he was suddenly a sick old man, he somehow found an accord with the member of the family who so far had meant least to him. It is certain that during this trip to Europe Alberto moved very close to his father, and exchanged the awe in which he had so far held him for a more normal affection, one that was to develop into a reverence for his memory. He needed some-one to admire, and he felt only conventional love for his mother.

The family landed at Lisbon, and went on to visit the three daughters, Maria, Gabriela, and Virgínia, in Oporto. Alberto was delighted to see his favourite sister again, living like a grand lady in her own house by the sea. The family reunion was a happy one on the level of the younger generation, though Henriques' ill-health and Dona Francisca's pursed lips, which

tightened perceptibly at the sight of too much joviality, cast
some shadow over the occasion. There was a great deal of speculation about what Papa would do with the proceeds of the sale of
the Fazenda Dumont, but on this subject Henriques kept his
own counsel.

Glad as he was to see his sisters, Alberto was avid for Paris. It
is almost impossible to overstate the magnificence of the French
capital, seen through the eyes of the South Americans of
European descent. The real Paris was splendid enough. But the
image of power, wealth, culture, science, fashion and glitter,
conjured through the imaginations of people who lived in a
rich but primitive continent, where the jungle and the sierra
leaned heavily against the plantation boundaries; this was the
image of Eldorado indeed. Alberto took his place on the train
in a fever of excitement. On to Paris!

The arrival at the Gare d'Orléans was all that he had imagined,
but the excitement died down when Alberto found himself confined in the stuffy house of some dull cousins, instead of staying
at one of the many fine hotels. But nothing could spoil the first
glimpse of the enchanted city. Alberto was dazzled. An
acquaintance speaks of him staring open-mouthed at the teeming
traffic, rolling his expressive and rather protuberant eyes at the
avenues and buildings, the bridges and monuments; the many
marvels of the loveliest city in the world.

A city full of vitality of every kind; but first in Alberto's eyes
was the dramatic evidence of scientific splendour. Across the
river, across the *quais* and the grand streets and the avenues
of Haussmann, across the graceful buildings, the shadow of the
new Eiffel Tower swung daily from West through North to
East. Its wonder and immensity took Alberto's breath away,
and he sat gazing at it, for hours at a time, from a seat on the
Right Bank. He must have dreamed that he had indeed come
amongst a race of giants, to whom any mystery must give way,
and any world surrender. The men who had built this marvel
must be capable of anything.

He was therefore surprised to discover, when he made
enquiry in Paris, that the conquest of the air was far less advanced
than he had imagined, in fact it could hardly be said to have
begun. He had given too much credit to the stories of the earlier
air pioneers, and too little to the ripe imagination of M. Jules

Verne. The actual facts of achievement up to the 1890s were modest enough, and can be briefly summarised.

After the aviation theorists, of whom the greatest and certainly the best-known was Leonardo da Vinci, practical experiment had followed two paths, that of the glider and that of the balloon. In the first category a number of unfortunates, supported on frameworks less or more practical, had launched themselves from high places, with the almost inevitably fatal results. Young Santos may have paused to consider the fate of the Brazilian monk Bartholomeo Lourenço de Gusmão, who actually came from São Paulo. He was reputed to have produced a flying machine in 1709, and ascended in it at Lisbon. The description of his craft gives little probability of it ever leaving the ground, but he is said to have had so much success that he was subsequently condemned as a sorcerer by the Inquisition, and put to death.

The balloonists were more fortunate. As is well known, the first real successes were achieved by the Montgolfier brothers. Having the notion that because smoke rises it must lift a balloon, they attempted to fill a balloon with smoke, consequently filled it with hot air, and achieved the same result. In 1783 their balloons ascended at Versailles, in the presence of the Sun King himself. Close on their heels came other hot air balloonists, and so rapid was the progress in lifting agents that hydrogen was used only a year later.

In 1784 the famous Lunardi came to London with a hydrogen balloon and rose from the Artillery Ground, Moorfield. The flight, watched by a crowd of 200,000 Londoners, was a great success, comment coming even from the ageing Doctor Johnson.* Free ballooning (i.e. drifting with the wind in a lighter-than-air craft), passed rapidly from a pioneering stage to a craze. Large numbers of ascents were made with increasing success; by aeronauts ranging from savants and true explorers to the intrepid lady who rose weekly from the Parc de Montmartre, reclining on a settee and playing a violin.

By 1852 the observatory at Kew had carried out a series of

* "The vehicles, Sir, can serve no use until we can guide them . . . the first experiment, however, was bold and deserved applause and reward. But since it has been performed, and its event is known, I had rather now find a medicine that can ease an asthma." (Boswell's *Life of Johnson*.)

scientific ascents, using a balloon of 85,000 cubic feet to make
physical and weather measurements; and the same balloon
covered 500 miles in one flight, and reached a height of 23,000
feet. Over 60 balloons left Paris during the siege of 1870-71.
But there the science had stopped.

More recent attempts to control flight—which will be
mentioned in their place—had been far from successful. Young
Alberto found that the "Clipper of the Clouds" was still a far-
off dream. Free ballooning had become a sport and an entertainment, the province either of wealthy amateurs or of horny-
handed practitioners who gave performances for a fee, and
were content to regard aerostation as a completed technique,
akin to small-boat sailing.

During his tours around the city, interspersed with visits to
relatives, museums, and exhibitions, Alberto absorbed these
facts without any properly-formed idea of what he personally
meant to do with them. For one thing, he was barely seventeen.
And anyway, there was so much to see and do and think of, that
the status of man's conquest of the air was only one facet of the
extraordinarily diverse world of science and technology that
unfolded before his wondering eyes.

Paris was in the throes of a series of exhibitions—off-shoots
of the Great Exhibitions of 1878 and 1889, which culminated
in the building of the Eiffel Tower and the Palais Royal. In the
Palace of Industry was an exhibition of science and mechanics,
and Henriques took his son to see it, leaving Dona Francisca to
go the rounds of the churches. As they walked through the aisles
Alberto stopped, fascinated, before a working exhibit of an
internal-combustion engine, the first he had ever seen. It was
a single-cylinder piston engine, of one horse-power, driven by
petrol, made of polished iron, steel, and brass. There it stood,
chugging away purposefully on its stand, like some neat little
gnomish god, alive in its functional sanctuary.

Henriques had gone on. He found himself alone, and went
back to the stand. There he discovered his son, mesmerised, his
large dark eyes fixed on the little god of power, the top of his
cane to his mouth, entranced. It was so small, so neat; compared to the great steam engines; it was light, natty, twinkling,
like little Alberto himself. He fell in love with it.

"I stood still before it just as if I had been nailed down by

Fate. I was completely fascinated. I told my father how surprised
I was at seeing that motor work, and he replied: 'That is enough
for today'."*

A heavy paternal answer, no doubt, but Henriques came
back from this day's trip deep in thought, more silent even than
usual. He spoke seldom, this hard old man living in the shadow
of death, not even to Dona Francisca, but it is certain that in the
preceding weeks he had begun to glimpse some hint of the
restless and scarcely-balanced mechanical genius lying dormant
in the round head of his son, Alberto. Otherwise his subsequent
actions are inexplicable, even by the standards of rich parental
indulgence; a fault which could not so far be laid as a weakness
to his account.

That night, while dining with the heavy cousins, Henriques
broached to them the possibility that he might next year send
Alberto back to Paris alone, to complete his studies. He asked
them to look after him and to guide his steps, and see that he
did not fall into frivolity. He must have placed great trust and
reliance on their influence if his half-formed plans were to
mature, or perhaps he misread the degree of his son's docility.

For years Alberto had kept his thoughts to himself. He had
given his parents no hint, which they would have been quick
enough to understand, of what really went on in his mind. He
now wanted to go further than the museums and libraries, and
with great initiative he discovered, through the City Directory,
the name of a professional balloonist. He carefully eluded his
family and arranged a meeting with him. The aeronaut, whose
name does not survive, looked gravely at the skinny youth.

"You want to make an ascent?" he asked, fingering his
ample moustache. "Hum! Hum! Are you sure you have the
courage? A balloon ascent is no small thing, and you seem so
young."

Alberto poured out assurances of his courage and the sincerity
of his purpose. At last the balloonist was convinced, and agreed
to take him "for a short ascent". But it must be for not more
than two hours, on a sunny, windless afternoon, and the
"honorarium" would be 1,200 francs.

"And you must sign me a contract," he went on, "to hold
yourself responsible for all damages we may do to your own life

* O Que eu Vi, O Que nós Voremos. A. Santos-Dumont.

and limbs and to mine, to the property of third parties, and to
the balloon and its accessories. Furthermore, you pay for railway
fares for transporting the balloon and ourselves, from where
we land, back to Paris.''

This was too steep, particularly since the gentleman in
question, a notorious crasher, had already once knocked down
a factory chimney, and on another occasion had descended on a
peasant's house and set it on fire, when the gas from the balloon
ignited from contact with the flue. Young Santos asked for
time to reflect, for though he could lay hands on this sum, he
would be spending everything he had been given for the Paris
trip on one afternoon. He summed up to himself, charac-
teristically.

"If I risk 1,200 francs for a couple of hours' pleasure I shall
find it either good or bad. If it is bad the money will be lost.
If it is good I shall want to repeat it and shall not have the
means." With this brisk mental exercise he dismissed the
aeronaut, and looked about him for other ventures.

When he had made his son a very generous allowance Henriques
had taken note of Alberto's lack of interest in the bright lights
and the Moulin Rouge, normally first targets for rich Latins in
their teens. Alberto had justified his faith by showing no signs
of spending his money in the classic way. Nobody knew that he
had considered parting with it all for one balloon ride. So there
is little wonder that the stern parental eyebrows were raised to
their highest at his next move.

Alberto ferreted out the automobile works of Peugeot, which
were concealed in a dusty shed at Valentigny, and bought a
three-and-a-half horse-power car. Before driving it away he
made the builders explain its working, down to the most precise
detail, over and over, until they were glad to see the last of him.

This was a greater sensation than the balloon trip would have
been. The year was 1891. The Peugeot firm, which now turns
out hundreds of cars a day, was one of the very first builders,
and in this year they made only two cars all told. That Alberto
secured one shows that there was no clamour to buy. His
"roadster" had four wheels with thin metal spokes and solid
tyres, it was steered by a tiller, and fitted with a Daimler-Benz
single-cylinder engine (imported from Germany), installed
behind and beneath the driver. This engine was extremely

difficult to control, while the steering was rudimentary, and it had no brakes worth mentioning. Henriques' first sight of his son mounted on this apparition almost brought on a recurrence of his old trouble, but he recollected himself, and ignoring the laments of Dona Francisca, became positively benign. It is not impossible that his wife's unqualified opposition had something to do with his own approval.

At least Alberto was untroubled by the need for vehicle or driving licences, since even in Paris a car was almost unknown. And since practically nobody but the owner and the makers knew how it worked, and since it needed a great deal of persuasion to make it run at all, it kept him happily busy for all of his spare time for the rest of his stay.

The fact that he had one of the very few cars in the world did not give Alberto a clear road. Paris was crammed with horse traffic, and driving was not much less dangerous then than later. Though its maximum speed was about 10 m.p.h. his car was barely controllable, and much the same could be said of the horse traffic also. The public sensation caused by his passage through the streets was a danger in itself, and he was forbidden by the police to stop at focal points, such as the Place de l'Opéra, for fear of attracting great crowds and holding up the traffic.

Henriques' indulgence now knew no bounds. He was first reconciled to the Peugeot, and then himself enthusiastic. This was the spirit that had sent the young engineer out to tame the wilderness of Brazil. He warmed to his son more and more, but though Alberto now felt a true affection he warily maintained his reserve. Now and later he showed himself capable of keeping his own counsel and biding his own time. Summer came to an end, and the family Santos-Dumont packed their trunks for the journey home. They had been in Paris seven months, and though Henriques had enjoyed the trip, the Paris doctors had given him little satisfaction.

They said goodbye to the cousins and took their place on the *rapide* for Lisbon. In a truck behind the guard's van, carefully wrapped in dust-sheets, rode Alberto's precious roadster. He had talked Henriques into taking it home to Brazil.

Back in São Paulo Henriques passed an uneasy winter. Inaction vexed him, and he was increasingly unwell. Alberto had made up his mind (for the time being) to become an automobile engineer, and was blissfully happy with his new car. If it had been a sensation in Paris it was ten times more so in São Paulo, for it must have been the first automobile ever to be seen in South America. Henriques' respectable friends, watching the palsied advance of the "roadster" through the dusty streets of São Paulo, themselves shuddered with mixed feelings of horror, envy, and reluctant admiration. Trust the Dumonts to pick up the latest mechanical fads!

Early in 1892 the problem of what Papa would do with his money was resolved at last, and that much to his credit. He had made up his mind long before. He now gathered his wife and children about him, and announced that the Fazenda Dumont fortune was to be divided. He and Dona Francisca were to keep a third; the remaining two-thirds was to be divided equally amongst the children. This decision was well received, as indeed it deserved to be. Alberto was the only minor in the family, and to make a clean sweep of the bequest, Henriques declared that he would emancipate him forthwith.

Accordingly, on his eighteenth birthday, he took him to the office of a notary-public in São Paulo, where the necessary deeds to effect his majority were drawn up and signed. After this ceremony the pair returned home, and Henriques waved his son into his study. It was a solemn moment. Opening his large safe, he withdrew a bundle of revenue bonds, to the value of Alberto's entire portion. These he gave his son.

"I have already given you your liberty today," he said, "here also is this capital. I have still some years to live; I want to see how you conduct yourself. Go to Paris, a most dangerous place for a boy. Let's see if you make a man of yourself. I would rather you did not become a professor. In Paris, with our cousin's help, find a specialist in Physics, Chemistry, Mechanics, and Electricity. Study these subjects, and don't forget that the world's future is in Mechanics."

He paused. Alberto looked in wonder at the papers in his hands. "You have no need to worry about earning a living," Henriques continued; "I will leave you enough to live on."*

This strange speech, exciting enough in itself, made a deep impression on Alberto's mind. To the very last Henriques'

* *Dans l'Air*. A. Santos-Dumont.

purpose was not clear, and his son must have remained an enigma to him. He was obviously worried by the boy's staid and serious ways, and by his lack of interest in girls. By pushing Alberto in at the deep end, loading him with money to spend as he wished, and leaving him to sink or swim in Paris of all places, Henriques may have been arranging himself something interesting and amusing, to enliven his declining years. It has even been suggested that he wanted to loosen Dona Francisca's grip on her youngest son. His glimpse of Alberto's genius can have been no more than a glimpse. Any suggestion that he could have foreseen his son's future eminence is a romantic notion, but flatly contradicted by both their characters.

He never saw his plan unfold. In the summer of 1892 the family sailed once more for Portugal, but when they reached Oporto Henriques was too unwell to continue to Paris. He sent Alberto on ahead. Then he grew still worse, and an overpowering desire arose in him to return to Brazil. Dona Francisca put him aboard the first ship leaving for South America, and he managed to win to the shores of his native land. But he went no farther than Rio, where he died on the 30th of August.

Alberto could not get home in time for the burial, and was left to mourn in Paris. Dona Francisca stayed on in São Paulo, where she was near her elder sons, and during the years of her widowhood she made frequent trips to Oporto to visit her daughters, the Villares, and her grandchildren. On one of these visits she died, and was buried at Oporto. Alberto had never been close to his mother, and saw little of her during her last years, while there is no record of her visiting him in Paris. But much later he felt a remembrance of the strong affection that his two pioneering parents must have held for one another, and the struggles and adventures they had shared in a lifetime together.

Years after Dona Francisca's death he obtained the approval of the rest of the family and had her body taken back to Brazil, where it was laid to rest beside Henriques. The stern partnership of their lives continued in death, in the Cemetery of St. John the Baptist in Rio de Janeiro.

Chapter 3

☆☆☆☆☆☆☆☆☆☆☆☆☆☆☆☆☆☆☆☆☆☆☆☆☆☆☆☆☆☆

The Serious Student

In the spring of 1892, suddenly fatherless at the age of 18, Alberto began his advanced studies in Paris. He had been delivered into the hands of his relations, and he faithfully accepted this part of Henriques's arrangements, at least for the time being. But his father's chosen instruments were no more than cousins, and he never grew any nearer to them, neither had he any close relative or friend in the city. This sudden launching on the world was a turning-point in his life. He was afloat in great waters.

He could have enrolled at any one of a large number of institutions, from the Sorbonne downwards, but his sharply individual nature did not relish the communal grind of the routine student. His background and travels, coupled with the gradual realisation of his wealth and independence, made him adopt a critical attitude towards the possibilities spread before him.

He therefore made inquiries for a free-lance tutor, who could direct a programme of studies to whatever channel pleased his pupil, but who would not prove oppressive if young Santos wished to depart from the normal paths of a conventional French education. Through his cousins he contacted a number of professors in this category, mostly retired savants who were not averse to picking up a little money by such part-time methods. They were somewhat disconcerted to find themselves interviewed by a small, immature-looking schoolboy, and briskly dismissed when they failed to satisfy him.

At length Alberto was brought into touch with a Monsieur Garcia, a highly qualified professor of engineering and science, who was at a loose end. M. Garcia was of Spanish descent, and was tactful enough to make a good impression. Alberto, always sensitive to ridicule, realised that his teacher would have to know about his ambitions towards aviation. M. Garcia seemed less likely than the others to greet such a confession with the mixture of alarm and condescension that was normal. And in every way he fulfilled the requirements of Henriques' injunction.

Monsieur Garcia was tall and gaunt, and the high top-hat he habitually wore, coupled with his rather mournful moustache, made him seem even taller and gaunter. But he was practised in physics, mechanics, electricity, and chemistry. Later Santos wrote: "I could not have been luckier; we discovered M. Garcia, a respectable preceptor, of Spanish origin, who knew everything. He taught me for many years."

He now settled into a studious life, of what he intended should be serious application. After the first few months he moved out of his cousins' house and took comfortable rooms in the best part of Paris. There was never anything flashy or ostentatious in his nature, and he waited several more years before equipping himself with a proper house and establishment of his own. His money was safely invested in Brazilian stocks, which steadily increased in value, to a degree that was satisfying, though not sensational. In the meantime, modesty of living became him.

Monsieur Garcia would visit him daily, either for individual tuition or for discussion of the last lecture Alberto had attended at a convenient academy; and also to progress the scheme of work which they had mapped out between them. With all Parisian educational life to choose from, he could pick his way from one course to another, or even attend at single lectures.

His "respectable preceptor" may possibly have known everything, but he shows signs of having been a dull man. Except for Alberto's one testimony quoted, he makes no other reference to him, and very little has survived about a character who, according to convention, should have made a powerful impression on his young pupil's mind. It is difficult to avoid the feeling that he was relegated to the position of a sort of educational secretary, charged with the donkey-work of arranging tuition, and explaining it when that was necessary, but lacking the character and natural authority to keep Alberto's nose to the grindstone, or to have any great influence on him.

The result was what might be expected from this butterfly technique. Though his education was wide and enthusiastically pursued, it had a certain superficiality. The somewhat uncritical accounts of his early years, which have been written in his native country, have followed the exasperating method of judging his youth from a heavy bias produced by his mature achievements. He is represented as a golden boy made solemn by consciousness of his own genius, working systematically to equip himself for his destiny, with the faithful figure of M. Garcia ever close beside him.

The truth was strange enough. Here was a youth from Latin America, rich and independent, at large in Paris with no censorious eyes upon him, no admonitory voices in his ears more effective than the nebulous cousins (who seemed to take remarkably little notice of him), and whose greatest danger of adverse comment might be the fear that they would report his doings to Dona Francisca, far off in Brazil. By all the rules he should have ignored education completely, at any rate of the conventional kind, in favour of the more traditional targets for young men with money to spend.

He would have received only formal reproach if he had spent his time at the Moulin Rouge and the Moulin de la Galette, the Tabarin, Elysées-Montmartre, Jardin de Paris, or Salle Wagram (entrance fee: gentlemen one franc, ladies twenty-five centimes). All these palaces of delights featured stage spectacles beyond the wildest dreams of the Americas, with daringly displayed actresses ranging in beauty and accomplishment from the incomparable La Goulue (a little past her prime, but still a favourite) and Nini Patte-en-l'Air, to the equally spirited but coarser cocottes of Les Milles Colonnes, in the rue de la Gaieté. In addition they provided bars, promenades, and salons, within sight and hearing of the stage, in which the patrons could stroll and drink and flirt and gossip, to a delectable social pattern which is now utterly lost.

If Alberto could resist all this (and it was difficult to sample it without diving in headfirst), there was a whole life of the café-club student, with more or less money to spend, that roared and boiled around a thousand bars and cellars, varying in degrees of respectability from those patronised by the faculty of the University of Paris, to the Gravilliers, noted by a guide as *"surtout fréquenté par des malfaiteurs, souteneurs et filles de bas étage"*.

Even if his tastes had been inexplicably more refined than would be judged natural by the standards of the day, there were still distractions in plenty. The Paris Opera and Ballet, which combined culture and amorous adventure in a mixture practically unrepeatable since those times; the serious theatre, headed by the Comédie Française; the countless concerts and *soirées* and *levées*, all competed for his attention.

The serious social round of Paris was a full-time occupation. Breakfast might be a formality not much more important than cleaning one's teeth, but thereafter the day was crowded. One promenaded in the Bois from 11 a.m. to midday: lunch was from midday to 2 p.m.; one paid visits between 4 and 6 p.m. (*"L'heure des five-o-clock"*); in the Bois again from 6 to 7 in summer and 3 to 5 in winter; dinner was from 7 to 9 p.m., and then the night's entertainment was just beginning. Thursday was *"Le jour élégant"*.

To balance the gaiety and the glitter: the poor, the hopeless, and the miserable were almost as numerous and as much in evidence as ever, and the anarchists, with a certain Gallic abandon, were exploding bombs to such effect that half Paris was terrorised.

Yet despite all the various levels of life seething around him Santos ploughed steadily on at his studies, guided by the inconspicuous M. Garcia. He may have turned aside occasionally to visit the theatre, or even a music hall, but such diversion must have been rare indeed, from the lack of any traces or records that survive. M. Garcia might have been dull and academical, but we know that Alberto was not. Yet he seemed possessed by an iron solemnity. It is impossible to deny him a certain wry admiration for his persistence in self-education, while admitting that his studies would have been more valuable if they had been directed by someone who was not himself under the direction of Alberto. And it is just conceivable that some harmless junketings in his youth might have given him a better balance later.

The four years between 1892 and 1896 passed quickly in this routine, with Alberto learning, by his own methods, all that study and attention to M. Garcia could teach him. Once a year he returned to Brazil for a holiday, and to pay a dutiful visit to Dona Francisca. He was able to answer her anxious enquiries about his respectable behaviour with a completely clear conscience, and her injunctions about religious observance with at least a semblance of attention. He was a good, conventional Christian, but lacked the stern devotion that would have satisfied his mother; a quality she found lacking in all her children.

Apart from these visits his programme allowed him no frivolous travel, though surprisingly he made one voyage to England. In 1894 all France was convulsed with the drama of the Dreyfus Trial (not as yet the Dreyfus Scandal). As the melancholy figure of Captain Dreyfus was embarked for Devil's Island, Santos too was leaving France, to take the cross-Channel packet for Dover.

He was enrolled at the University of Bristol as an "occasional student" or "listener", a rather typical piece of Santos educational planning, and attended a number of lectures on technical and scientific subjects. Whatever impression his English tutors and lecturers might have gained of him was unfortunately lost, when the entire records of the University were destroyed during an air raid on Bristol.

The urge to explore the air was still fermenting in his mind. Without confiding in his relatives or his learned preceptor, he consulted the Bottin *Year Books*, those admirable French volumes of reference, that classify every known activity, and its practitioners. From them he obtained the names and addresses of all the balloonists in Paris, and began systematically making appointments to see them, with the object of finally achieving his cherished and long-postponed trip in a balloon.

Some of those he interviewed no longer went in for ballooning, while others still tried to frighten him with stories of the dangers of the air. They were a phlegmatic and professional body, making their business pay by highly-priced ascents at fairs and exhibitions, and when they would consider the proposition at all they adopted the same attitude as the aeronaut whom Santos had consulted on his first trip to Paris. They quoted what they considered to be an impossible price, with no special desire to get Alberto's custom, and shrugged their shoulders when he refused to pay. "Evidently," he observed, "they had decided to keep aerostation to themselves, just like a secret of state." Alberto could now have paid their price, but would not. His remarkable care with his money extended to this, his heart's desire, as much as to the more ordinary snares of the metropolis.

He found another outlet for his urge for adventure. His Peugeot "roadster", which he had taken to Brazil, and then back again with him to Paris, was already out of date. Its high spindly structure and feeble engine, combined with rudimentary steering and eccentric brakes, could do little more than show that a man could move on the road, in a vehicle with no horse attached.

In Paris a number of firms were building small motor-tricycles, in which a simple air-cooled petrol engine was coupled directly to the two driving wheels behind, while the daring rider sat on a saddle and steered the one wheel in front by handlebars. With much less dead weight than the horseless carriages the tricycles had a better performance, and could streak past the Peugeot's 10 m.p.h. at a spanking pace of twice that speed. The engines were more reliable, which usually meant that the driver had only one breakdown per journey, instead of several.

Alberto sold his Peugeot, and bought one of the new models, a De Dion. Flushed with enthusiasm, he began exploring the thrills of controlling a vehicle travelling at more than twenty miles an hour. The motor-tricycles had caught on, and for some time they were a distinct vogue among the more wealthy and adventurous young Parisians. Santos found a wide acquaintance among these enthusiasts, with whom he could discuss mechanical matters, and match his own vehicle against other makes, such as the Bollée tricycle; and against different riders. If this sounds not unlike a modern motor-scooter club it should be remembered that it was a most expensive hobby, patronised by the young, wealthy, and dashing, and that these society swells were strongly of the opinion that the ownership of a *voiturette* made them "fast" in a double sense of the word.

This movement soon progressed sufficiently for several small rallies and meetings to be arranged, at all of which M. Alberto Santos-Dumont was a starter. In a knickerbocker suit, cap, and goggles, he would leave the starting-line with his saddle vibrating furiously under the onslaught of the engine mounted immediately behind it, and vanish up the road in a clatter of chains and a twinkle of nickel-plate, leaving a pungent cloud of castor-oil smoke behind him, while an occasional ear-splitting report would send flocks of pigeons whirring into the air.

The tacit disapproval of M. Garcia was ignored, while since the circles in which his cousins moved could not possibly intersect those of the automobilists, he had little to fear from them. He began to think about organising a real race, a contest in which his friends could try their hardest; without interference from horse-carts, vegetable barrows, and the Paris police.

He decided that the best available track was the *vélodrome* in the Parc des Princes, normally devoted to the bicycle racing which has always contributed so splendidly to the more frenzied side of French sporting life. (At this time it was occasionally visited by Toulouse-Lautrec, to sketch the crowds and the cyclists.) He went to see the directors of the track. They were amazed at the notion. Alberto pleaded. They were doubtful. At last he hired the *vélodrome*, at a stiffish fee, for an entire afternoon, and announced that a race would be held there. Other voices were joined to those of Messieurs les Directeurs, who had been persuaded against their will, prophesying the most lamentable disasters. A track designed for bicycles would be fatal to the motor-tricycles. They would overturn and wreck themselves. There would be many dead, and a still larger number of injured. Conversely, said the prophets, launching suddenly into technicalities, the banking on the corners would spoil the uprightness of the carburettors, stopping the tricycles and thereby causing them to topple inwards on the bankings, when nothing could save their rash conductors.

Alberto was still young enough to quail under this weight of pessimism, but he refused to give up his idea. He organised the meeting, offered the prizes (and therefore had to stand down from the contest), and was rewarded by the enthusiastic support of his new friends. The directors hedged, by the mysterious tactics of forbidding the race on Sunday afternoon, and then washed their hands of further responsibility. Santos brought the date forward to Saturday, and the controversy, as controversies often do, brought out a good crowd.

The meeting was a novel and delightful spectacle, providing a new topic in the salons and restaurants for some time to come. The little tricycles ran well, picking their way daintily round the track in the sunshine, and swooping off the banking in a way that kept the crowd on its toes. No-one was hurt, and when Santos presented the prizes he had himself provided he was voted a fine fellow, and his race a great success.

By 1896 Alberto's education petered out. He was a rapid learner, and had learnt all he considered necessary. Indeed he had worked hard in spasms, and faithfully fulfilled his father's injunctions. Monsieur Garcia was becoming tiresome, and in addition Alberto was homesick for Brazil. His detachment from Parisian life, which we have already noted, had started as a certain rather humourless concentration on the duties of a student, and had become something of a habit. He did not yet feel that Paris was his home, and he was also afflicted with an odd restlessness, the first signs of a malaise that stayed with him all his life.

Most important of all, he had made no progress with his plans for exploring the air, and so the mainspring of his ambitions had found nothing to drive on. He was stale and depressed, as he boarded the steamer for Rio. He had completed his education, but to what purpose? He had picked over the accumulated wisdom of the centre of the world, but for what end? He did not have to earn a living. The breath-taking prospect of Rio harbour, as his ship steamed into the bay, filled him with the gentle melancholy of early manhood. "I regretted bitterly that I had not persevered in my attempt to make a balloon ascent", he wrote. "At that distance, far from ballooning possibilities, even the high prices demanded by the aeronauts seemed to me of secondary importance."

Of all sad words. . . . But Santos was at home, and the fine wide skies of Brazil, recklessly flooded with golden sunshine, were the consolations he had expected them to be. He visited his relations, and imprinted a kiss on the formidable cheek of Dona Francisca. He made the rounds of his old friends. He talked gravely with his father's elderly contemporaries, and boasted more gaily with the young people of his own age. He not unnaturally found them painfully provincial.

The countryside was his great consolation, a consolation for he knew not exactly what, but probably for the pleasant sadness of being young, and rich, and living half in dreams. He was able once more to lie under a great tree, gazing, with his dark eyes unfocused, to where the green branches gave way to the sky, to the deep blue and the castles of the towering clouds, and the eagles flying.

He stayed on through the end of the year, and well into the next, through the hot sleepy summer of the southern latitudes. He looked into various activities which he thought might interest him, but nothing took root. His absorption in plantations had gone with his childhood, and any other conventional ideas were soon dislodged from an imagination continually returning to the navigation of the air.

After a few months he was bored, and began to long for Paris. Nothing remained in Brazil to detain him, except the plain love of the country where he was born. He had distressed the eager mamas of São Paulo by his apparent lack of interest in their numerous smiling daughters, and thus had shown no signs of taking refuge in the family-raising that was the traditional occupation of the Brazilian (and other) nineteenth-century gentlemen, of no profession but substantial income. His mind was unsettled, but made up in one direction at least, and he was going back.

While waiting for the ship to sail from Rio he visited the bookshops to equip himself for the voyage, for he was always fond of reading. One of the books he bought, inevitably, was the recently-published *Andrée—To the North Pole by Balloon*, by MM. Lachambre and Machuron, and opening this volume on the steamer he instantly became so engrossed that he paid no attention to the gradual dwindling of the Sugar-Loaf Mountain into the southern sea. He read on, rigid and absorbed, as once he had been by the sight of the little engine.

The authors of this work, Messieurs Lachambre and Machuron, were engineers and balloon constructors, who already catered to the practising aeronauts of France when they were approached by the Andrée Expedition. Henri Lachambre, born in 1846, fought in the Franco-Prussian war, after which he became interested in *aérostation*. In 1875 he set up his Aérostatic workshop in Vaugirard, Paris, and sold balloons and balloon-handling equipment to the governments of Spain, Japan, Holland, Belgium, Portugal, Rumania, Russia, and the U.S.A.

He was joined by his nephew, Alexis Machuron, in 1889. Machuron did his military service in the Balloon Corps at Grenoble. He became an expert balloonist, and he and his uncle, hearty, jolly men, ran their strange business very cosily, varying their special projects with, for example, a line of small grotesque carnival shapes, made of inflated gold-beater's skin, for which they were famous all over the world, selling some 150,000 every year. But the polar balloon was their masterpiece.

The expedition to the North Pole by balloon had been conceived by Salomon August Andrée, a forty-year-old Swedish scientist. He became interested in ballooning during a stay in the United States, and worked out his ideas for the trip while he was head of the technical department of the Patent Office in Stockholm.

He was another dedicated man, of a type which seemed to be particularly attracted to aviation—devoted to his mother, indifferent to women, blind to the arts, passionately curious, careless of self-interest. He wrote in his diary: "Dangerous? Perhaps. But what am I worth?" And again—"It is altogether too great a risk to bind oneself to a condition of things where another individual would be fully entitled—and what right would I have to repress this individuality?—to demand the same place in my life that I myself occupied. As soon as I feel any heart-leaves begin to germinate I am eager to uproot them, for I know that the feeling, if I ever allowed it to live, would become so powerful that I should not dare to submit to it."*

In 1893 a Swedish fund bought him a balloon, with which he made a number of practice ascents in Sweden. By 1896 his North Pole project had been accorded Governmental backing, after a substantial contribution from Alfred Nobel, and he had persuaded (one suspects ever so slightly against their will) two companions to complete his team. They were Nils Strindberg,

* *The Andrée Diaries.* E. Adams Ray.

a physicist and expert photographer, and Dr. Ekholm, assistant meteorologist at the State Central Institute.

Strindberg spent the spring of 1896 practising ballooning, under the guidance of MM. Lachambre and Machuron, while *Eagle*, the polar balloon, was building. It was a large and elaborate craft designed to carry the three explorers, a boat, sledges, tents, carrier-pigeons, scientific instruments, cameras, provisions for four months, and Arctic equipment on a lavish scale. It was fitted with sails, and by using these against the reaction drag of a guide-rope Andrée hoped to be able to deviate as much as 30 degrees from the wind direction. A spirit cooking stove was carried, hung 25 feet below the basket for safety, lighted by remote control, and fitted with an inclined mirror to show the cook above what was happening.

On the 7th of June, 1896, the balloon and its equipment, with Andrée, Strindberg, Ekholm, M. Lachambre, and a handling crew, left Gothenburg by steamer, headed for Dane's Island, on the desolate north coast of Spitzbergen. There they set up a base by a house belonging, rather surprisingly, to an Englishman called Pike. When all was ready they sat down to wait for a wind that would carry the balloon across the Pole to the Bering Straits, a distance of 2,300 miles, which they hoped to cover in about six days. Unhappily no such wind had appeared by the end of August, and the expedition returned to Sweden.

This might have been taken as a bad practical omen, but Andrée was adamant. Dr. Ekholm's place was taken by Knut Fraenkel, a young and adventurous civil engineer who had some experience of ballooning, and Andrée was ready to try again in the following year.

This time it was M. Machuron's turn, and he went with the expedition when they sailed again, on 18th May, 1897. They established themselves at their old camp once more, and by early June they were ready to start. They had to wait for six more weeks for the favourable wind that might, perhaps, now have been assessed as a dangerous rarity.

But on July the 11th it blew from the South. Andrée, whose iron determination had carried everything up to this moment, showed a sudden doubt when the moment came to make the decision to go. There was a strange air of doom in the camp.

The adventurers entered the basket at midday. M. Machuron supervised the final preparations, filled with a sudden foreboding.

At last all was ready. M. Machuron stood by the basket. Strindberg leant out and asked him to give his love to his fiancée. The Frenchman was much moved, and there was some turmoil among the launching crew. "Wait a moment! Keep calm!" shouted M. Machuron, and finally he reported to Andrée that all was ready. Andrée called "Cut away everything!"

The *Eagle* rose slowly, dragging its trail-ropes, and as it moved over the bay into the desolate Polar sea a large section of trail-rope was seen to fall off into the water. The basket barely cleared the waves, and M. Machuron watched anxiously, while the balloon grew smaller and smaller, until it faded into the misty unknown of the chartless North.

It was never seen again.

Surely this was a sad and tragic story to inspire a young man, dreaming of his own conquest of the air. The book, and the character of Andrée, had a lasting effect on him. But Santos was immersed so deeply in the technical details of the construction methods, and Lachambre and Machuron's part in it, that he was little influenced by the dark mystery of the fate of *Eagle*. The story remained unsolved for another thirty-three years, until near the end of Santos-Dumont's own life, when the world was startled by the discovery of the pathetic remains of the Andrée Expedition.

On the north-west coast of Spitzbergen, 150 miles from their starting-place, lies desolate White Island, only twice ever visited by sailors. There a Norwegian scientific expedition, embarked in the *Bratvaag*, found the remains of the last camp of Andrée, Strindberg, and Fraenkel. Their skeletons rested where they had lain down for the last time, and their diaries were recovered and read. The photographic plates they had exposed thirty-three years before were developed and printed, and the mystery was solved.

It seemed that *Eagle* had made good progress for twenty-four hours, covering 160 miles to gain 82 degrees North. The Expedition was in good heart, and released carrier-pigeons with observations of their progress (though only one ever got through). But on the second day the wind, which had already demonstrated how seldom it blew from the South, failed completely, and the balloon became shrouded in fog.

Freezing mist formed ice on the basket and ropes, and the *Eagle* came to rest on the pack-ice. After twelve more hours it floated clear once again, and a vagrant breeze carried it erratically East and then North-West. But its buoyancy dwindled, as the ice and snow gained on the envelope, and to keep it drifting they were obliged to throw out all the ballast, much equipment, and even some of the provisions.

At last, on the third day, it came down on the ice, and would go no farther. It landed at a position 82.56 North, 29.56 East, after 65 hours' flight, 216 miles from its starting point. The work of the loving hands of MM. Lachambre and Machuron lay, borne down by ice, a startling black sphere in a world of desolate whiteness, and the passengers broke out their equipment and prepared for the return journey on foot. With many backward glances, they left the *Eagle* behind them.

It was a terrible prospect. The pack-ice was jagged, slushy, and filled with pools. Struggling along pulling heavy loads, using their boat to get themselves and their sledges across the numberless water barriers, they managed no more than a mile or two a day. All the time the pack-ice was drifting, in a direction opposing their line of march. Through July and August and September they toiled on, gradually winning Southwards, but becoming ill and exhausted, while the fearful Arctic winter grew nearer.

On the 5th of October they staggered off the pack-ice on to White Island. They knew their position, but they could go no farther, and they planned to spend the winter there. But the iron cold gained on them, before they could make preparations for it. First Strindberg died, and the other two buried him. The diaries stop at the 17th, and some short time after that Andrée and Fraenkel lay down in their flimsy tent, to a sleep from which they never woke.

The three explorers rested, while the ice collected over them, the gales blew and the blizzards howled, the Northern Lights glimmered down and the sun melted the ice in the spring; over and over again. Their sleep was not disturbed for thirty-three years.

Chapter 4

☆☆☆☆☆☆☆☆☆☆ ☆ ☆☆☆☆☆☆☆☆☆☆☆☆☆☆☆☆☆☆

La Belle Epoque

The Santos-Dumont who dismounts from the Lisbon express at the Gare d'Orléans, in the autumn of 1897, is a new man. As he hurries through the patches of light and shade under the station roof, with his small mountain of heavy luggage trundling behind him, it is time for us to examine him more closely, and to memorise a face and figure that will come to be among the most celebrated in all Paris.

He stands now outside the station in the sunlight, fishing elegantly in his waistcoat pocket for a franc or two for the porters, his frock-coat thrust back to show light grey trousers with turn-ups, cut rather short in the leg; shiny patent-leather button boots; a pleated silk shirt with a high starched collar; and a broad grey silk tie fastened with a pearl pin. His top-hat is glossy, he carries his light-coloured gloves with an assurance which marks his station, and he holds himself with the perkiness of his twenty-three years.

Alberto Santos-Dumont stands 5 feet 5 inches in his boots, which, avant-garde like the turn-up in his trousers, include the innovation now known as "elevators". He is very sensitive about his small stature; but his light weight of 50 kilos will be a help to him as an aeronaut; he keeps down to it carefully, and he will use this lightness and spareness later as the main principle of construction for his flying machines.

His face is attractive, in a rather abstract way. He has a large head, with a wide forehead above dark brown, somewhat protruding eyes, accentuated by strong eyebrows. His hair is brown, darkened almost to black by the use of pomade, and parted in the middle. This middle parting is another innovation in Paris, for Santos can by no means be accused of excessive conformity. He has a strong nose, ears that stick out from his head, and a full clipped moustache set off by large white teeth. His skin is clear and light, but tans quickly in the sun.

When he brings his attention to bear on any subject his gaze is penetrating and sometimes slightly malicious, and he can snap and sparkle with all the animation and force of character of the powerful spirit which moves him; at other times he is moody, withdrawn, vague, and apparently indecisive. At these two extremes he seems to be two totally different men.

He is always very smartly dressed, to the point of dandyism, usually preferring dark materials with vertical stripes. His clothes are closely cut to accentuate the slimness of his figure, and to fortify his natural trimness he adopts the habit, after his thirtieth year, of wearing a broad thin leather belt under his waistcoat.

For those who rejoice in the deceptiveness of appearance (a deception less common than is generally supposed), Alberto shows little signs of the great qualities that will make him famous, as he whirls away from the station in an open fiacre. His physical strength, agility, courage, and pertinacity are hardly evident in what appears to the casual observer as an undersized and perhaps over-dressed Latin-American traveller, probably on his way to a season of hand-kissing in the drawing-rooms of the capital. But in fact he is well equipped for the schemes now gathering impetus in his large round head. His curious education has not been unfruitful.

He speaks Portuguese, his native language, and also French, English, and Spanish. His quick intelligence has absorbed a surprising amount of practical science. He has never been particularly taken by the classics, reads little outside textbooks, and never writes a letter if he can send a telegram or a *pneumatique*. This habit is the cause of one of the many difficulties of his biographers, and to make matters worse the only information of the diary type he is known to record are the technical details of his work. But he has learnt enough outside scientific subjects to complete the education of a gentleman, and to make him acceptable in the most civilised circles.

The society he is now entering as a grown man has been long established as the brilliant beacon whose light reaches across the seas and continents, to tens of millions who see it as the Mecca of all things desirable. Only England, solid, prosperous, and self-satisfied, can make some show of deprecating the admiration and envy which France inspires in the rest of the world. For this is one of her most glorious periods, splendid more in brilliance and contrast than in the solider virtues, though not lacking those in full measure: *La Belle Epoque*, the last years of the nineteenth century.

The Third Republic was soaring into its apogee. "At no time since the reign of Louis XIV has the genius of individual French-men and Frenchwomen been more brilliantly displayed, or in a greater variety of fields, than this period."* Talent, and par-ticularly innovation, was swarming in every part of France. As ever, Paris was more than the capital; it was the focus, the heart, and the inspiration of the nation. Pioneers of every kind were thick on the boulevards and voluble in the cafés. In literature Zola, Victor Hugo, Anatole France, Proust, Barrès, De Maupassant, Verlaine: in painting Toulouse-Lautrec, and the great impressionists, Pissaro, Degas, Manet, Cézanne, Monet, Renoir, Matisse, Van Gogh, Gauguin: in science Henri Poincaré, Pasteur, Pierre Curie, Ampère, Berthelot: in engineer-ing Eiffel, André Citroën, Panhard: in music Debussy, Fauré, César Franck, Saint-Saëns, Massenet: in the theatre Sarah Bernhardt and Ida Rubinstein: these formed the pinnacles of European culture. The names ring like bells. It was a back-ground composed of the ultimate in sophistication, a pool where the fish were so large, so many, and so active that only the most scintillating could hope to make a ripple.

Amongst all these intellectual splendours, unknown but simmering with ambition, young Santos was safely established once more in his comfortable rooms, his baggage unpacked; firm in his resolve to seek out at once the builders of the Andrée balloon. He lost no time in locating the workshop of MM. Lachambre and Machuron. As soon as he met them he felt that

* *The Development of Modern France.* D. W. Brogan.

all would now be well. The aeronauts impressed him from the first as men with no nonsense about them, practical constructors and capable navigators. In his turn M. Lachambre seems to have taken to the little Brazilian, with his eager, rather shrill voice and earnest manner, who attempted to cloak his excitement with an assumed air of casualness.

"When I asked M. Lachambre how much it would cost me to take a short trip in one of his balloons his reply so astonished me that I asked him to repeat it.

" 'For a long trip of three or four hours,' he said, 'it will cost you 250 francs, all expenses and return of balloon by rail included.'

" 'And the damages?' I asked.

" 'We shall not do any damages!' he replied, laughing."*

This was good enough for Santos. He closed with the offer on the spot, and M. Machuron agreed to take him up the next day.

In the fine pearly haze of a calm May morning Alberto accordingly made his way to Vaugirard, near the Porte de Versailles, where the ascent was to begin from the Parc d' Aérostation. His eagerness was so great that he journeyed by horse-cab, not trusting even his beloved tricycle for so important a rendezvous. He arrived well before the time for the ascension, so as to miss none of the preparations.

The balloon envelope, which had a capacity of 750 cubic metres, was spread out flat on the grass, with the gas-pipe laid ready to the entry valve. The two aeronauts were in attendance, calm and jovial, in comfortable clothes, looking like two middle-aged fishermen off for a day's sport by the river. At an order from Monsieur Lachambre his men began to fill the envelope with gas, and in a little while the bag rose from the ground like a giant mushroom, growing fast, until it formed an enormous sphere.

At 11 o'clock all was ready. The balloon was held only by its mooring rope, and a fresh, gentle breeze rocked the wicker basket. Santos sprang aboard, anxious to be off, and stood eager but uncertain, holding a bag of sand ballast. M. Machuron stood beside him, and M. Lachambre made a final inspection from the outside, walking all round the balloon. The moorings were unfastened, and held only by the workmen.

* *Dans l'Air*. A. Santos-Dumont.

"Let go all!" cried M. Machuron. There was a slight jerk as the men released the balloon, and then it moved smoothly upwards. At the same time the breeze that had been ruffling Alberto's hair stopped, and there was a dead calm in the basket. The balloon was moving at the speed of the wind that was now its own element, and not a breath stirred M. Machuron's small pennant, which hung limply from the suspension ropes.

This was the first great impression that ballooning made on Santos; the stillness and smoothness of the movement. Infinitely gentle was the illusion of the forward and upward progress, and it seemed as if it were not he and M. Machuron that travelled, but the earth which sank down and away from them.

The balloon rose fast. At 4,500 feet Santos looked down into an abyss of space, and for the first time saw the earth like a concave saucer beneath him, the horizon seeming to lift up to a rim that melted into the hazy sky. The thousand details of the great scene laid out beneath him made his head spin, but his own phrasing of what has been written so many times since still has a clear and luminous freshness, just as the scene itself first came before his wondering eyes.

"Villages and woods, meadows and châteaux, file before us like pictures on wheels, out of which the whistling of loco-motives throws sharp notes. These faint, piercing sounds, together with the yelping and barking of dogs, are the only noises which reach one through the depths of the upper air. The human voice cannot mount up into these boundless solitudes. Human beings look like ants along the white lines that are highways, and the rows of houses look like children's play-things."*

Santos was recalled from the enchantment of this scene by a new and practical fact. A cloud passed across the face of the sun, and the balloon above him cooled in the colder layer of air where now they floated. Before M. Lachambre had launched them he had ensured that the weights of M. Machuron, and Santos, plus their ballast, was slightly exceeded by the lift of the gasbag, as it was while moored on the sunlit grass of the Parc d'Aérostation. The cooling now caused the envelope to contract, wrinkling slightly, and it began descending, gently at first and then faster. The aeronaut and his passenger threw out

* *Dans l'Air.* A. Santos-Dumont.

sand, emptying two bags unconcernedly on the citizens below, and the balance was restored. M. Machuron consulted his barograph, and declared himself satisfied.

The balloon now rode steady at some 8,000 feet, no trifling altitude, and Alberto's breath came faster, as much from lack of oxygen as from excitement. A higher current of air carried them over a solid platform of cloud, and the sun cast their shadow on this screen of dazzling whiteness. Around their profile, thus projected below, they could distinguish the three concentric circles of a triple rainbow. As they could no longer see the earth, all sensation of movement ceased. They could be travelling at the speed of a storm and not know it. The compass gave them orientation, but could not give them their heading. They had no idea of the direction in which they were moving. . . .

As a final touch the aeronauts now heard, faintly from below the clouds beneath them, the bells of the noon-day Angelus ringing from some village steeple. "*Il faut déjeuner!*" exclaimed Monsieur Machuron, glancing keenly at the basket by Alberto's feet. A true son of France, the aeronaut had no time for sandwiches or other uncouth makeshifts for the midday meal, and as soon as Santos unstrapped his basket M. Machuron tucked a white napkin into his collar.

They shared a substantial luncheon of hard-boiled eggs in aspic, cold roast beef and chicken, cheese, ice-cream, fruits and cake, champagne, coffee, and Chartreuse. Since these delicacies were conveyed from the picnic-basket straight into the aeronauts, no alteration was caused in the trim of the balloon. Nothing, thought Santos, could be more delicious than lunching like this above the clouds. "No dining-room could be so marvellous in its decoration. The sun sets the clouds in ebullition, making them throw up rainbow jets of frozen vapour like great sheaves of fireworks all around the table. Lovely white spangles of the most delicate ice formation scatter here and there by magic; while flakes of snow form, moment by moment, out of nothingness, beneath our very eyes, and in our very drinking-glasses."*

The balloonists were finishing the coffee in Alberto's flask, and draining the last drops of liqueur, when they noticed that this snow was on the increase. As they packed away the poor

* *Dans l'Air*. A. Santos-Dumont.

remnants of the luncheon, casually dropping the chicken bones and cheese rinds over the side of the basket, they realised that a curtain had suddenly fallen on this wonderful stage setting of sunlight, cloud billows, and azure sky. The barograph rose by 5 millimetres, showing that the balloon was falling. It had become loaded with snow on its upper surface, and in a few minutes it sank into the bank of stratus below.

The cloud vapour enveloped them in a fog. They could see the basket, the instruments, and the part of the rigging nearest to them, but the netting that held them to the balloon faded away a few feet above, and the gas-bag itself had entirely disappeared. For a while, silent and heavy with luncheon, the navigators experienced a disagreeable sensation of hanging in the void without support, of having lost their last ounce of weight in a limbo of nothingness, sombre and portentous.

With one eye on the barograph, M. Machuron let go more sand, and shortly afterwards they emerged under the clouds, at a height of 1,000 feet, the balloon still losing altitude, but more gradually. Once again the scene was transformed. The weather had changed. The wind had freshened to a stiff breeze, and the first village they sighted fled away and was gone before they could identify it. Little gusts nudged the balloon left and right, and up and down. To steady them M. Machuron let out his big trail-rope, 300 feet long, which served the important purpose of arresting the balloon's descent as the rope's heavy length was increasingly transferred to the ground.

The aeronauts got out their maps and compared them with the natural map below, and used their compass to read the direction of the wind. Soon they could identify the roads, villages, forests and railways that hastened towards them from the horizon. Monsieur Machuron was now concentrating on his speciality, the art of balloon pilotage, and bade his passenger watch closely. The basket was almost down to tree-top height, and half the trail-rope dragged along the ground behind them. Steadied by this, and relieved of its weight, the balloon kept a constant height, and whenever an obstacle appeared ahead M. Machuron instructed Santos to throw out sand. This, coupled with the updraught over trees, small hills, and buildings, caused the balloon to leap up and over the dangers in its path. Fortunately these did not include, at that time, the high-tension

electrical cables which would now certainly render the same
manoeuvre fatal within a mile or two.

M. Machuron was not intending to play the part of an instructor, but Santos was watching with all his eyes, and kept up a
constant stream of questions. He was particularly intrigued by
the action of the trail-rope.* They had now decided to keep to
a low altitude for the rest of the trip, and whenever the balloon
rose slightly, the extra length of guide-rope lifted off the ground
gave them more ballast, until equilibrium was restored, while
when they approached the ground the contrary effect was
produced.

In spite of the threatening weather the pilot remained un-
perturbed, and his passenger so absorbed as to have no thoughts
for danger. "During the whole flight I observed the pilot at his
work, and comprehended perfectly all that he did. It seemed to
me that I had really been born for aeronautics. Everything that
I saw was very simple and easy to do; I did not get giddy, or
frightened."†

If this sounds like bumptious over-confidence, it was well
justified in later years, and one must remember that this was an
age in which half the fearsome experiences of present-day travel,
which are now taken for granted, would then have sent strong
men into hysterics, or reduced them to quivering wrecks. The
modern and commonplace delights of the speed and hideous
noise of road, underground train, or aeroplane travel, had not
yet begun their assaults on the ears and nerves of the late
nineteenth century.

In the meantime the guide-rope had betrayed one of its less
attractive characteristics. It had been dragging along over fields,
hills, and valleys, roads and houses, hedges and meadows, giving
a series of violent shocks to the balloon and its occupants. Just
after they passed over a clump of trees a savage jerk flung them
to one side of the basket. The balloon had stopped short, and
swayed in the wind gusts at the end of its guide-rope, which
was curled round the head of an oak. There they stuck, with the
wind increasing in force, and the balloon shaking them, "like
salad in a salad-basket".

* Always called a "guide-rope" by Santos-Dumont and so referred to
hereafter.
† *O Que eu Vi, O Que nós Veremos.* A. Santos-Dumont.

Attempts to free the rope proving fruitless, M. Machuron released more and more ballast to increase their lift and tear them away. After fifteen minutes of struggle the rope suddenly came loose, and the lightened balloon made a tremendous leap upwards, piercing the clouds "like a cannon-ball". This rapid gain in altitude was dangerous, and the pilot had to adjust the other side of his balance of forces, by hastily releasing some gas from the manoeuvre valve. It was in this way, by balancing gas against ballast, that the balloon pilot operated, and when he had released all the ballast his power to control the balloon was gone, and his flight must end.

So this vital principle of lighter-than-air flight, which Santos noted carefully, went as follows: when a balloon rises, the gas inside it expands. If the bag is not to burst some gas must be released, manually or through the open "neck" at the base of the gas-bag. Therefore when the balloon descends again it has less lift, and ballast must be thrown out to keep it afloat.

M. Machuron soon had the balloon down to guide-rope height again, his long experience allowing for its delay in responding to his actions, and since there was little sand remaining they had to make up their minds to land. The north-east corner of the Forest of Fontainebleau came into sight, and hurried only too quickly towards them. They were travelling too fast for a good landing, and the pilot's first concern was to work them into some shelter where the wind would be less strong.

He noted a tongue of trees which jutted out from the forest athwart their path, dropped the last of the ballast to clear it, and then immediately valved gas, shouting to Santos to throw out the anchor. This was a normal small boat grapnel, on the end of a strong cord. A moment after Alberto had flung it over the side the basket touched the grass, at no more than walking speed, and tipped gently over. With a final dramatic gesture M. Machuron pulled the emergency gas release cord, and the balloon subsided downwind of them.

As the sphere deflated, Santos dragged his photographic apparatus from the basket and took a number of "instantaneous pictures". For a few minutes the envelope flapped and billowed in a variety of strange and ugly shapes, then it lay still and flat on the ground. The two aeronauts folded the envelope, like chambermaids clearing up after a rowdy party, and packed it carefully in the passenger basket, with its netting removed and folded alongside.

They found they were in the grounds of the Château de la Ferrière, owned by M. Alphonse de Rothschild. They had been more than two hours in the air, and had covered 60 miles since leaving Paris. The farm workers who came running were sent to the village for a conveyance, and half-an-hour later a horse-drawn brake came, and the balloon was packed into it. They drove triumphantly to the railway station of La Ferrière, where their apparatus, which weighed a total of some 440 lbs., was put on the next train for Paris. At the Gare de Lyon they parted in the best of humour, and were home by nightfall.

The first flight had been an unqualified success. Santos had enjoyed every minute, and vowed himself to further lessons and adventures. He was truly launched upon ballooning, or as expressed in a leaflet published in his praise in Brazil during 1901: "His ascensions then commenced, and for same nature had endowed him admirably; to his intellectual accomplishments Santos-Dumont associated a notable collection of physical aptitudes: the agility of an athlete, the skilled touch of a machinist, expertness in jumping, and he only weighed 50 kilograms!"*

Alberto's life now had a focus indeed. On the very next morning he was back at the workshop of Lachambre and Machuron, to ask them to construct him a balloon. The partners said that they would be happy to oblige, and all three of them started at once on the discussion of details. They suggested the normal size and construction, similar to the craft in which Santos had been initiated; but they soon realised that they had an entirely different customer from their normal clientele, when he coolly disagreed with all their proposals.

They suggested a balloon of 750-1,000 cubic metres in size, with conventional basket and rigging. Santos was obsessed with the idea of lightness and smallness, and asked for one of 100 cubic metres. MM. Lachambre and Machuron threw up their hands at the idea. With so little lift the gas-bag would never carry the rigging and basket even, far less a crew. Santos ex-

* *Santos-Dumont and the Conquest of the Air.* A. Napoleão, translated by d'Oliviera.

plained that he wanted a one-man balloon anyway, and that he had ideas about the materials of construction which he would like to discuss. He suggested that the envelope be made of varnished Japanese silk, the rigging as light as possible, the basket to a new design, and all the accessories to scale. Lastly he pointed out with more enthusiasm than tact, that he himself was barely half the weight of M. Machuron.

So concerned were the partners that they dragged Santos to their works, and let their own artisans tell him where he was at fault. To their surprise, and in fact his own, Alberto held his ground. They protested that the gas-bag at least must be properly made of heavy treated silk, or taffetas. Santos went and produced a specimen of Japanese silk, such as he had seen used for kites, and they tried it on a tensile rig. To the exasperation of the experts it withstood a load of 700 kilogrammes to the linear metre—stronger than the conventional material.

Finally MM. Lachambre and Machuron gave way, and agreed to build the balloon to Alberto's specifications. It would be the smallest man-carrying balloon ever known to have been made. The entire envelope would only weigh 8 lb., although three coats of varnish would bring this up to 31 lb. The whole craft would come out at no more than 72 lb., and most of it could be packed up and carried in a valise. In full cry after his destiny at last, Santos had no qualms about expense, and the constructors were ordered to make everything of the best.

In the meantime it was necessary to gain experience. MM. Lachambre and Machuron were sufficiently like the rest of the aeronauts of the day to make whatever they could out of fairs, exhibitions, and displays. Santos came to an arrangement whereby they accepted him, at a blanket figure, as a crew member under training during these flights. This worked out cheaper than if he had ordered the trips solely for himself, and gave him a wider experience of different parts of the country.

While his balloon was building he made a number of ascents in this way, and finally graduated to a solo trip in one of the firm's balloons. By the end of this practice period he had made some twenty-five flights, and reached a new agreement by which he paid only the expenses and damages of the trips. He sometimes deputised for the partners as an exhibition pilot, while they drew the fee for their balloon's appearance. It was an agreement that worked to the complete satisfaction of both parties.

These activities, which involved a lot of travelling around France and Belgium, took up a great deal of his time. He was becoming increasingly devoted to *aérostation* to the exclusion of almost all else. Though his few friends and acquaintances in Paris were of a similarly *sportif* character, they had not invaded the balloonist's province, and had to admit that Alberto had largely forsaken them, and that the new craze had quite carried him away. The cousins had given him up as hopeless.

He did not come through his apprenticeship without some hair-raising experiences. In the autumn of 1897 he engaged to make an ascent at a fair at Péronne in northern France, deputising for M. Lachambre in one of his balloons. The weather was threatening when the time approached for the ascent, with thunder grumbling in the distance. Some of the crowd, who knew he was an amateur, begged him not to go, while the majority kept quiet and hoped for some excitement. But the feeling that he held the centre of the stage and the audience was waiting and must be satisfied, the feeling that was to bring him later so near to his undoing, first made itself evident at Péronne. He brusquely turned down the wounding suggestion that he take a more experienced rival aeronaut with him, and set off in a gloomy twilight.

Soon he had cause to regret his rashness. His balloon was carried into a thunderstorm, where he was not only subjected to the unnerving effect of flashes of lightning at close quarters, such as the modern air traveller must endure, but also to the deafening claps of thunder, which the aeroplane passenger cannot hear. Night was gaining upon him, and the wind was increasing, carrying him he knew not where.

At first, he confessed, he was very frightened. Then his mood changed. "On, on I went, tearing through the blackness. I knew that I must be going with great speed, yet sensed no motion. I heard and felt the storm. I realised I was in great danger, yet the danger was not tangible. With it there was a fierce kind of joy. What shall I say? How shall I describe it? Up there in the black solitude, amid the lightning flashes and the thunder-claps, I was part of the storm."*

* *Dans l'Air*. A. Santos-Dumont.

Should these brave words, which were written some time afterwards, provoke any feelings of unworthy scepticism, Alberto's later history undoubtedly proved him to have great physical courage, while the unique property of the free balloon, to feel itself a part of its environment instead of an intruder thrusting through it, gave some grounds for the observation. And nothing could be more characteristic than this half-bombastic, half-obsessed declaration of delight in a nerve-racking experience, as if he had some internal demon of doubt, that must constantly be exorcised by a passion of bravery.

Throwing out ballast, he rose through the storm and above it. It was night when he emerged, inheritor of an endless empty universe, with a vault of stars above him, and a cold carpet of cloud below. He was astounded and awe-struck. Beneath his feet the clouds still lit up and faded with the reflections of internal lightnings, and the sullen rumbling of thunder welled upward from the depths. But above him the crisp stars were bright and steady, and the shape of his balloon cut a firm curve of black against the sky. The basket rode evenly, and he was alone.

He found that he loved solitude. He did not love it enough to become a hermit, but when chance threw it in his way, he embraced it. So through this night he rejoiced, with the storm past and behind him. He let the balloon descend again, to where he could watch the sleeping earth, and note the flash of moonlight on a river, and the curl of mist that followed its course. He watched the bright flares from the fireboxes of railway locomotives, and how the lights tracing their path changed from emerald to red. He gazed in wonder at the clusters of brightness that marked cities.

He saw the black night pale to grey, and the stars go out; marked the bands of colours that ebbed slowly back into the eastern sky, and saw the sun return to flood the world with light, and to strike the sphere above him and turn it to gold.

Soon after dawn he touched ground, in a still morning. It was an easy landing, and he was in Belgium.

Chapter 5

☆☆☆☆☆☆☆☆☆☆☆☆☆☆☆☆☆☆☆☆☆☆☆☆☆☆☆☆

"Number One"

Santos-Dumont fast became an experienced and accomplished balloonist, and his enthusiasm flourished on his experience. Indeed the advice he wrote at the time, in an article for a weekly magazine, has the hallmark of the single-minded. "Say that you are a young man who would roam, who would enjoy adventures, who would penetrate the unknown and deal with the unexpected—but say that you are tied down at home by family and business. I advise you to take to spherical ballooning!"

This was not very practical advice for the Parisian *petit bourgeois* of the day, though there seems no reason why, with modern transport and construction methods (and away from electric power lines), it should not now be very good advice indeed. A branch of the same spirit is responsible for the great present-day popularity of gliding.

Alberto's small balloon, which he had already christened *Brazil*, was taking form in the workshop of Lachambre and Machuron, every component needing to be made specially, with Santos continually imploring the workmen to "build in lightness". This phrase, which would seem an obvious enough requisite of the making of all aircraft, has rung in the heads of every aircraft designer ever since, but a glance at the sketch designs of proposed flying machines of a few decades before

Alberto's time shows that it was much less self-evident than one might suppose.

His adventures piloting the Lachambre balloons were being digested into a mass of information, carefully recorded in his own hand, on airmanship and the vagaries of the air. The balloonist and the glider are both uniquely equipped to get the feeling for this basic understanding. The weather and the behaviour of air masses, the effects of different kinds of land or water below, the winds, and the up and down air currents, all affect them so strongly and immediately that they must sense them with the intimacy of complete comprehension. As the old sailing-ship mariner knew the sea, so must the balloonist or glider know the air; not as a medium but as a whole new world, whose ways must be understood, followed, and *loved*; if he hopes to live in a dominion properly belonging to the birds.

Even after he had begun to build and fly airships he continued to gain experience with free balloons. In 1898 he invited four of his friends from the Automobile Club of Paris to ascend with him from Vaugirard. The balloon was a large one which he had ordered after his experience with *Brazil*. They rose majestically, equipped with cameras, field-glasses, and copious supplies of provisions, ready to cross frontiers and explore new continents if necessary. Unfortunately there was a dead calm, and the balloon remained stationary over Paris.

Santos threw out ballast and went up to ten thousand feet, seeking a wind, until his guests began to cough and pant. Nothing. He valved gas and went down to roof-top level. Still nothing. He went up and down again and again, each time using ballast and gas, while hours went by; but the balloon remained obstinately over Paris. Finally he had used up all his ballast, including his reserve for landing. His power to manoeuvre had gone but, due undoubtedly to the presence of his friends, he had passed the point at which he should have landed. The balloon began to drift at last, but his one idea now was to get down.

He thought of landing in the square before the Gare de Lyon, but decided it was too dangerous. To persuade the balloon towards the wood next to the zoo at Vincennes he was obliged to throw overboard everything loose, the ballast-sacks, the cameras and plates, the field-glasses, and all that was left of the food. He was considering asking his passengers to strip, when he finally dumped the basket safely on to the ground. The guests dispersed in a much less genial spirit than that in which they had set out. It had been a trying day.

A totally different adventure, in the following year, showed him the other face of the air ocean. During a stay at Nice he made a solo flight, with the promise of a gentle breeze from the sea, to admire the mountains and beaches of the Côte d'Azur. He rose from the Place Masséna, and for a while all went well. After an hour or two, however, a storm sprang up, and he employed his previous tactic of rising above it. At the higher altitude he saw, to his dismay, that the wind would carry him out to sea, and he hastily valved gas to land.

He sank to within a thousand feet of the ground, near the mouth of the Var River, and found to his great surprise that he could go no lower. He released more gas, but he was actually rising. More gas still, and the balloon rose to a height of ten thousand feet. He felt the icy clutch of terror which comes with the knowledge that control is lost, and then he realised for the first time that he was in a powerful up-current. This was at least understandable, and he composed himself to see what would happen. He dared not release any more gas.

Fortunately the wind no longer blew out to sea, and presently he drifted out of the up-current, and the balloon descended fast. As he came close to the ground he threw out large amounts of ballast, and saw that the gale was whipping at the trees and shrubs in a way that boded ill for his landing. Before he could realise how fast he was moving, he was within a few feet of the ground. Desperately he threw out his anchor. The basket bounced from tree-top to hedge, the grapnel would not hold, and in a moment he was being dragged through avenues and copses, rattled in the basket from side to side, his face cut and bruised, and the clothes all but torn from his back. If any solid trees or building had been in his path this would have been his last flight, but just as he gave himself up for lost the anchor held, the basket tipped violently over, and he was shot out of it on to the ground, where he lay unconscious.

When he came to, the balloon was gone, nor was it ever seen again. Santos had to stagger more than a mile until he met some peasants, who helped him back to Nice, where he was stitched and doctored and put to bed. The product of this exploit was another careful page in his notebook.

His working experience went into his new balloon. At last *Brazil* was ready. Taken to Vaugirard and inflated, it looked little bigger than a child's toy, and MM. Lachambre and Machuron still looked at it uneasily, even as they enthusiastically quaffed the champagne which Santos had provided in honour of the occasion. The rigging was unusually long, to steady the tiny basket beneath, and this made the little sphere look even smaller than it was. Only 66 lb. of sand ballast was on board, but the lift calculations were vindicated, and when Santos called "Let go all!" one man was enough to release the mooring rope, and the balloon rose bravely into the air, with the small silken pennant of a Brazilian flag hanging from the rigging.

Santos made a large number of flights in *Brazil*, mostly over Paris and the Ile de France. He found it completely practical, very simple to control and handle, so far as a balloon can be controlled, and particularly convenient in the ease with which it could be set up and flown, and then later packed up and carried home. Balloons were filled with comparatively expensive hydrogen, and this envelope-full of gas was usually lost on every trip, when the aeronaut pulled his rip-cord on landing. *Brazil* needed about one-seventh as much gas as the more normal balloons then in use.

Although he was only one of many aeronauts, his little balloon caught the imagination of the young blades of the Automobile Club, and he began to be known outside the immediate circle of his acquaintances. The novelty of his background and nationality provided still more interest, and an article on him appeared in a Paris magazine. His first trials confirmed in him the belief that lightness and simplicity were the keys to success, though as he himself was undoubtedly the lightest aeronaut flying at the time he had no imitators of this aspect of construction. He still looked with disfavour on his 66 lb. of ballast, considering it to be so much wasted pay-load, and he sketched out an idea, which he put into practice much later, to use a propeller, turning in a horizontal plane, to give a balloon an impulse upwards or downwards.

By the end of the year he decided that he must have a proper home, and he looked about for a house in Paris. To follow his

chosen star he realised that he must spend money, and perhaps
this is the place to emphasise that, although he was comparatively rich, his purse was by no means bottomless. The money
coming in from Brazil, though well invested, did not put him
in the really wealthy bracket, by the standards then prevailing,
and indeed over the next ten years he consistently spent rather
more than his income. The general impression in Paris, that
he possessed fabulous riches, arose from the fact that he spent
money lavishly on his chief interests; but he did not have the
expenses of a family, and he watched his spending carefully in
all other respects. Bearing this in mind, the open-handedness
he showed later becomes more genuine, instead of being ascribed,
as it often was at the time, to the actions of a man to whom
money meant nothing.

After careful investigation he obtained the lease of a house on
the corner of rue Washington and the Champs-Elysées, near
the Arc de Triomphe and conveniently central in Paris. This
house still stands, part of a dignified block of five storeys with
large and well-proportioned living-rooms, but now, because of
its frontage on to the Champs-Elysées, no longer a private home.
The ground floor is a showroom for a refrigerator maker, and
the first floor is occupied by the office of the newspaper Le
Parisien Libéré. But it is not too hard to imagine it as it was, a
dignified, honey-coloured house of pleasing lines, with a pair
of small orange-trees in tubs flanking the front door.

Here he engaged a cook, two maids, and a valet, and for the
first time enjoyed the benefits of a proper establishment. His
staff were soon made aware of the more unusual aspects of their
new master, with the furnishings of the dining-room. In addition
to the normal items, Santos installed a small dining-table which
he had suspended from the high ceiling by wires, so that it hung
six feet from the floor. A chair was likewise fastened, and rigged
close to the table. Alberto reached this chair by mounting on
stilts, and when seated and swaying slightly on the wires he
would have a meal served to him by his valet, who handed up
the food on a tray held high above his head. When the ceiling
showed signs of collapsing he achieved the same result by a table
and chairs with legs some ten feet long.

By this system Santos intended to accustom himself to eating
meals high up on an unstable foundation, as in a balloon or air-

ship, but it can hardly be denied that it showed the beginnings of a certain charming eccentricity, which increasingly became an engaging part of his character. He had already the calm acceptance of all great natural eccentrics, which never for one moment allows them to doubt the complete normality of their behaviour.

Fully organised at home, and now able to spend on his motor-tricycle any time that he could spare from ballooning, Santos could think seriously about the next major stage in his great dream—powered and controlled flight. The progress, or lack of progress, up to the year 1897, which had so surprised him when first he came to France, should now be briefly summarised. This is not a history of early aviation, but if we are to understand Santos-Dumont we must understand his problems and his starting point.

Ever since the Montgolfiers, and indeed long before, ideas had been projected for the construction of lighter-than-air ships that could be moved and steered with sails, oars, and other fantasia; the inventors sometimes, with outstanding optimism, drawing pieces of ordnance and castles on to their designs. The Andrée balloon had actually made use of sails. But the first really powered and steerable ship to take the air had been the elongated balloon of Henri Giffard. In 1852 this French inventor of the steam injector, who was the foremost designer of steam engines in Europe at that time, built an engine of three horse-power, weighing only 350 lb. all told. He then constructed an elongated balloon envelope, 144 feet long and 40 feet in diameter, slung the engine below it, fitted a propeller to the engine, and added a rudder for good measure. He realised that his craft was safe only in a dead calm, and choosing such a condition he made a successful flight from the Hippodrome in Paris. He achieved a speed of 6 m.p.h., together with some cautious changes of direction.

His airship, which poised a large bag of hydrogen just above the steam engine's furnace, was much less safe than a fused bomb, and since he could not increase the power of the engine he was obliged to give up hope of improvement. A German engineer, Paul Haenlein, attempted an airship with a gas engine, but this also was a failure. In 1883 the French brothers Tissandier constructed an airship with an electric motor working from batteries. This flew successfully, and was a great deal safer than Giffard's machine, but it was still too feeble to fight even the laziest breeze.

The Tissandier principle was much improved, in 1884, by the Frenchmen Renard and Krebs, when they produced their electrically driven airship *La France*. This was constructed of a bamboo framework covered by Chinese silk, but the 8 h.p. electric engine was made in France. It made several successful flights, including a round trip of five miles at Chalais-Meudon, but once again it was clear that no improvement could be hoped for, due to the weight of the motor and batteries.

While Santos was pondering on the work of these pioneers, and forming his own plans, in Germany David Schwarz was building an airship with a hull of light alloy girders covered with aluminium sheeting, and driven by a petrol engine. This was the forerunner of the famous line of Zeppelins, and marked an early German deviation on to a course which Count Zeppelin followed so successfully thereafter. Although very advanced in theory, it was a practical failure, due to troubles with the machinery, and it was not until 1900 that LZ-1 flew with some success.

So it was that the field was clear. Nobody had produced any aerial vehicle which could be steered in the desired direction, which was not also helpless and in danger of destruction at the first breath of wind, and which showed any hopes of improvement. After *La France* a lull had fallen, which lasted nearly fifteen years.

The balloonists were doing quite nicely at their own art, and saw little prospect beyond it. M. Machuron, certainly among the most experienced and progressive of them, had addressed Santos on this very subject, while they both lay battered in the basket of his balloon, caught by the guide-rope, on the trip to Fontainebleau described in the last chapter.

"Observe the treachery and vindictiveness of the wind," he shouted between the thuds and crashes. "We are tied to the tree, yet see with what force it tries to jerk loose." (Here they were both thrown violently to the bottom of the basket.) "What screw propeller could hold course against it? What elongated balloon would not double up and take you flying to destruction?"

Good questions, M. Machuron, as Santos was to find out.

Alberto himself was convinced at the time. He confessed that his faith in the steerable airship was often shaken afterwards, in the course of his adventures with free balloons. But one evening as he rode home to No. 9 rue Washington, he reflected that his tricycle's De Dion engine was very light and comparatively powerful, and he became convinced that therein lay the secret. In this as in a number of other developments, Santos was not the only man to have the idea; but he was the first to act, and the first to succeed.

"If I make a cylindrical balloon long enough and thin enough, it will cut the air. . . . I could use the light and powerful petrol motor, and if the wind is too strong, shall I not be as a sailing yachtsman, who is not criticised for refusing to go out in a squall? Giffard had no such opportunity." So he mused, and inevitably discussed the idea with his automobile and ballooning friends. They were horrified.

"If you want to commit suicide," remarked one of his well-wishers, "why not sit on a cask of gunpowder with a lighted cigar in your mouth?" Santos mildly pointed out that Giffard's airship, filled with hydrogen and spitting smoke and sparks, had survived its test trips, while he meant to use an engine from one of the *velocettes*.

"In that case your craft will shake to pieces," went on the adviser. "The ground steadies the structure, and with it the engine. Lifted off the ground it will rattle like dice in a box." Santos was not sure about this, and when he was not sure about anything he liked to try it and find out.

He therefore arranged for Charles, his valet, to hire two workmen with ropes, and instructed them to meet him in the Bois de Boulogne. He himself set out on his tricycle, and selected a large tree with a stout branch jutting out close to the ground. He then directed the workmen to throw their ropes over the branch and make them fast to the tricycle. Fortunately it was early morning, and there were no witnesses.

Santos started the engine, mounted the saddle, and gave the order to heave. The De Dion, with its rider hanging on to the handlebars, rose five feet into the air, and Santos opened the throttle wide. Charles glanced nervously around. There were not so very many prohibitions in the Bois, compared with some parks, but he felt that this would certainly be one of them, if

anybody were to think of it. His master, immaculate and unconcerned, thought of nothing but the matter in hand.

Alberto found, to his delight, that the vibration was less when
he was off the ground than when he was on. The engine seemed
to have nothing to vibrate against, and though it could scarcely
be claimed that it was smooth, it was certainly less rough than
on the road. The party dispersed, and Santos rode home in
triumph.

Back at rue Washington he took a large sheet of squared paper,
and laid down the lines of his *Airship No 1*. "I have always been
charmed by simplicity, while complications, be they never so
ingenious, repel me." With these words he started work, and
in this precept lay the germ of his success.

He decided to have a motor constructed out of two cylinders
of the De Dion tricycle engine, and he calculated that this
would give $3\frac{1}{2}$ h.p. and weigh sixty-six pounds. Then he needed
to know the weights of the propeller, fuel, rigging, controls,
and lastly his own weight, and so decide the minimum size of
envelope that could hold enough gas to lift all this. Everything
was to be small and light. Besides being sound aviation practice,
he reflected, it would be cheaper.

After a few days of work he took his sketch designs to
Monsieur Lachambre. There was another bout of expostulation,
as the good aeronaut bent over the papers. The combination of
gas and petrol was madness. Did his young friend want him,
Lachambre, to have his blood on his conscience? Throwing out
his arms he demanded whether Santos had not studied the
lessons of history, and if not whether he had at least listened to
M. Machuron? He flatly refused. He would have nothing to do
with the project.

Once more Santos had to talk him round, and at last he gave
way. It was agreed that the envelope and its rigging and spars
should be constructed by Lachambre and Machuron. Santos
himself would design and construct the motor, propeller, and
basket. For this he would need a workshop and mechanics.
Some enquiry among his mechanical friends led him to a small
establishment in the rue de Colisée, which specialised in the
repair of the few automobiles and motor-tricycles that came its
way. Santos brought two engines and his plans to this *atelier*,
where after much poring over sketches, and sucking of mous-

taches and pointing with grimy forefingers, the mechanicians agreed to do the work.

The man put in charge of the job was named Albert Chapin, a solid, careful, highly-skilled member of the brand-new corps of petrol engine mechanics. His broad country face, short powerful body, and thick capable fingers, conformed to a type which has brought comfort to many tourists in France, when they limp in their expiring motor-cars to the doors of some rural garage. As the work went forward Santos grew to like the resourceful Chapin, who also found the young Brazilian a man of sense and understanding. In due course Santos took him on his own staff, and Chapin became his chief mechanic.

By the spring of 1898 the engine was running, though there was much development still to do. Santos used the extraordinary system of mounting a second cylinder above the first, with the top piston linked to the lower by a rigid connecting-rod, through two gas-tight joints. This was certainly light and simple, if far from smooth-running. There was no hurry, for the rest of the airship would take several months. Santos had some time on his hands, and decided to fit the new engine to his dismembered tricycle, and show the Automobile Club a thing or two.

The great sport of motor racing began almost with the birth of the motor-car. At first, the only sort of contest was to drive from town to town, the almost uncontrollable cars panting and lurching over dirt roads made for horse traffic, bumping and swaying through the potholes in clouds of dust and grit, until the disastrous Paris-Madrid race of 1903, where "the crashes turned the course into the semblance of a battle-field", brought these early epics to a dramatic end.

In 1895 the Paris-Bordeaux race was won by Emile Levassor at an average speed of 15 m.p.h.,* and in 1896 the winner of the Paris-Marseilles-Paris race (a fearful ordeal of over a thousand miles) recorded 18 m.p.h. In 1897 the course was shorter: Paris-Amsterdam. Alberto's tricycle was not eligible to enter, but he tuned up the engine, and shortly after the start swung out of a side-road and joined the competitors. To his delight he found that he could keep up with the leaders, and he would have persisted to Amsterdam itself, if he had not feared

* Sixteen petrol and seven steam-powered vehicles were entered.

that the road would ruin his fine motor. He turned back, regretful but exultant, leaving the mastodons to rumble on north-eastward down the long French roads, past the creaking farm-carts and the waving rustics.

This experience revived his love of automobiling. With his precious engine back in the workshop he had no more use for the tricycle, and he bought instead a new 6 h.p. Panhard. It was winter time, and he fancied a short holiday in Nice. True to himself he decided to make the journey the hard way, and taking only a valise he drove South, night and day, with only an hour's rest, and completed the distance of 600 miles from Paris in 54 hours. At a time when the average automobilist thought seriously before driving ten miles this was a feat indeed, but the alert young gentleman who strode into his hotel on the Promenade des Anglais looked no more than a little dusty.

His money, his polished manners and obvious charm, and his wide acquaintance in Paris, easily won him new friends on the Côte d'Azur, and of course many designing female eyes inspected the wealthy young bachelor; but it is typical of Santos that the only reference he afterwards made to a holiday like this, where there was no opportunity for aviation, concerned the dubious delights of the gruelling drive down from Paris.

When he got back he found that his new work took up so much time that he could no longer take his Panhard far into the countryside. For short journeys in Paris it was too much trouble for a man who could not give it his full attention. His eye was caught by a small, handy electric brougham. It ran on batteries, started at once and never gave trouble, and it was silent and effective. Santos bought it and kept it for several years. His days as an "automobilist" were over, and he was now merely a sophisticated driver.

All through the spring and summer of 1898 the construction of *No 1* went on, under the increasingly detailed supervision of its owner. The airship was in no sense a rigid, or even a semi-rigid structure. It was simply an elongated balloon, with rigging lines attached to thin horizontal wooden rods, which were sewn directly into the fabric so as to dispense with the weight of the usual balloon net. From these lines a basket hung, well below the gas-bag, and the motor was mounted on the basket. Santos tested the basket and the motor assembly by suspending them from the roof of his workshop, starting the motor, and measuring the pull of the propeller. He found it to equal 25 lb.

The triangular rudder, made of silk on a steel wire frame, was attached to one of the rigging lines, and as its movement could be controlled only coarsely, and the turning movement it then imparted was transmitted to a structure as pliable as a rubber hose, it was obvious that steering was going to be a chancy business. For changing direction up and down he devised a system of balance weights hanging fore and aft. By pulling one of these into the central basket he could alter the centre of gravity, and so tip the nose up or down. He hoped that this ability to "drive the airship obliquely" would save him from carrying ballast, except that needed to "weigh off" his craft at the beginning of the flight.

In all other respects *No 1* was a balloon, but its differences were sufficient for every part to need special handwork. So it was not until September of 1898 that he was able to make the final inspection of the whole assembly in the workshop, declare himself satisfied, and order the stripping and transport of the airship for its first trials.

Chapter 6

☆☆☆☆☆☆☆☆☆☆☆☆☆☆☆☆☆☆☆☆☆☆☆☆☆☆☆☆

"I Had Navigated the Air"

The Jardin d'Acclimatation, the new Zoological Gardens in the Bois de Boulogne, was chosen as the scene of the first trial of *No 1*. On the 18th of September, 1898, the gas-bag and rigging, and the basket with its motor, were carefully laid out on the turf amongst the trees, by Santos, Lachambre, Machuron, and Chapin. A small crowd gathered when the news of the trials got about, a pool of dark clothes on the olive-green autumn grass, dotted with the bright colours of the ladies' summer dresses, and topped with a creamy froth of panama hats and straw boaters. The weather was sunny, with a gentle breeze.*

The presence of most of Alberto's aviation and motoring friends ensured a fine babel of conversation and counsel, amongst which he strove to concentrate on the affair in hand. Those who insisted that the whole idea was lunacy were shouted down by some of the more encouraging balloonists, who reminded Santos that he must be sure to ascend from the upwind end of the clearing, so that he could avoid the trees at the down-wind end.

Hastily acknowledging this profusion of advice, he ordered the inflation of the gas-bag. Hydrogen storage had been arranged,

* In an interview with *Lectures pour Tous* in 1913, Santos declared that this flight took place in February, while snow was falling!

and the airship was slowly filled with 180 cubic metres of gas, at a cost of one franc per cubic metre. It floated high above the basket, and soon only the mooring-ropes restrained *No 1* on the ground. Chapin turned on the petrol, and moved the square, thin sails of the propeller, which looked more like a windmill than an airscrew.

The precious engine started easily. After warming up it was allowed to run for a moment at its full speed of a thousand revolutions, so that the twinkle of the propeller's metal sails became a bright blur in the sunlight. Then it was throttled down to idling, and the airship was walked over to the up-wind side of the clear space, and faced down-wind. The aeronaut jumped into the basket. The moment had come, and in these last seconds there was no hesitation. "Let go all!" shouted Santos at the top of his voice, above the popping of the engine.

Machuron and Chapin released the mooring ropes. Santos opened up the engine. *No 1* started to rise, but her own tiny power, working with the wind, carried her forward into the trees, before she could climb enough to clear them. There was a rending sound, the engine stopped, and in a shocked silence she crumpled to the grass. Everybody let out their breath in a subdued groan.

Santos hopped out at once, for he had not even been jarred. But he was extremely vexed, and inclined to lay the blame on the balloonists who had advised him. He angrily told them he had known all along that he should have started into wind. There was a slight altercation, from which Santos learnt nothing except that he would be better advised to use his own judgement in future, or that if he did otherwise it would be useless to hold the consequences against the well-meaning advisers. The incident helped to make him exceedingly stubborn.

Machuron, Lachambre, and Chapin examined the airship, and found the damage to be slight. It was quickly hauled back to the workshop, and after two days' hard work was as good as new. On the 20th of September, 1898, the team was back again at the same position, hoping for a calm day for their second attempt. But the pennant on the large captive balloon of M. Lachambre, tethered nearby, still showed a slight wind in the clearing, and Santos gave the order to position the airship on the down-wind side, facing into the breeze.

Once more the preparations went smoothly. For the flight Santos wore a normal dark-coloured formal suit, with a red silk tie emerging from the bottom of a very high stiff collar, button boots and a cloth cap. He was tense with the hopes and fears of nearly twelve months. When the engine was running properly he called for the release, and this time No 1 went slowly ahead into wind, rising steadily. He hauled in his forward ballast and she pointed for the sky, and an audible gasp came from below as she cleared the trees. Santos trimmed her level, and at once pulled on one of the rudder lines. To his intense joy, and the excitement of the crowd below, she answered slowly to her helm. She steered! She bent and flexed, and her maze of cordage thrummed and twanged, but she came round; and airship and pilot made a triumphant circuit of M. Lachambre's captive balloon.

Despite the surge of sheer delight that flooded through Santos, he kept his head, and gingerly circled round the trees. His small delicate hands and agile brain were working fast and carefully. No 1 must have been the least rigid airship ever to fly, and controlling her like trying to waltz with a jelly-fish. But he made her turn left and right in response to the rudder, and to slant up and down according to the displacement of the two adjustable sacks of ballast.

His motor ran steadily, pushing the basket forward, and in effect pulling the gas-bag after it; and indeed, because of the length of the rigging, if the engine had produced more power Santos in his basket would have found himself well out in front of the rest of No 1. But everything was in equilibrium, and for some minutes more he circled first this way and then that, with his red tie fluttering over his shoulder.

Made reckless by excitement and success, he jockeyed the nose of the airship up, and climbed it to more than a thousand feet. At this height he headed for the Longchamp racecourse, marvelling at his ability to go where he willed. He was prudent enough to stay over the Bois. But when he started to descend near the turf of Bagatelle he had the first taste of a trouble that was to follow him for long after.

The shape of No 1 depended entirely on the pressure of the gas inside it, and we have already noted that any balloon which rises must lose gas. No 1 had a special relief valve for this purpose, but to maintain the pressure inside the envelope, under all conditions, an airpump was fitted to the motor, which replaced lost gas with air. Thus, though the airship might lose lift, it should not lose shape. Unfortunately this airpump was not up to its job.

As he descended, the envelope began to shrink and sag; and because it was a cylinder this caused it to bend in the middle, so that the tensions on the rigging lines became uneven. The rudder jammed, the ballast weights became unmanageable, and Santos found himself falling, with no means to check his speed.

Below him on the grass some big boys were flying kites. His guide-rope touched the ground near them, as they stared upwards in amazement.

He acted by instinct, leaning from the basket. "Pull it!" he shouted at the top of his voice, "Pull it into wind!" The rope, and his voice and gestures, acted like a conditioned reflex on the kite-flyers. They seized the guide-rope and raced against the wind. The check was enough to arrest the fall of No 1, and she sank gently to the grass, like a huge kite landing. Santos leapt nimbly out of the basket and scattered francs liberally among his gratified helpers. With their assistance he packed the deflated airship and its equipment, and when his anxious technical team joined him he had already hailed a couple of cabs, and was loading them for the return to the workshop.

Neither this abrupt landing, nor the earlier fiasco, produced any cooling of his elation and ardour. He had not yet overtaken the accomplishments of the Renard/Krebs electric airship, but he fully realised that the potentialities of his design went far beyond it. He was on the right track at last, with a source of power that would constantly improve, making success certain in the end. "I had performed every evolution prescribed by the problem. . . . I had mounted without sacrificing ballast. I had descended without sacrificing gas. My shifting weights had proved successful, and it would have been impossible not to recognise the capital triumph of these oblique flights. . . . The sentiment of success filled me: I had navigated the air!"*

One of Alberto's more endearing characteristics was this bouncing cockiness. Truth to tell, the first flights of No 1 were

* Dans l'Air. A. Santos-Dumont.

little advance on the feats of 20 years before. But they caught everyone's imagination from the very first, as if his dynamism had made it obvious that this was only a beginning. The Parisian man in the street began to hear of him for the first time, and sensed and responded to the ardour and courage of the little Brazilian. He himself was back in his workshop, deciding that he must do something drastic to prevent a recurrence of the mishap at Bagatelle, and already considering the design of *Santos-Dumont No 2*.

But this first attempt had aroused the greatest enthusiasm. The feeling had been abroad for some time that controllable flight was very near, and the sight of Santos steering *No 1* had brought expectancy to tip-toe. The professional aeronauts were still none too sure, but the South American world, and especially Brazil, was delirious with pride, though the official account from that country, written many years later, modestly records: "Said early experiments, as the Brazilian airman confesses, were very interesting, because it was the first time for the humming of a (petrol) motor to be heard in the air."*

He found himself something of a celebrity and a minor social figure, praised for his skill and daring, and more acceptable to the hostesses of Paris than the rougher and more grimy pioneers of his day, who had neither his accomplishments nor his social graces. Santos has been accused (if this is an accusation) of having a powerfully-developed flair for publicity, in which some said he gloried unduly. This sounds like simple envy. He unashamedly enjoyed the publicity which came his way, not being hag-ridden by the enforced modesty of the Anglo-Saxon; and sometimes he pandered to his public to an extent that hazarded his own life (though never, it should be noted, that of others). But he seldom went out of his way to gain credit. He was always markedly reserved, and sometimes painfully shy. He performed his experiments in the air over Paris because he lived and worked there, and also for good reasons which will emerge later; and it was therefore inevitable that he appeared before the largest and most brilliant grandstand in the world.

The Paris papers and magazines began to take notice of his feats in the autumn of 1898. While busy back in his workshop,

* A. Napoleão, translated by d'Oliveira.

considering the next steps, he was photographed and caricatured, the best-known sketches of him being drawn by the
well-known artist "Sem". This was the professional name of
Georges Goursat, at that time the most fashionable caricaturist
of famous men. Goursat struck up an acquaintance with Santos,
whilst drawing him in his workshop, and this soon became a
friendship closer than any he had made outside Brazil. It was a
little surprising that Santos should choose a man like this as an
intimate, rather than someone more in line with his own
devouring interests, for this was the most single-minded period
of his life, and now he lived and breathed only for aviation.

Georges Goursat, the son of a provincial grocer, was born at
Périgueux, in the Dordogne. He was thirty-six years old at this
time; ten years older than Santos. As a young man he tried his
luck as a cartoonist, first in Bordeaux, then in Marseille. He was
successful enough to come to Paris, where his style was quickly
appreciated and accepted. He was one of the first cartoonists to
use a strong characterisation of his own, rather than attempting
a portrait, and he caricatured the whole figure of his subject,
instead of concentrating on the face. He used no captions for
his drawings, another innovation at this time, and he considered
himself an expert on fashion. He took very seriously his self-
imposed role of adviser on this subject.

Later he also became a reporter, beginning with an article on
"Dogs' Island", off the Turkish coast, where the unwanted
dogs of Constantinople were deported to die. He followed this
with a sensational exposé of the clandestine dancing halls in
Paris, where society ladies could (and apparently did) meet
apaches, thugs, and prostitutes. He did not marry, and in spite
of his boundless opportunities for dalliance he appears to have
made no use of them. Naturally, he was a bon vivant, and a
keen man around town, in a harmless sort of way.

Santos too was fond of good food and good wine (though he
seldom drank except with his meals), and as he began to move
into the status of a minor celebrity he formed the habit of
meeting his friends at Maxim's, the famous restaurant in the rue
Royale. More than sixty years later the reputation of this great
establishment is as high as ever, and its décor has not changed in
any but the minutest details. In the dimly-lit interior dark wood
beams are supported by pillars heavily carved. Mirrors are let

into the walls, and wood and glass is etched with elaborate whirlicues, while those wall panels which do not reflect the diners are covered with paintings, of a type that in England would be attributed to the pre-Raphaelite influence. (This rich and sombre effect is now known to irreverent Parisians as *"Style Métro"*.) Each table is lit by a candle with a red shade, and the only other lighting comes from the ghostly blue flames of the little spirit stoves, as the ultimate cooking rites are performed before the bulging eyes of the patrons.

Here Santos might easily be imagined even now, at the corner table which is still remembered as his own, sitting with one or two companions enjoying the drawn-out courses and continuous conversation of a superb Parisian dinner. The bluish light would flicker on his glistening stiff front and high cylindrical collar, picking out his white teeth and sparkling eyes, his prominent shirt-cuffs and his white button-hole, while his high excited voice and expressive hands dominate the conversation, or he sits silent and remote, listening or wrapped in his own thoughts. At other tables men lean forward until their heads touch the cheeks of their dinner companions, to whisper and nod; and then ladies' heads turn, casually, carrying round with them a glitter of jewels or a high feather head-dress. Santos would pay no heed.

In 1899 he was twenty-six years old, and still unmarried. There is nothing particularly strange in this, for a young man with a mission in life. But he never was known to have even the most innocent flirtation, and he died a bachelor. In these coarse post-Freudian days we must face the question that is always asked in a case like this. Was Santos sexually normal? The answer admittedly is totally irrelevant, if we are only considering his flying exploits, but it is of the most vital importance in the portrait of him as a man.

Already there was some speculation among his acquaintances, and some enemies hinted that he was a homosexual. Havelock Ellis had just begun to publish his *Studies in Psychology of Sex*, and there was a good deal of ill-digested theory at large, avidly discussed in high society. The downfall of Oscar Wilde had been as great a sensation in France as in England, and Wilde himself was living in Paris.*

* Under the name of "Sebastian Melmoth".

Santos, if only by his dress and manner, laid himself open to suspicion. Careful research, however, into both his life and his character, utterly destroys this suggestion. Whatever may be the superficial opinion, that of the experts is entirely against it. His devotion to his father; his scientific and mechanical interests, and his indifference to the arts; above all the fact that, in a city where nothing could be kept secret for long, he lived continuously for sixteen years with a blameless character; all this is decisive.

He said himself, "that he never married because if he had the responsibilities of the head of a family, he would not feel able to hazard his life, in the venture which he had chosen as his lot".* This is scarcely good enough, and has certainly never weighed very heavily on even the most dangerous-living men, if they really wanted to marry. He was fond of children, and lacked the harsh asceticism of an Andrée, deliberately hurling temptation out of his path. He had, as his Brazilian biographers proudly point out, "the Latin temperament". He was sufficiently rich. Moreover, the problem was not merely that he did not marry, but that he seemed entirely disinterested in one half of the human race.

It seems conclusive, therefore, that Santos was that not uncommon, though seldom described type of man, not infrequently found among the wealthy and successful, who is sexually neutral. This blind spot had its advantages. It saved him time, emotional energy, involvement, responsibility; even, on the lowest level, money; but it greatly increased his nervous strain, and forced him to hug his burdens to himself. Later, when he had to face his last and greatest crisis, he faced it alone.

The causes of this condition, unless due to some obvious physical defect, are very obscure. It is significant, though, that in many cases there is a domineering mother somewhere in the past history. An extraordinary natural shyness, increased by parental repression, coupled with an almost pathological fastidiousness, may be just enough to keep the subject isolated. It seemed to do so in his case, but remembering his money, his opportunities, and his "Latin temperament", it must have been a very powerful repression, with some flavour of mystery to this day.

* Quem deu Asas ao Homem. H. Dumont-Villares.

It is probable that he was entirely unaware of this type of speculation, and would have been outraged by it. He was furiously busy. *No 1* had shown him that his first principles were right, or sufficiently so for him to go on. But after he had made sufficient flights to prove these principles he decided to build another airship, to incorporate the improvements that flooded into his mind. He realised, none better, that so far he had not done more than repeat the achievement of the Renard/Krebs airship, though indeed he had made more flights.

In the spring of 1899 therefore, *Santos-Dumont No 2* began to take shape under the eyes of Alberto, its designer, and the skilled hands of Chapin and the small team of mechanics which now worked permanently for him. He had recruited Gasteau, another general fitter, and Dozon, a *cordier-arrimeur* (rigger), plus two or three semi-skilled assistants. The pay-roll of his employees had to be satisfied from his own income, for nothing was being earned; and he had to be careful. Thus he did a great deal of practical work himself, rolling back his cuffs and filing and fitting with his workmen. They found this a likeable trait, and became very devoted to him. They saw that he did much of the work, and took all of the risks; that he understood everything better than they themselves did, and that he was always courteous, patient and clear in his instructions.

No 2 used a great deal of material from *No 1*, which therefore disappeared into the new model. The engine, propeller and basket were transferred complete. The gas-bag was larger, giving another 44 lb. of lift. But the great concern was to safeguard the arrangements to keep the airship taut. So he doubled his engine-driven airpump with another, and he also decided that pumping air into the hydrogen-filled envelope was not a good system.

He therefore designed an interior ballonet, which was sewn inside the gas-bag, intended to receive the pumped air, and by its inflation keep the main envelope tight. (See diagram.) The gas-filled part of the envelope had automatic blow-off valves, and so had the ballonet, but the latter's valve lifted at a lower pressure. By this means the air pumping into the ballonet maintained the pressure throughout the envelope, while if (as when ascending) the combined pressure of gas and air became too great, the air valve would lift and release air pres-

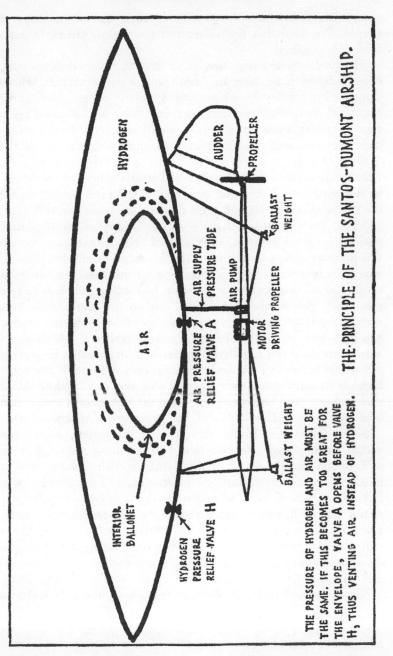

THE PRINCIPLE OF THE SANTOS-DUMONT AIRSHIP.

HYDROGEN

INTERIOR BALLONET

AIR

HYDROGEN PRESSURE RELIEF VALVE H

AIR PRESSURE RELIEF VALVE A

AIR SUPPLY PRESSURE TUBE

RUDDER

PROPELLER

BALLAST WEIGHT

AIR PUMP

MOTOR DRIVING PROPELLER

BALLAST WEIGHT

THE PRESSURE OF HYDROGEN AND AIR MUST BE THE SAME. IF THIS BECOMES TOO GREAT FOR THE ENVELOPE, VALVE A OPENS BEFORE VALVE H, THUS VENTING AIR INSTEAD OF HYDROGEN.

sure, without loss of hydrogen. It was an ingenious system, and simple. Provided that the valves and the pumps did their part, it would be effective.

The professional aeronauts, galvanised by his modest success, began talking of forming an Aero Club, a conception in whose timing one cannot avoid sensing a desire to produce some organised competition to the young Brazilian, who showed every sign of gaining a substantial lead over all his rivals. In the meantime they renewed their entreaties to him, to be careful of the dangers of explosion. M. Lachambre was as vehement as ever. "Do I dare strike matches in the basket of a spherical balloon?" he demanded, throwing out his arms. "Do I even permit myself the solace of a cigarette on trips that last for many hours?"

Santos, who smoked hardly at all, and that usually after periods of great tension, only smiled. His sole concession to this point of view was to ensure that his motor's exhaust pointed straight downwards. His confidence in himself was at high level, though his first taste of fame had lately induced him to wear dark glasses when he walked out on the boulevards. This showed, perhaps, some over-estimation of his celebrity status, and a curious mental confusion towards publicity, which alternately attracted and repelled him. He had little reason to worry, for at this moment Paris had attention only for one of the most burning controversies ever to convulse the city. While *No 2* was building, the Dreyfus Trial, after the wretched Captain had been five years on Devil's Island, had become the Affaire Dreyfus.

Santos-Dumont and his airship were forgotten, while the verbal battle raged. No-one talked of anything else. On 16th of February the President of the Republic, Félix Faure, died at home in slightly mysterious circumstances, and the anti-Dreyfus faction, of which he was known to be a member, promptly stated that he had been murdered by the pro-Dreyfus elements. The official story was that he had perished of a stroke, but a still stronger rumour suggested "that the President had simply died from over-exertions of a type dangerous to one of his age and physique".*

Santos refused to be drawn into these arguments. It was at a

* D. W. Brogan. His successor, President Loubet, was attacked at Auteuil ïaces, on June 14th, by Baron de Christiani, an anti-Dreyfus man, who smashed his top-hat with a walking stick.

time like this, when his nature, which hated cruelty and spite, withdrew him even further from his surroundings, that he felt himself more intensely a stranger in a foreign land. His love of his own country, and insistence on his nationality, grew more pronounced. For *No 2* he had another Brazilian flag made, and spent more time in the company of his principal Brazilian friend in Paris, Antônio Prado, son of the Ambassador. This minor estrangement, though temporary only, did not go unnoticed by the French aeronauts.

The first test of *No2* was set for the 11th of May, 1899, at the captive balloon station in the Jardin d'Acclimatation. The day dawned with rain and wind, but to Chapin's surprise Santos sent word to inflate the airship, and appeared shortly after this had been started. As there was no shed, the work was done in the open, and the long shape of *No 2* was soon filling out, bright yellow, and glistening with moisture. It was obviously going to be a vexatious day, with every kind of delay and difficulty, and once Santos had to speak sharply to one of his workmen, who had failed in some simple preparation.

First the inflation apparatus gave trouble; then a valve leaked and had to be dismantled, wasting a quantity of hydrogen. When the airship finally floated clear and the gas-filling trunk was removed, the engine was wet and refused to start. The spectators stood mute under a roof of dripping umbrellas, and everyone was damp, uncomfortable, and bad-tempered.

This must have been the chief reason for Santos persisting in his plan to fly that day; irritation swamping his better judgement. He also doubtless experienced a feeling, familiar and dangerous to test pilots in later years, that a long and tedious train of preparations must culminate in some action, come what may. This mental state has accounted for many a good airman; but even with these two excuses his decision to go on and fly was still wrong, though understandable. A last consideration was that if he postponed the flight until the next day he would have to sacrifice his fill-up of hydrogen.

Coughing and spluttering, the engine was coaxed to run, until it was hot enough to deal with the damp; when it hammered away bravely. It was raining harder than ever, and the wind was gusty. Ignoring the gloomy looks of Chapin, Santos mounted on board, and gave the order to cast off. As with every airship launch, the last job had been to ballast her so that she had just positive buoyancy; that is, a gentle impulse to rise. But weighed down by water, No 2 rose slowly. A fresh shower of cold rain rattled on her envelope, cooling the hydrogen and causing it to contract faster than the two pumps could inflate the air ballonnet to compensate.

The airship started to shrink, before even it had cleared the trees. Faster than No 1 had done, it began to fold in the middle. Before Santos could do anything at all a gust of wind seized it, doubled it up, and cast it into a row of trees. The engine stopped with a jerk. The wrecked airship slid slowly to the ground, in a sound of tearing silk and snapping branches. The rain drummed down on the debris. The first and only flight of No 2 was over.

Santos was very angry, and badly shaken. He was even more depressed, knowing well that the débâcle had been no-one's fault but his own. Back in the house on rue Washington he sat late and alone, brooding on the waste of time and money, and the probable reactions of his critics. These were not as sharp and wounding as they might have been, had the aeronauts not been passionately arguing, like everybody else, the pros and cons of the Dreyfus Affair.

In a matter of days, however, Santos displayed that buoyant recovery of spirits which served him so well for the best periods of his life. He began translating the fiasco into data for the building of the next airship. He worked still harder, and sat longer in his study, shading the gas-light to his desk, as the hours of darkness marched by. He went out seldom.

Antônio Prado, visiting him one evening, talked of the dangers he had already survived in his short career as an aeronaut. "Do you ever feel afraid?" he asked. Santos answered, yes, he did. "What do you do, then?" persisted Prado. Santos said: "I grow pale, and try to gain control of myself by thinking of other things. If I do not succeed, I feign courage before those watching me, and face the danger. But even so I am still afraid."

Chapter 7

☆☆☆☆☆☆☆☆☆☆☆☆☆☆☆☆☆☆☆☆☆☆☆☆☆☆☆☆☆

" Le Petit Santos "

The combined workshops of Lachambre and Machuron, and Santos-Dumont's own establishment in the rue de Colisée, spent most of the hot summer of 1899 working on the building of *No 3*. Far away in Dayton, Ohio, young Orville and Wilbur Wright, bicycle mechanics in a small way, had just discarded the idea that they might attempt to manufacture an automobile. The horseless carriage seemed a passing fad and an impractical idea to them, and they decided instead to turn their spare-time efforts to experiments with gliding.

Santos was satisfied with everything in his progress so far (proof of a durable spirit, in view of his record), except for the problem of rigidity. Conversely, the line of airship development in Germany had no difficulty on that score, but instead was grappling with a design that was rigid enough, and therefore too heavy to fly. It is strange to note, while examining this period of aviation, how little experimenters in different lands knew about each other's work. There were few learned bodies to disseminate information, and fewer journals and reviews. Though neither Santos nor his fellow-pioneers were particularly secretive, they heard next to nothing of those details which would have been so mutually helpful to them. The importance of this, to Santos in particular, will come out later.

No 3 was much shorter and fatter than her forebears, but with 500 cubic metres of gas space she had nearly three times the lift of *No 1*. Santos hoped that this would allow him to use the cheaper domestic coal-gas, instead of the more costly hydrogen. It would also free him from the indifferent service for filling with hydrogen, given by the balloon station at the Jardin d' Acclimatation, and allow him to refill at any point that had gas laid on. In the Paris of that time, this was to say almost anywhere.

He had likewise experienced more than enough of his envelope folding up on him, and determined that *No 3* should keep her shape. He hoped that the plumper gas-bag would be less liable to bending, and since the compensating airpumps had twice let him down he abandoned them. In addition he arranged short rigging lines from the envelope to be fixed to a longitudinal bamboo pole that lay close beneath it, running for most of the length of the airship. The basket was slung from this pole. Thus the airship had a backbone, though neither the envelope above nor the basket beneath were rigidly attached to it.

Otherwise it was very similar to *No 2*, with the same motor and propeller once more, so that *No 2* followed the fate of *No 1*, and was swallowed up in the next machine. With nothing new but the different envelope and rigging, and in fact simpler than *No 2*, the airship was easy to build, and ready for flight on the 13th of November, 1899. With only 48 days of the nineteenth century left to run, *No 3* was taken to Vaugirard and inflated with coal-gas.

Chapin was full of confidence in the new craft, and told his patron that he himself would like to fly in it. Santos patted his shoulder affectionately, but they both knew that none of the Santos-Dumont aerostats would carry more than one man, even if there were room for the burly Chapin in the passenger compartment, which was not much bigger than a laundry-basket.

No 3 made a good first take-off, in dull and chilly weather, and climbed easily upwards, heading towards the Champ de Mars. Though Chapin could not go, it is not too difficult to hover in imagination close behind the aeronaut's back, and follow him in the piloting of an elementary airship. The most successful flight to date is the best opportunity.

As the airship slopes upwards the pilot is already letting out his

forward balance weights, to bring her to an even keel. The
increased effectiveness of the weights, now rigged to the
bamboo pole, astonishes him, and he almost stands No 3 on her
tail in the first minute. The little engine chugs faithfully away,
clamped to the bracket just behind him, and the square-bladed
propeller pushes the engine and basket forward. Santos is
glancing quickly round, at the rigging, the envelope above,
back at the rudder, to see that all is well. The first moments of
flight with a new ship are even more critical in these early days,
when no established theory can give confidence to the aeronaut
before he leaves the ground.

Steady in level flight our airship builds up to a speed of about
12 miles per hour, though there is no exact way of measuring
the speed. The fat gas-bag above slides easily through the air,
demonstrating that a good streamline shape can be much thicker
for its length than was then suspected. Santos can see, by looking
upwards, that his basket is straining forward appreciably on its
rigging, and drawing the envelope along with it.

Over the Champ de Mars the pilot looks down. Here is the
big open space he needs for his test manoeuvres. He pulls on
his rudder-strings, and the large rudder leans far out to one side.
As it is placed outside the propeller wash the airship responds
sluggishly, but round she comes at last, Santos watching anxiously
for signs of strain or distortion in the rigging. Everything creaks
and bends alarmingly. The cords of the rigging stretch and
contract under the changing stresses.

He tries her left and right several times, skidding considerably
in the turns, his eyes sparkling as the gentle breeze of his passage
ruffles the hair beneath his cap, and bravely extends his small
flag. He can see people below, running and pointing; a tug on
the river blows a greeting on its siren, and the smoke of
November fires drifts up from ten thousand chimneys. Driving
No 3 to climb and dive, he masters the use of the shifting weights,
until he can control her better than either of the first two airships.

All the while he watches, screwing up his eyes, for the first
signs of misbehaviour from the gas-bag. She holds her shape well,
and gradually he relaxes. She wallows and pitches in a fashion
which would be disagreeable to most people, but Santos, who
is never seasick, makes nothing of it.

"I know that what one feels most distressingly at sea is not so much the movement . . . as the smells of the paint, varnish, tar, mingled with the odours of the kitchen, the heat of the boilers, and the stench of the smoke and the hold. In the airship there is no smell—all is pure and clean—and the pitching itself has none of the shocks and hesitations of the boat at sea. The movement is suave and flowing. . . . Indeed, I cannot describe the delight, the wonder, and intoxication of this free diagonal movement onward and upward or onward and downward, combined at will with brusque changes of direction horizontally when the airship answers to a touch of the rudder.''*

This last sentence may be attributed to poetic licence, or to a parental affection for his own brain-child. Truth to tell, by any normal standards (if any had existed) *No 3* must have been a pig to control. She lurched and skidded, and had a periodical pitching movement.† The piloting experience that Santos built up on these early airships eventually made him a master of touch, feel, anticipation, and lightning reaction. He was the first man ever to learn the advanced pilotage of a powered flying machine.

His musings, on this flight of 13th November, were cut short by the sudden consciousness that before him, grey, gaunt, and menacing in the cold light, the Eiffel Tower stretched its thousand feet into the wintry air. He shaped a course towards it at about half its height, and using it as a mark flew round and round it, at a respectful distance. Then he headed towards the Parc des Princes, scene of his tricycle race, and so unknowingly covered the course of the test which would later give him so bitter a struggle.

The airship was still behaving perfectly, so he did not land at the Velodrome. He turned for Bagatelle, where the kite-fliers had saved him a year before, and came gently down to the ground level, where his guide-rope was seized by a dozen eager hands. As he stopped the engine he heaved a sigh of pure happiness. It was the first time, after three dangerous and humiliating crashes, that he had ended a trip by stepping with dignity from the basket of a whole airship. He had cruised over Paris at his will, and landed safely at the place of his choice. He tasted some reward at last, for his pertinacity and courage.

* *Dans l'Air*. A. Santos-Dumont.
† Known to early aviators as "*Montagnes russes*".

Everyone who knew Santos had some different view of him; some opinions bewilderingly varied and even contradictory. But all were at one concerning his physical bravery. He managed to combine this with a curious primness, like a maiden aunt going over Niagara Falls in a barrel. The man who could say "I feign courage . . . and face the danger", not only proved his words a hundred times over, but gave a very important clue to the tensions and stresses within him, of the fight between the animal instinct that says "Go back!" and the mind that insists "Go on!" The unfortunate beginnings of his flying career put his courage to the iron test.

After he alighted, *No 3* was kept for a while floating at her mooring rope. She was fit to fly again immediately if necessary, thought Santos. The crowds surrounding her grew, while his friends and helpers arrived breathless, to load him with a thousand congratulations. "Such effortless ease!" they cried, "And on the thirteenth too!" Santos-Dumont smiled more widely at this. He had no superstition about the thirteenth, but for some reason which he would never divulge he dreaded the number eight instead.

As there was nowhere to put her safely away, the crew now had to release the gas from *No 3*. This was the first time they had ever done so, the other airships ending in a state where the emergency rip valve had been operated, to reduce them quickly to a shapeless and tangled mass. But watching *No 3* deflating, Santos realised for the first time that if only he had a shed he could park her like a car in a garage. She had lost no gas in her flight, and it hurt him to see it go to waste now. With him, to see was to think, and to think was to act. He determined to build an airship hangar.

The Aéro Club de France had been finally founded in 1898, under the Presidency of Comte Albert de Dion, who had earlier founded the Automobile Club.* It need hardly be said that Santos was an early and most enthusiastic member. The Club's first action was to buy land at the Coteaux de Longchamp at St. Cloud, to be used for general aviation purposes, and this opportunity fixed his attention. He was riding on one of his periodic peaks of optimism: "I foresaw that I was going into

* Other founder members were Prince Roland Bonaparte, Gustave Eiffel, M. de Fouvielle, Comte Henri de la Vaulx, and the Comte de la Vallette.

airship construction as a sort of life work." He needed a proper workshop, a balloon and airship house or hangar, a hydrogen plant, and connection with the gas mains. Leave it to Santos-Dumont. It will all be arranged.

Meanwhile there were more trips with *No 3*, widely spaced because of the winter weather, and because he had learnt caution in defying the wind and the rain. He could now fairly claim to have greatly surpassed the Renard/Krebs airship. As the twentieth century dawned, to the tune of rejoicings which might have been stilled if the revellers had known what was in store during the next fifty years (though in fact the customary centennial prediction of the end of the world was not omitted), the fat shape of *No 3* became a familiar sight over Paris, and the fame of its designer knew no bounds.

He had arrived. Everybody talked of *"Le Petit Santos"*. His suits were copied, and his hats and ties. His high white collars were known as "Santos-Dumonts". His life was examined, and the details printed, but since this was before the refined technique of the journalistic "profile", the results are disappointingly meagre. He was interviewed and quoted, and duly predicted the coming of great aerostats as large as liners, plying between the continents, heavily decorated with mirrors, candelabra, and plush, with every luxury furnished to the fortunate passengers. Or if he did not say exactly these things, the journalists supplied the deficiency.

His friends too were interviewed, and rose nobly to the occasion. "He has the agility of a cat, the sure feet of a climber, and the hands of an engineer," graciously explained the Marquis de Soriano to an attentive reporter. "He is always very smartly dressed, he has a shrill, eager voice, an extraordinarily restless manner, a pale, refined face, and large, serious-looking eyes."

"He is assertive, sure of himself, and argumentative to a degree," stated one informant positively. "He will not brook opposition, and if someone makes a statement he disagrees with he will tell him brusquely that if he doesn't know he had better shut up. He is not immediately attractive as a personality."

"He is extremely shy and reserved," countered Georges Goursat. "He is always the soul of courtesy, and so unsure of himself that he would rather face a firing-squad than speak a few words in public."

It is the fate of celebrities to be misrepresented, but there were honest reasons for these contradictions. There was a certain amount of jealousy at large, due in some degree to his being a foreigner, but it was not excessive, and most of the many statements to the press were sincere. He was indeed a complicated and many-sided personality, already just a shade unbalanced, and apparently almost as much a mystery to his contemporaries as he is to the present day. He adapted himself so well to different sorts of company that each section thought it knew the real Santos-Dumont. Probably none of the mirrors held up to his reflection gave a true picture of the solemn, dedicated young man of twenty-seven years, alone in No 9 rue Washington, working late over his papers at a desk with a shaded light.

"I foresaw that I was going into airship construction as a sort of life work." In the same practical way as he had organised his private life, Santos now decided that he must organise his chosen destiny. He duly obtained permission from the Aéro Club to build an airship base on their land at St. Cloud. They were a little reluctant, but he went through them like a buzz-saw through softwood. Before they had realised exactly what had happened, his pegs were in the grass at the new location, and he was at work on the ground-plans. When they realised the full extent of his project, jaws dropped and beards were tugged in anguish. But it was then too late.

He positioned the hydrogen-plant, engine workshops, storage buildings, and experimental workshop, and most important of all, the airship hangar. This he called an "aerodrome", following the loose current use of Greek compounds including "drome", to mean enclosure. It was not until later that the meaning of the word spread to embrace, as in the present Oxford Dictionary definition, an airfield with all its buildings and hangars.

The great airship shed was his masterpiece, and cost him more money than even he could well afford. It was designed of wood, 100 feet long, 25 feet wide, and 36 feet high. It was to hold his present and immediately projected airships, fully in-flated, and Santos designed large sliding doors which would open up one end completely, so that the airship could be walked out ready to fly. He remarked rather ingenuously that he had to undertake all this entirely at his own expense, forgetting perhaps that the land purchased by the Aéro Club was almost immediately dominated by his airship station, and that while he was undeniably ahead of his rivals he was not, by a very long way, the only pioneer in the field. There were even some grumbles among the members, that the Aéro Club seemed to have been created for the convenience of M. Santos-Dumont.

He was in fact very much of a lone hand. He did not encourage equal co-operation with others in his work, and his money freed him from the need to consult financial backers. He therefore showed a certain understandable, if irritating desire to have it both ways, when he treasured his independence while at the same time deploring that he was not receiving any financial assistance. He never put this problem to the test by making definite advances to official or semi-official bodies for funds. It is unlikely that such approaches would have succeeded with French institutions, which would certainly have preferred to back a Frenchman, had one been available. And if he had succeeded in arranging some financial backing, the chances are strong that he would speedily have regretted it, and quarrelled with his backers.

This appears to be the inevitable relationship between genius and its support, since the end of the great days of patronage by high persons. The genius is a special sort of person, and the public body that controls money is definitely a special (and usually dreary) sort of creature, and the two are as antipathetic as oil and water. When the genius in question has nearly enough funds of his own, the effect is still worse. Despite his wistful glances at the big money-bags, Santos was probably fortunate to avoid entanglements at this time. And it must be emphasised, in fairness to him, that though he rejected collaboration he did not make any secret of his own methods, and neither now nor later (except in one special case) did he take out patents, or make any of the conventional moves to turn his work into a financial advantage.

After his personal qualities, this independence was probably his greatest asset and the reason why he kept a short head in front of those others who were now in the race to fly a controllable machine. For it must never be forgotten, as his own

Henriques Santos-Dumont
(*Courtesy of A. Dumont-Villares*)

Dona Francisca
(*Courtesy of A. Dumont-Villares*)

The serious student—Santos-Dumont at 19   (*Courtesy of A. Dumont-Villares*)

Number One in flight
(*Courtesy of A. Dumont-Villares*)

Santos-Dumont with basket and motor of *Number One*

Santos-Dumont with M. de Rothschild after first accident to *Number 5*
(*Courtesy of A. Dumont-Villares*)

The end of *Number 5* in the light-well of the Trocadero
(*Courtesy of A. Dumont-Villares*)

The Deutsch Prize

Number 6 passing the Eiffel Tower, and approaching the finish line

(*Courtesy of A. Dumont-Villares*)

Number 9 in rue Washington   (*Collection Exempler*)

Number 9 at the army review   (*Collection Harlingue*)

Santos-Dumont in front of the Neuilly hangar (*Radio Times Hulton*)

Santos-Dumont driving an ostrich and trap (*Library of Congress*)

The Evolution of *Number 14 bis*   "A monstrous hybrid"
(Courtesy of A. Dumont-Villares)

Before the first flight   *(Courtesy of A. Dumont-Villares)*

Before the flight of November 12, 1906. Note Chapin, left, and the new ailerons
(Courtesy of the Science Museum, London)

country's officially-sponsored accounts inevitably do forget, that he was not the only airship pioneer. In Germany, while Santos was building his "aerodrome", LZ-1 was almost ready to fly; a large (420 feet long) fully rigid airship, with two Daimler-Benz motors. A Frenchman named Gaudron had flown a powered balloon at the Alexandra Palace, north of London, in May 1898, admittedly to no great effect; and attempts in the same direction had been made by Spencer in England, Carl Myers in U.S.A., and Sauter in Switzerland.* The stimulus of the potted power of the internal combustion engine was having its inevitable effect everywhere. Man, that busy little animal, was persistently at work, rooting out the secrets that would give him the means for his further glory and destruction.

The first spring of the new century (or the last spring of the old, as some pedants insist) saw a great upsurge in scientific progress in France, where the threads of many separate lines of advance, not solely in aviation, now mingled and flowed forward to practical advantage. It was to be the year of the Great Exposition, designed to outshine those of 1878 and 1889. It was, moreover, the year in which flying ceased to be the wild dream of madmen, or at best eccentrics, and (in France at any rate) focused the attention of substantial citizens of wealth and standing. While Santos-Dumont's workmen laboured at St. Cloud, and the inventor himself divided his time between excursions in his electric buggy to the scene of the building, and flights above it in No 3, on to the centre of the scene came one of the first members of the Aéro Club de France.

Monsieur Henri Deutsch de la Meurthe was a rich man with many interests, chief of which was the refinement of oil, paraffin, and petroleum. He was a shining example of a type of Frenchman (the Comte de Dion was another) of which France may well be proud: wealthy but highly intelligent, broad-minded, and visionary. He was born into a powerful Jewish family of engineer-financiers, who laid the foundations of the French oil industry; but his abilities while still a student showed that he had no special need of this flying start.

He was an accomplished sportsman, an excellent shot, and a

* This relationship between the different lines of airship invention is best set out in *A History of Flying*. C. H. Gibbs-Smith.

musician who fostered struggling composers,* himself compos-
ing a number of symphonic works, and an opera (*Icare*) which
was produced at the National Academy of Music. He very
quickly understood the potentiality of the petrol engine,
founding a Petroleum Museum, and publishing a book on the
subject. In 1887 he sponsored the building of an "explosion
motor". He presented one of the first petrol automobiles ever
to be made, to President Carnot. As early as 1889 he publicly
stated that ". . . in the petrol engine lies the solution to the
problem of aerial navigation". His keen and brilliant brain and
boundless enthusiasm were engagingly blended with a volcanic
and highly excitable temperament.

At a meeting of the Committee of the Aéro Club, in April
1900, M. Deutsch de la Meurthe made an announcement. To
commemorate the start of the new century, which would undoubtedly see the dawn of a fresh era, of inestimable benefit to
mankind; and inspired by the example of the forthcoming
Great Exposition, he offered a prize of 100,000 francs (about
£6,000) for an aeronautical achievement, the details of which
he would work out with the Scientific Commission of the Club.
The President of this body was no less a celebrity than Prince
Roland Bonaparte, and after suitable consultation it was announced that, "the prize would be awarded to the first dirigible
balloon or airship that between 1st of May and 1st of October
in 1900, 1901, 1902, 1903 or 1904 should rise from the Parc
d'Aérostation of the Aéro Club at St. Cloud and, without
touching ground and by its own self-contained means on board
alone, describe a closed curve in such a way that the axis of the
Eiffel Tower should be within the interior of the circuit, and
return to the point of departure in the maximum time of half
an hour." Breathless but triumphant, the Commission beamed
on the members who had assembled to hear this announcement,
and M. Deutsch himself was warmly congratulated by everyone
present. Santos, pressing forward to add his own tribute, wrung
M. Deutsch by the hand, while registering a mental vow that
the prize would be his.

Putting this large sum up for competition caused an immediate

* An enterprise in which he was linked with H.S.H. Prince Albert of
Monaco, and the Comtesse Greffulhe (a lady who later served as the model
for Proust's Duchess de Guermantes).

sensation. The Scientific Commission added, as an afterthought, that if the prize remained unclaimed the interest on the money deposited by M. Deutsch would be awarded, year by year, to the flying achievement which the Commission deemed most creditable. This was named the Encouragement Prize.

Santos returned to his study in a fever of plans and projects. He rapidly calculated the distance to be covered in the course for the Deutsch Prize (7 miles). To do this in under thirty minutes he would need a speed of 14 m.p.h. in still air. *No 3* was too slow. He must design a new and faster airship, and he must have his aerodrome completed as quickly as possible, for he wanted to build the new model there, and have all his organisation about him. He therefore pushed on the construction as fast as he could, but found to his chagrin that the builders, who refused to work night-shifts, did not have the devotion of his own team of mechanics.

Meanwhile he must gain all possible experience with *No 3*, and he flew her on every available day. But he realised that she was too fat and clumsy, and his faithful little motor, which had served him in three airships, was too weak for the speed he wanted. So when he lost his rudder on the last of these trips, and was compelled to descend, softly but out of control, on the plain of Ivry, he decided not to repair her. Everything must be concentrated on the building of *No 4*, as soon as the great hangar was ready.

He was becoming more intolerant of advice. And he seems to have taken a strong dislike to his building contractors. "Even here" (at St. Cloud) "I had to contend with that conceit and prejudice of artisans which had already given me so much trouble at the Jardin d'Acclimatation. It was declared that the sliding doors of my aerodrome could not be made to slide, on account of their great size. I had to insist. 'Follow my directions,' I said, 'and do not concern yourselves with their practicability!' Although the men had named their own pay, it was a long time before I could get the better of this vainglorious stubbornness of theirs. When finished the doors worked, naturally."

The last sentence is pure Santos.

Chapter 8

☆☆☆☆☆☆☆☆☆☆☆☆☆☆☆☆☆☆☆☆☆☆☆☆☆☆☆☆☆

The Great Exposition

Early in 1900, when a young and unknown Spanish painter named Picasso was arriving in Paris, the Great Exposition of 1900 started to gather momentum. Unlike other exhibitions held before it, such as that at the Crystal Palace in 1851, the showmanship was not confined to a single building, but spread on both sides of the Seine, from La Concorde to the Trocadero, and from Invalides to the Champs-Elysées. The main exhibition gate at the Place de la Concorde (there were 35 other gates) was an enormous Persian-Byzantine arch, surmounted by a statue, 6 metres high, representing *"La Parisienne"*. Her dress was designed by Patou.

The Grand Palais was filled to bursting with the scientific and industrial genius of France, while there were pavilions in the shape of pagodas, castles, and temples, and a wealth of cupolas, domes, campaniles, spires and minarets. Three large stone bears decorated the roof of the Finnish Exhibition, while the Dutch pavilion was guarded by sitting idols (one bearing the plaque *Avertisseur d'incendie* affixed by the Paris Fire Department). In the Madagascar Pavilion the orchestra of the Queen of Madagascar played the waltz from *Faust*. The Palace of Electricity, a rococo monster of shattering vulgarity and magnificence, glittered with gilding by day and with electric lamps by night.

An immense Wheel, 300 feet high, with wire spokes so thin that they were nearly invisible, carried passengers in forty cars to a height where they could see the floodlights illuminating the principal buildings of *La Ville Lumière*.

The new Paris *Métro* was opened by President Loubet, and the thousands of visitors could also use a surface electric train (whose driver, to the horror of the Académie, was called "*le wattman*") to carry them round the pavilions. In addition there was a rolling pavement, which moved at 5 m.p.h.

A new bridge over the Seine, in the heart of Paris, so adorned with triumphant statuary as to seem one great exclamation mark, was named "Pont Alexandre III" for the Tzar of Russia, and opened by the President and Prince Ouroussoff. Among the hundreds of lesser exhibits were a complete Dahomey village; a representation of the Algerian Casbah, seething with leather workers, copper beaters, and carpet makers; a Cambodian sacred mountain and pagoda, a Siberian village, and a British Indian pavilion where, among carpets, ricebags and silks, a mechanical piano, sculpted with Hindu deities, played jigs. There was an upside-down manor with the furniture fixed to the ceilings, a Swiss village, a Boer village, and every kind of national theatre and dance-hall. It was the fair of fairs.

Monsieur Picard, Commissaire-Général of the Exposition, outlined its objective: "The Exposition of 1900 must epitomise the feeling and the philosophy of the age, which is a compound of grandeur, grace, and beauty; which reflects the clear genius of France, showing herself, as in the past, the foremost nation in the march of progress."

"This noble dream" went on the *Guide Officiel de l'Exposition*, discarding all false modesty, "is now realised. In the perfect programme, precisely arranged, our eyes can behold that which the thinker has conceived, and the engineers have wished for. Never before has so splendid a spectacle been offered for human admiration. Never has our country better shown the fecundity of her resources, the strength of the efforts of those who serve her, both artists and technicians and also simple workmen, united into one splendid demonstration."

One imagines the writer letting out his breath, at the end of this intoxicating sentence, and draining a *fine* before resuming his task. "At the head of the programme one places education and teaching; for it is by these that man enters upon the world; it is the source of all progress. Immediately after come the works of art and genius. We give third place to literature and science, and after them come the great manufacturers of today, the most powerful agents of industrial progress. We will show the construction and decoration of houses and public buildings; spinning, textiles and clothing, the chemical industry, and all kinds of diverse manufacture." The *Guide* continued with a catalogue embracing most of the man-made features of the existing world.

Reading through this prospectus of material Paradise, Santos was delighted to see that an Aviation exhibition was included. He could also find mention of balloon developments; experiments in colour photography, in radio; and even a guarded prediction of the future possibilities of television. Electricity was queen of this city-wide ball. "Once an elusive fairy, electricity has become an all-powerful sovereign, invested by human genius with an infinite might . . . for the central motive of the Palace, admirably created by Monsieur Henaud, Electricity, like Phoebus Apollo, launches herself through space, conducted by a horse and a flying dragon . . ." The *Guide Officiel* is almost airborne itself, on barely controllable wings of rhetoric.

The many groups of exhibition sculpture followed the pattern hallowed by custom. Regal and scantily-draped females, and muscular-torsoed males, represented Agriculture, Industry, Astronomy, and so on. One of these groups depicted Physics and Petroleum presenting the Internal Combustion Engine to Aviation, under the benign eye of a correctly-dressed gentleman who might have been Science, Achievement, or even President Loubet.

On the 14th of April, 1900, the President of the Republic opened the Exposition. Nothing was ready. It had rained the night before, and the officials had to jump over puddles while making their tour. Workers had been feverishly active until the last minute, and some of the scaffoldings had been taken down and hidden inside the pavilions. The next day they were put up again, and many buildings were not opened to the public for another six weeks.

This was such a summer as Paris had never known before. The Old World still supported a score or more of costly crowns upon royal heads, and most of them came to the Great Exposition. Only England, embarrassed by the Boer War, and sombre in the last years of the great Queen, held aloof from the fair.

Santos was in his element. He could spend his mornings at St. Cloud with his workmen, drawing, explaining, arguing with Chapin, or rolling back his large shirt-cuffs to pick up a tool, and file or saw some special fitting. When the morning grew hot he could leave the sheds and mount again on to his reliable electric buggy, and with the simple pressure of one foot send it whirring away down the road, to luncheon with a friend at a restaurant in the Bois.

After an excellent meal, at which he would pick his dishes carefully (being now rather faddy about food and careful of his figure), he could sit over coffee and a cognac and discuss the latest mechanical wonders spread out in such profusion throughout the Exposition. And later still he could be away, with Goursat or Prado, to visit a lecture, or to examine some particular exhibit more closely, or to meet a visiting savant.

In the evening the demands of society claimed him more and more. At the countless receptions and soirées he was very definitely The Thing, one of the lions of this season-of-all-seasons. His charm and his exquisite manners ensured his popularity, while his periodic reluctance to talk about his exploits could be overcome without unduly tedious difficulty. Yet while he bowed and chattered with the best, and twirled his gloves and paid his compliments, it cannot be denied that he was a bird of a different colour, whose difference stood out even in that variegated company.

Parisian Society, headed by its Arbiters of Elegance, Le Comte Boni de Castellane and his American Comtesse, had long worn that air of "fast" brilliance which was later to transmit itself, through the Paris-loving Edward VII, to Edwardian England. Social historians were to see in it much the same pictures of golden pleasure as haunt the memories of those who can recall England in the first decade of the twentieth century.

"It was the time of a Europe joyful, opulent, rich, undisturbed, living for amusement in the happy dramas of adulteries and sensual restlessness, whose tender epics made the heart beat. Enshrined in placidity and engulfed in peace, the women dreamed of love, and the men thought of pleasure. Passion was in general inhibited in women by the constant presence of a cruel jailer; the corset, tragic armour of iron and ugly whalebone. Tender meetings were made complicated or impossible, when the lover could not always possess the necessary skill of an expert lady's maid."*

Allowing something for journalistic licence, this still sounds hardly the milieu for a Santos-Dumont. But he took it all in his stride, moving confidently from ball to supper-party, restaurant to salon, dexterously and almost unconsciously evading the tentative advances that must have come his way. Indeed one is tempted to assume that if any lady had complained to him of the tightness of her corset he would have excused himself with perfect grace, returned to his study in the rue Washington, and sketched out a design for an improvement. Yet all the while his thoughts were fixed on the Deutsch Prize, and his new airship.

Santos-Dumont No 4 was a compromise between the dangerously pliable forms of his first two designs, and that of the portly but reliable *No 3*. It was nearly twice as long as its predecessor, half the diameter, and had four-fifths of the cubic capacity. But it was intended to use the greater lifting power of hydrogen, for now that Santos had his own generating plant he no longer saw advantage in the use of coal-gas. And he wanted more lift for the more ambitious construction system of *No 4*.

The envelope still had the same attachment method for the suspension lines, and they were still rigged on to the bamboo spar from *No 3*, to give semi-rigidity. But there was no basket slung below; instead the longitudinal spar was equipped with cross-pieces and verticals, on which were mounted the engine, fuel-tanks, ballast and controls. The propeller, turning at 100 r.p.m., was a new design, of fabric stretched on a frame-work, and was much larger than his old ones. It was mounted, as a pulling or "tractor" airscrew, at the forward end of the spar, and had the engine connected to it by a long shaft.

This appeared to leave no place for the aeronaut, and in fact it seemed almost as if Santos had forgotten about himself, until the very last moment. He overcame this deficiency by mounting, on the spar, an ordinary bicycle saddle, which was to be his position while flying. MM. Lachambre and Machuron, those

* *La Haute Société.* Gabriel-Louis Pringue.

sturdy traditionalists, were aghast at the very thought of this arrangement, but they were required now only to fulfil the designer's specifications.

"I was obliged to sit in the midst of the spider web below the balloon on the saddle of a bicycle frame which I had incorporated into it. Thus the absence of the traditional balloon basket appeared to leave me astride a pole in the midst of a confusion of ropes, tubes, and machinery. Nevertheless, the device was very handy, because round this bicycle frame I had united cords for controlling the shifting weights, for regulating the motor's speed, for opening and shutting the balloon's valves, for turning on and off the water-ballast spigots, and certain other functions of the airship. . . . For steering, my hands reposed on the bicycle handlebars connected with the rudder."*

This terrifying arrangement, which must have been anything but reposeful, had a very definite appearance of the fantastic, particularly when it was seen that the inventor's feet rested on bicycle pedals, with which he intended to turn the engine if he needed to re-start it in mid-air. However, it was practical enough, provided no bumping or swaying threatened to unseat the rider, and provided the rider had the courage of a Santos. In practice his precarious perch, clinging to the bicycle, seemed to cause him no concern, but he found that he did not have the freedom of action permitted by a basket, and the saddle was left out of his later models.

The main envelope was pointed front and back, and the internal ballonet, that villain of the earlier airships, was restored once more, together with the pumps to inflate it. Santos was now more confident of his machinery and valves, and he could not rely on the slimmer shape of No 4 staying rigid without some help. The pointed bow and stern were visible proofs of the current lack of understanding of basic aerodynamics; and this in turn raises one of the minor mysteries of early aviation.

Why did the pioneers pay so little attention to the science of ship design? It is true enough, and it was well understood, that air and water do not obey the same laws, but there was a great deal to be learned from hydrodynamics, and it is not unreasonable to suppose that the early aeronauts might at least have looked at the subject. It would have been more valuable still to

* *Dans l'Air.* A. Santos-Dumont.

the heavier-than-air researchers. They could at least have deduced the elementary fact that the rudder works best at the rear of the ship.

To drive *No 4* a new motor had been constructed, on much the same lines as the old faithful, now finally put aside. It was placed just in front of the handlebars, where it annoyed its natty owner by sprinkling him with hot oil. This first experience with a tractor airscrew and engine in front was going to be dirty, windy, and noisy, and the antithesis of most of the things which Santos enjoyed in airship travel.

But by August of the Exposition year he was able to show *No 4* assembled and ready, in his own airship shed at St. Cloud. She was the first move in his avowed intention to win the Deutsch Prize, but he was also most anxious to show her to the meeting which for him would be the high spot of the Exposition: the International Congress of Aeronautics, sponsored by the Aéro Club de France. Her first flight was successful, and the inventor and his team had the delightful experience of walking her out of her new shed, already inflated, launching her on her test over Paris, and finally recovering her and walking her back into the hangar again.

This was practical flying at last. After the test she floated in the shed, still taut with hydrogen, as unconcerned as a horse waiting in its stable for the next outing. To Santos this achievement was the fulfilment of his first dreams, and worth any amount of noise and discomfort.

He made a number of ascents with *No 4*, in August and September, to the immense enthusiasm of the visitors to the Exposition and, in fact, of the residents of Paris also. The Congress of Aviation began in September, one of 130 congresses held in the Congress Palace: (they included a Vegetarian Congress, a Peace Congress, a Socialist Congress, a Firemen's Congress; a Medical Congress with 12,000 doctors, and a Feminist Congress which broke up in disorder during the final banquet). Naturally enough the star of the Congress of Aviation was the Brazilian aeronaut overhead. For while they were reading papers on aerostation and gliding, navigation and power plants, controls and materials—some wildly inaccurate (one expert flatly insisting that heavier-than-air flight would never be possible) Santos was above them, controlling and navigating his materials and power plant—misguided and mistaken enough in many of his ideas, but trying, making practical attempts, sometimes succeeding and always learning.

Many interesting characters participated in the International Congress of Aeronautics. They ranged through simple crackpots and earnest bigots, to wealthy and influential industrialists beginning to take an interest in aviation, like Deutsch and Archdeacon, and practical scientists who wanted only luck or a little more application to solve the enigma of heavier-than-air flight. The brothers Wright were not there, being hard pressed to raise the price of a railway ticket from Dayton, Ohio, to North Carolina, where they were just beginning their gliding experiments.

But a prominent American had come, none other than Professor Langley, whose experiments brought him so near to success that he is assessed by C. Gibbs-Smith as "the unluckiest aero-inventor in history". Samuel Pierpont Langley, mathematician, astronomer, and Secretary of the Smithsonian Institution in Washington, now in his sixties, had been experimenting with model aeroplanes for fifteen years. He had built more than thirty models powered by elastic, conducted experiments with aerofoils on a rotating table, and in 1891 had published *Experiments in Aerodynamics*.

Undeterred by many failures, he had adapted small high-performance steam engines to bigger and bigger models, until in 1896 he succeeded in flying an unmanned model for three-quarters of a mile. The United States Government, which so far had placidly ignored him, was galvanised by the Spanish War into making him a grant for the development of a full-size machine. He chose a petrol engine for this project, and was working on it when he appeared at the Congress.* He can certainly be counted as a very scientific, experienced, and well-informed delegate.

This wealth of aviation talent was as anxious to see Santos in action as he naturally was to show his paces. Unfortunately the proceedings of the Congress were very ponderous, and it was therefore only free for one day after *No 4* was ready. By bad luck the 19th of September, the day in question, was rough and windy, and even Santos did not dare let the airship off her

* *A History of Flying*. C. H. Gibbs-Smith.

mooring ropes. Indeed, while he was running up the engine outside the hangar, a gust swung her against a cable and broke off the rudder. However, he had been able to show that she could hold her own by engine power against the strongish wind then blowing, and the members of the Congress declared themselves much impressed. They had seen Santos before in flight, passing far above their heads.

He showed them all around his workshops, as a consolation for the cancelled flying, and Professor Langley was sufficiently interested to ask for a separate visit. He therefore returned alone three days later, watched Santos make a short test flight, lunched with him at the workshop, and spent the afternoon discussing aviation.

Their respective researches lay along very different lines. Langley had given little effort to lighter-than-air craft, and Santos had barely considered heavier-than-air. This contrast between the rather grim old man from the Smithsonian and the mercurial young Brazilian was less interesting, perhaps, than the difference between the two approaches to their problems. Langley was a sound, practical engineer, whose contributions to the discovery of flight can hardly be overestimated. Santos was practical too, but he was also a dreamer and visionary, and his work was so erratic that its value to the conquest of the air is very debatable. Yet he was flying, and Langley was not. It is true that Langley was an old man, and an unlucky one. But it seems as if fortune keeps some special prize for the Doers, which she denies to the Thinkers, even if, as in the case of Andrée, the prize is only a dramatic end.

Professor Langley congratulated Santos warmly, and gave him "the heartiest kind of encouragement", and then they parted, and Langley sailed again for America, where he was to meet his last and bitterest disappointments.

No 4 was out and flying on almost every suitable day. Santos found her handy and not too difficult to control. While his means for going up and down was still based on the shift of centre of gravity by sandbags, his main ballast, and that very little, was contained in a water tank, which he could empty by merely turning a tap.

More and more the citizens below were subjected to the unnerving sight of *No 4* chugging by overhead, with the inventor clearly visible apparently riding a bicycle below the envelope, steering by the handlebars, and by winding his ballast bags in and out, and seemingly not far removed from Blondin on his tightrope. There is no record of any safety-strap or harness ever being incorporated in this frightening rig. It is not surprising that the testimonials to his courage were so many and so sincere.

He was busily experimenting: with controls, motor, techniques of landing and of rising from the ground, and general handling. But the goal for all this work was to be the Deutsch Prize. After a few weeks he decided that *No 4* was still not quite fast enough. She could win the prize in theory, but in practice the margin was too small. He was going to need yet another airship.

He started by fitting *No 4* with a new engine of four air-cooled cylinders constructed for him by M. Buchet, to an arrangement of his own design. He found, however, that this was too heavy for the airship, and he would need more gas to lift the more powerful engine. He therefore cut the envelope of *No 4* in half, and let a new section into the middle, as was disastrously done to the British dirigible *R.101* thirty years later. Next he realised that his hangar was too short to hold the enlarged airship, and he had to build fourteen feet more on to it. The Exposition year was running out, and Santos and his men worked like demons. The engine fitting, the airship envelope lengthening, and the addition to the hangar were all finished in fourteen days.

They were spurred by signs of the final phase of the summer's junketings, inaugurated by President Loubet's banquet to the Mayors of France. For this monster repast, held late in September in the Tuileries gardens, 36,000 mayors were invited, of whom some 22,000 turned up. The organisers supervised the setting of the tables by going round in an automobile. 22,000 hat-racks were built, so that each mayor could hang his hat next to his place at table. The waiters were instructed to pass every dish twice, and to be very generous with the wines. The mayors devoured hors-d'oeuvres, salmon, fillet of beef, duck, roast chicken, pheasant, salad, ices, cheese, fruits, petit fours, coffee, cognac, and rum. The affair was a huge success, and Santos, returning from St. Cloud, was held up for several minutes by the 22,000 mayors, very convivial, who were escorting the President home to the Elysée Palace.

Before saying goodbye to *No 4* it is worth mentioning that she received so much publicity and was photographed so often, in the Exposition autumn, that most of the world's newspapers used her picture for illustrating later news items about Santos, despite the fact that the stories may have involved a totally different airship.

There were more modifications to come, in the gradual process of turning *No 4* into *No 5*, but when the main alterations were done Santos had her inflated in the shed, and made ready to fly. The Exposition was still open. But now a period of impossible weather set in, and day after day he was compelled to watch gloomily from the window of his workshop, while the high winds and rains of autumn cut the leaves from the trees, and whirled them in arabesques across the sodden grass of St. Cloud.

The Exposition, too, was staggering slightly, as its appointed period drew near. It was beginning to suffer the hangover common to large fairs, in their last days of life. The exhibits looked worn, and when they needed attention it was no longer worthwhile to repair them. The main ceremonies were over, and the most important delegates gone.

After two weeks of waiting, Santos gave up for the year. He deflated his airship and removed the engine and propeller assembly for test in his workshop. He wanted speed, and he meant to boost the power. He therefore rigged up a longitudinal pole taken from the airship, complete with all its attachments, in a pair of slings beside his sheds, and went to work making adjustments, and measuring the pull of the whole assembly against a spring balance.

To make the reading right it was necessary, he decided, that everything must be exactly as when in flight, and this included his own presence on the bicycle saddle. In cold, wet weather he sentenced himself to sitting in the rig in the open air while the engine was run, and adjusted by Chapin, and run again. The tractor propeller blew an icy gale about his ears, which increased in violence when Chapin triumphantly increased the propeller speed to 140 r.p.m.

Santos never seemed to extend his originality of design to his own personal equipment. Ordinary suits and hats, and for that matter high stiff collars, appeared to be wildly unsuitable for aviation, and an ordinary topcoat did not make things much better. A few days of this and he took cold, and shortly a doctor was summoned to rue Washington, who declared that he had pneumonia.

This was a serious ailment, in the days before the sulpha drugs and penicillin. In the early part of November he was very ill. A nurse was engaged to live in, who worked under the supervision of Charles, the valet. When at last he could sit up and receive visitors he was ordered to take a proper rest in a warmer climate. Accordingly he packed his trunks, his papers and books, a quantity of special tools, and his electric buggy (which went on a railway truck) and set out for Nice to recuperate.

He was no armchair convalescent. English residents in his hotel, sitting stunned by the news of the death of the old Queen at Osborne, raised heavy eyes in wonder, to see the mercurial comings and goings of this dynamic little man. He could not relax. It was one of his great defects. Soon he was fretting in Nice, thinking of the Deutsch Prize, sketching out ideas on sheets of squared paper, to bring *No 5* up to the standard that would get him over the course in thirty minutes.

One thing was certain. He would not have the propeller in front of him again, if he could help it, and he wanted his basket back. But he could not balance the basket on a pole, and he did not want to sling it underneath. Musing thus, he sketched a triangular-section built-up girder on his note-pad, consisting of three long thin members joined and spaced by short struts. The idea appealed to him, if he could make it light enough. That brought his convalescence to an abrupt end, and he sought out a carpenter's shop.

The proprietor was astonished at first, by this eccentric customer, but when he discovered that it was the celebrated M. Santos-Dumont he put everything at his disposal. Santos took off his coat and went to work himself. He made the framework of pine, with joints worked out of aluminium sheet, and to prevent distortion he braced it with piano wire. The result was a long, narrow girder of great rigidity, weighing only 90 lb., a fitting backbone for the extra power and manoeuvrability that would be required of the Deutsch racer. The engine, fuel, controls and basket would all fit inside its spaces. When it was finished it was dismantled and packed, in sections, with his voluminous trunks, and sent back to Paris. There the Customs Office (the *Octroi*, which levied taxes on certain goods brought into Paris from the provinces*) stopped the trunks, examined the spar, and kept it for a week while they decided how it fitted into the regulations. They then levied the maximum tax on it, as a fine piece of cabinet work.

* Not to be confused with the Douanes, which taxed foreign goods at the frontier. One of the scenes of *La Bohême* takes place outside a Paris Customs House. They were abolished in 1943.

Chapter 9

☆☆☆☆☆☆☆☆☆☆☆☆☆☆☆☆☆☆☆☆☆☆☆☆☆☆☆☆☆☆☆☆☆

The Santos-Dumont Prize

Good news awaited him in Paris. Back in his house, happy to
have his things once more about him, he found a letter from
the Scientific Commission of the Aéro Club. This begged to
inform him that the Commission had considered the disposal
of the Encouragement Prize, the sum of money to be awarded
annually so long as the Deutsch Prize remained unclaimed, and
found from the interest on M. Deutsch's 100,000 francs. It
had been unanimously decided that this award, for the year
1900, should go to M. Santos-Dumont, in recognition of his
valuable flights during the Paris Exposition.

Santos was naturally delighted. He immediately sent off a
pneumatique thanking the Aéro Club for the honour. His pleasure
was in no way abated by the undeniable fact that there was
practically no competition, at least in terms of achievement,
and that the Commission had reached a foregone conclusion
after weighty argument. There was indeed, except for the
conspicuous exploits of Santos, somewhat of a lull in European
air development, when compared with the efforts of the last
part of the nineteenth century. The only Frenchman who might
have had some claim on the Commission's attention was a
man we must hear more of in due course, Captain Ferber of the
French Army.

Ferber had become an aviation enthusiast when he was serving with an Alpine artillery brigade. He had made a hobby of experiments with gliders, using the steep rises and soft snow-banks to achieve some short glides (and comfortable landings). He followed the principles of Lilienthal. In 1900 he was still tentatively experimenting with gliders, but without enough success to put him in the running with the Commission. His importance will be seen later, when he used his chief asset, a burning belief in the future of aviation, to initiate the spurt of activity which suddenly put France in front of the world.

After gracefully accepting the 4,000 francs Encouragement Prize, Santos did some rapid thinking, and his next action was swift and rather tactless. He returned the money to the Aéro Club, to found another award, which he christened the Santos-Dumont Prize, which would be presented to the first aviator to fulfil the conditions of the Deutsch Prize, but with certain significant differences.

The main difficulty facing him in his attempts to gain the big award was the time limit of thirty minutes. This had been cunningly calculated by the Commission (so as to stimulate development), as being beyond the powers of anything then flying. Santos now stated the conditions of winning his own prize, in a letter to the Commission:

"The Santos-Dumont Prize shall be awarded to the aeronaut, a member of the Aéro Club, and not the founder of this prize, who between 1st of May and 1st October, 1901, starting from the Parc d'Aérostation of St. Cloud, shall turn round the Eiffel Tower and come back to the starting-point, at the end of whatever time, without having touched ground, and by his self-contained means on board alone."

This gesture caused a good deal of raised eyebrows and shrugged shoulders in the Aéro Club. In the first place it seemed to criticise the conditions laid down by the Commission, on behalf of M. Deutsch. Secondly, though the donor was mag-nanimously excluded from the award, it hardly seemed probable that anyone else was in a position to try for it, and in fact it was never claimed. Unless it has been converted to another purpose the money rests in the Club's treasury to this day.*

* If the condition as to dates can be set aside, there seems no reason why it should not be won, even now.

Some of the muttering was certainly caused by the impression that these careless dispensations had been made by a man too rich to bother with trifles. In fact Santos, with his ever more ambitious plans to finance, could have used the money. He had put up the prize in a genuine effort to encourage others. The fact that there was practically no-one to encourage, and that his conditions presented a situation very favourable to himself, if only he were eligible, escaped his perception. He had these occasional blind spots.

With the new girder type keel he was completing the transformation of *No 4* into *No 5*. Delighted with the strength, lightness and rigidity of the braced structure, he considered using piano wire for his main rigging also. "Then what turned out to be an utterly new idea in aeronautics followed. I asked myself why I should not use this same piano wire for all my dirigible balloon suspensions in place of the cords and ropes used in all kinds of balloons up to this time. I did it, and the innovation turned out to be peculiarly valuable." It was certainly a good move, but hardly worthy of the phrase "an utterly new idea in aeronautics".

All components for the propulsion and control of the airship were fitted into the girder. Forward was the basket, with controls led to it; amidships the engine, with fuel and water ballast tanks; while the propeller was where he much preferred it, at the stern. The design was completed with a larger and more effective rudder. The engine had once more been replaced, immediately Santos had glimpsed a wonderful new model in the *atelier* of Monsieur Buchet. It was a modification of a Daimler-Benz, giving 15 h.p. Now installed on the centre of gravity of the airship, it drew cries of admiration from the frequent visitors to his workshops.

"I should be afraid to ask the price of such a motor de luxe," declared Monsieur Georges. "It is more like a piece of goldsmith's work. I am ravished by the devices for the electric ignition." The exquisitely-built magneto was the envy of his motoring friends, whose early cars were fired by the hot tube, that demon of sinister memory to the pioneer motorist. Automobiles were now becoming more common on the roads, and electric ignition had recently been introduced, to banish the delay and drudgery of "heating the tube" necessary before the gallant driver could set out. But it was proving a mixed blessing. All over France cars were halted by the road while their owners peered dismally at an electric system that had mysteriously stopped working (which the hot tube hardly ever did), gloomily aware that they had not the first idea of how to put matters right.

This unreliable side of the magneto seems to have escaped Santos. He was no longer a practical automobilist. And in an engine of so much power, with four air-cooled cylinders, and weighing only 180 lb., he felt certain that he would have the extra speed needed for the Deutsch Prize. Why, the change to piano wire alone should halve the drag of his airship through the air. So he anxiously reasoned, and re-checked his calculations, seeking for lightness and speed.

During the winter M. Lachambre had worked on the envelope of the new airship, using most of the panel gores from No 4. The ends were made less pointed, producing a better shape. As with all the airships except the tubby No 3, an interior ballonet was fitted, with an airpump to keep it inflated. Both sand and water ballast were carried, for although it was found that water was better for trimming the airship before flight, sand could be thrown out more quickly, and the amount measured more accurately.

The new airship was finished without the help of M. Machuron. For some months he had been seriously ill, and he died in March 1901, leaving a young widow and an infant child. He was only 29 years old, and M. Lachambre was left to mourn a dynamic young nephew who had put new life into his business, and Santos to grieve for the loss of his first instructor, the man who had introduced him to the air. Even within his short life-time, poor M. Machuron, who could not believe in the steerable airship, had lived to see his pupil prove him wrong.

Santos now had sufficient status to gather like-minded men about him, if he was prepared to encourage their acquaintance. During the building of No 5 he became increasingly friendly with three enthusiasts who previously had been counted only among his numerous automobiling and aeronautical acquaintances. They were about his own age, and the first of them, Louis Blériot, whose historic flight across the English Channel in 1909 excuses him from any need for introduction, was a year older. Blériot, then a large bluff man with a wide smile, a virile moustache, and a loud voice, came from Cambrai, and had studied at the *Ecole Centrale des Arts et Métiers*, where he had occasionally run into Santos during their student days.

He had seized on the opportunities offered by the coming of the motor-car, and manufactured numbers of components and accessories. He was specially famed for his huge acetylene headlamps, a favourite item with the early town-to-town racers. He had known Santos when they were both members of the Automobile Club, and now, like everybody else in Paris, he shared the common knowledge of his celebrity.

Blériot had become interested in aviation as early as 1896, but he was not greatly attracted to ballooning and airships. He shared the common belief that they could never be practical, but he also held the far more uncommon opinion that heavier-than-air flight was possible. His enthusiasm gained Santos-Dumont's attention, and Blériot made a habit of coming out to St. Cloud, as did others of the band of faithful, to sit in the workshop and chat while Santos applied himself to his business. Their friendship continued for some years, but without any real warmth, for Blériot was a hearty, gusty man, who loved life, adventure, and pleasure, and it seems clear that though he admired Santos he rated him as a queer fish, not easily to be understood.

His other two friends of importance, with the same line of interest, were the brothers Henri and Maurice Farman. They were a year or two younger than he, born of English parents in Paris, nominally British citizens but indistinguishable from Frenchmen. (They could hardly speak English.) Henri, who was later to be perhaps the most important of the early European designers, had inherited, like Santos, a comfortable income. He studied painting, at which he had some minor success, before becoming a racing motorist. He and his brother Maurice were jovial young men, in a fair way to becoming what would later be called playboys, when they too were caught up in the popular hero-worship of the intrepid Brazilian. They joined the other pilgrims at St. Cloud, where they rubbed shoulders with Goursat, Blériot, Prado, the Marquis de Sorieno, Senhor Penteado, or even the Prince Roland Bonaparte, together with the rest of their host's wide and varied acquaintance.

When they knew him better they gave him all the technical

help they could, a difficult job with the self-contained Santos, and diluted his tendency to overwork by sometimes inducing him to come to a play or to the concert-hall with them. He found more enjoyment in these occasional visits than he had before he met his new friends, though to the end of his life he regarded such relaxings as social occasions, rather than as pleasures in themselves.

His other important acquisition was a staunch admirer, M. Emmanuel Aimé, Secretary-General of the Aéro Club. Of all the people who had an important influence on the promotion of early aviation, Monsieur Aimé has probably received the least publicity and credit. He started life as a poor mathematics professor, and at the age (in 1900) of 42 had still been unable, in spite of his passionate interest in aviation, to afford the price of a balloon ascent for himself. He wrote widely and well on aviation subjects, was the editor of L'Aérophile, and contributed to Auto, and the Journal. He gave lectures on the technical problems of aerostation, and became Secretary-General of the Aéro Club almost as soon as it formed.

He seems to have been that type of man who undertakes all the hard work that the rich and brilliant cannot bother with. In his scanty spare time he invented a number of instruments for use in aeronautics, made researches into the properties of whirlwinds, worked like a demon in a score of different ways, and finally, at the age of eighty, was awarded the Club's Silver Medal, which he had most richly earned.

Always referred to by the Press as "his devoted collaborator" poor M. Aimé gets no mention at all in Santos-Dumont's own writings (though he did a lot of his mathematical calculations for him), and he remains a shadowy Dr. Watson to a Brazilian Holmes. But with the great increase of activity that had come with the building of the "aerodrome", Santos needed someone a cut above the solid Chapin, and Monsieur Aimé stepped into the breech, unpaid. He was an agreeable companion, moreover, who could join the other, more brilliant friends, and make up a party for the evening, providing it was not too expensive. Sometimes they would all visit Maxim's, though this was distinctly above Aimé's standard of living, and Santos was usually the host.

Alberto never had the least difficulty in mixing the social

strata in which he moved with such confidence. He was accepted easily everywhere. He had no arrogance, either with rich or poor, and if he had taken any interest in politics he would probably have been a progressive Liberal. His father had deeply impressed him with respect and concern for his work-people, and he himself had a powerful social conscience, and a horror of want and misery. Like many other progressive liberals, he was wealthy and independent, but he told himself that he had a mission, for which his money was dedicated as much as himself. Cynical people might suggest that if this excuse for an easy conscience was removed, another could always be found; but of course if he were not dedicated he would not have been Santos-Dumont. And he had always to remember that he was a foreigner in a strange land, and his political opinions would in any case be unwelcome.

There was nothing specially intimate in his new friendships. There is not enough evidence to show that he ever had a really intimate friend, outside his immediate family circle, of which he saw little during these early years. But they gave him, with Goursat and one or two others, a circle of cronies who could meet and pass many happy hours of social conversation, and these first years of the new century were certainly the happiest of his life, as well as the most glorious. He was more at his ease, in and out of company. Even the nagging urge towards the Deutsch Prize could not hamper his spirits.

During this winter he visited the country house of a distant relative, Monsieur Georges, a wealthy gentleman who lived near Paris. As he was classed as a relation, Madame Georges had given permission for the whole of her large staff of servants to visit a fair in the village. Santos had hardly arrived when the good lady, a grande dame to her fingertips, was prostrated by the tidings that other, and unexpected guests were on their way. There was a flurry of horror and excitement, but Santos coolly took his host and hostess by the arms, and they all found their way, with some difficulty, to the kitchen. Here he helped their faltering efforts to prepare tea for the new arrivals.

He had brought his personal servant Charles with him in the buggy, for a gentleman could not travel alone, but when all was finally ready the man refused to serve tea, saying that he was the valet of Monsieur Santos, and not a footman to the family

Georges. This betrayal by the veteran of the Bois de Boulogne greatly incensed his master, who discharged him on the spot, ordering him to find his own way to Paris.

But all ended happily. A few days later Charles came to his house and asked to be taken back. Santos sternly reproved him, but Charles threw out his arms apologetically and said, "But it is you, Monsieur, who have spoiled me!" After this disarming statement all was forgiven, and the menage at rue Washington went on as smoothly as before.

No more than three years had passed since Santos first started his experiences in *aérostation*. In this short time he had run through one balloon and four airships, and was now ready with his fifth. He was a national character, and his fame had spread to England, Germany, and the United States, while in Brazil his name was already a legend. Since his rise to eminence he had not been home, and he knew that he could not go back until the Deutsch Prize had been won. Yet even now his example was stimulating other countries, where the beginnings of great events were stirring.

Far away from the limelight of Paris unseen rivals were closing up the distance by which he led them. On the misty surface of Lake Constance floated a huge airship hangar, and from this the first of Count Zeppelin's monsters had already taken the air. Its fully rigid, aluminium framework contained sixteen balloons, and it had two rudders, sliding weights to drive it up or down, and two engines turning four propellers. Technically, the Count was ahead of Santos already.

On the opposite side of the world, and working on opposite principles, the brothers Wright had just returned to their bicycle shop at Dayton, bronzed and fit after an autumn spent gliding in the sand-hills of Kitty Hawk. Although most of their trials used their glider as an un-manned kite, with strings to operate the controls, they had managed some successful piloted flights, pulled down the slope of a suitable hill leaning over the lower wing, kicking off with a last plunge, and achieving a few dozen feet of gliding under control. They were full of plans for the future, and well content with their progress. Casual, sardonic, and humorous, they were the very personification of the European's idea of the American engineer and man of the great open spaces. But there was nothing casual about their progress. Step by methodical step they were moving towards a success which, barring accidents, appeared inevitable.

To anybody living in Paris such rumours of these faraway goings-on as filtered through to the capital must have sounded like very small competition. In fact at this time Santos had not heard of the Wrights at all. It would be difficult for him to believe, if he had heard, that anyone could progress in so great an enterprise, when the massed technical skill and imaginative audacity of France was still baulked.

This comfortable feeling counter-balanced his impatience to win the big prize, when he first took *No 5* into the air. On the 9th of July, 1901, he made a polished departure from his "aerodrome", and anxiously watched by Lachambre, Aimé, Goursat, Chapin, and the rest of his team, rose easily above the trees and set course for Vincennes. After half an hour he was back, and glided neatly in to a landing. The big windmill sails of his propeller were idling round as he came down to earth, and stopped turning as the eager helpers grabbed his mooring-rope. Everything had gone to plan, the airship controlled easily, and after Chapin checked her over he was able to announce that all was well. Santos had her walked into the hangar for the night. It was as simple as that.

Early next morning he was off again, heading for the Long-champs racecourse, where he meant to run his serious trials over a safe open space. He had not actually obtained permission from the all-powerful Jockey Club, whose officials were some-what startled to see him careering round the course at low altitude. So great was his fame and prestige that they hastily took the hint, and four days later sent him a letter graciously placing their air space at his disposal. Santos was taken a little aback. He knew that the racing season was over, and it had not occurred to him to ask permission. He thought of the air as an unexplored ocean, wide open to the pioneer navigator.

His manoeuvring trials went off without a hitch. His friends on the ground were not so lucky. Aimé, Georges Besançon (director of *Aérophile* magazine), and M. Hermite, attending him below, were confronted by the frowsy figure of the race-course watchman. Did the gentlemen realise that it was 4.30 a.m.? And did that thing up there have a permit? Lying manfully, they assured him that Santos carried the permit in the nacelle with him, and the custodian withdrew, baffled.

Ten times Santos circled the racecourse, to a total distance of some 20 miles, each time stopping at a point of his choice. Pleased and satisfied, he next steered for the Ile de Puteaux, reached it, and made back towards Longchamps. He glanced round for the Eiffel Tower, that spectre always in his mind's eye, but it was hidden in the soft morning mist. But he knew where to find it, and he set his nose towards it, as if pulled by a fascination.

He was just glimpsing its outline when one of his rudder connections broke. He must land at once. Fortunately there was no wind, and he shifted his centre of gravity, drove No 5 downwards, and calmly alighted in the Trocadero Gardens, where workmen, running from all directions, seized his rope. They were delighted at this sudden arrival. Did Monsieur Santos want anything? Why, yes. He needed a ladder. No sooner said than done, and while two workmen held the stern rope of No 5, four more held a ladder vertically under the tail. He ran up it to the rudder, turned back his cuffs, and deftly repaired the broken connection.

The ladder was taken away, and Santos swung the propeller and leapt into the basket. On his sharp command they let go smartly, and No 5 was on her way once more, with the aeronaut waving his cap in acknowledgement of their help. He turned the Eiffel Tower in a wide curve, looking up sideways as it slid past him, and flew straight back to St. Cloud. Chapin was consulting a massive silver watch, his broad face puckered with worry, when the airship came in sight, flying at more than 500 feet. It had been absent for an hour and six minutes.

When it was safely put away Santos claimed that he had carried out the provisions governing the award of the Santos-Dumont prize, though of course he was excluded from competing. As he made rather a point of this it should be noted that his claim does not stand up, since the workmen and their ladder, in the Trocadero gardens, certainly invalidated the clause about "by his self-contained means alone", to say nothing of "without having touched ground". There was something faintly exasperating, to the members of the Aéro Club, about this putting up of the conditions for a competition and then claiming to fulfil them, as if to show how easy it all was. Panache, they hinted darkly, was a French invention.

For his own part Santos was getting worried about the conditions for the Deutsch Prize. Although he was pleased with his new airship, he could easily calculate how little speed he had in hand. A very small wind might spoil everything. The Scientific Commission had ruled that its members, who were to be the judges of all attempts, must be notified twenty-four hours in advance of the competitor starting. This would mean forecasting the weather twenty-four hours ahead, a feat even more difficult then than now. Nothing stronger than the lightest breeze would do. Worse still, he thought, when once a competitor had committed the formal act of assembling a Scientific Commission on a slope of the River Seine, so far from the centre of Paris as St. Cloud, he would be under a weighty moral pressure to go on with his trial, come wind, fog, or rain.

If it came to that, once the Commission was in place, even a small defect in the airship might have to be ignored. Lastly, as Santos confided pessimistically to a friend, he was barred by common courtesy from convoking them at the very hour most promising for airship flying—the calm of dawn. "The duellist may call out his friends at that sacred hour," he said; "but not the airship captain."

This delicate sentiment did not survive for long. The weather office assured him that the next day would dawn clear and still. With a good deal less than twenty-four hours' notice he sent out messages in all directions, and convened the Commission to attend at St. Cloud, at first light the next morning.

Chapter 10

✩✩✩✩✩✩✩✩✩✩✩✩✩✩✩✩✩✩✩✩✩✩✩✩✩✩✩✩✩✩✩

Calamity at the Trocadero

The morning of the 13th of July was still and gloriously beautiful. Through the summer haze the dew shone on every blade of grass, forecasting a day of brilliant heat.

Long before sunrise Santos arrived at St. Cloud in his electric buggy. He received the report of Chapin and his engineers, and with the mechanics checked the structure and engine of *No 5*. By 6.30 a.m. the members of the Scientific Commission of the Aéro Club were assembled, headed by M. Deutsch in person, magnificent in formal morning attire.

Santos supervised the starting of the engine, the delicate sails of the propeller being turned by Chapin himself. It displayed a certain amount of temperament (probably due to the dampness of the morning mists, said Santos), but after careful adjustment of the carburettor a series of earsplitting reports alerted the somewhat drowsy crowd and Commission, and it became apparent that the attempt was soon to start.

M. René de Knyff, a member of the Commission, and experienced in the ways of petrol engines (he had recently competed in the Paris-Berlin motor race) listened to the loud rattle of the motor, now running freely, and shook his head from time to time. "A sound like a pistol shot showed that everything was not all right," he said later. "It turned out that one of the cylinders was out of order."

But Santos decided that he could not delay. The Commission was waiting, a small crowd was eager for action, and a breeze might spring up at any time. He took his place in the tiny basket, barely large enough for himself, and impossibly small for a normal-sized man, and threw off his coat. He was wearing braces over a cream silk shirt with the usual high collar, a light-coloured tie with a pearl pin, topped off by a straw hat. An onlooker suspected that he had been reducing weight during the previous few weeks, though indeed he had little enough weight to reduce.

At 6.40, M. Deutsch approached the basket and once more shook hands with Santos. Though obliged to raise his voice to a bellow to make himself heard above the engine, he addressed him warmly, indeed affectionately, and wished him luck and a speedy return. M. Jeantaud began to count off the seconds by the chronometer. The crowd was silent. It was 6.41.

"Let go!" cried Santos.

"Good luck!" shouted back dozens of voices.

The engine popped and rattled under full throttle. Slowly *No 5* struggled upwards, and pointed for the distant Eiffel Tower. The guide-rope caught here and there in bushes and trees, and seeing the dangers of entanglement Santos let go water from his ballast tank. So delicate was the balance of the aerostat that this improved the climb, until she mounted above the park and set course for Paris, pursued by a group of cyclists.

The sound of the engine dwindled and died. "*Vive* Santos!" cheered the crowd raggedly, and the spell seemed to be broken, and a hum of conversation rose. Expert opinions were freely given on his chances.

But in his basket, Santos was uneasy. His engine was not giving full power, yet he was making good progress, and in fact he rounded the Eiffel Tower in the tenth minute. This could only mean that a breeze had sprung up behind him, which he would have to fight on the return journey. He did not know what was wrong with the engine.

His fears were justified. After the turning-point his ground speed came down to a walking pace, and his flagging engine reluctantly pushed him into a freshening wind. The second half of the journey took three times as long as the first, and it was forty minutes after the start before he came again over the dark knot of the Commission, grouped round M. Jeantaud. Ten minutes too slow!

At this moment his engine gave a last despairing cough, and stopped altogether. *No 5* lost way, and began to drift. The members of the Commission stared helplessly upwards. The aerostat was borne backwards over its course for about a quarter of a mile, losing height, until it caught in a high chestnut tree, and subsided stern-first in the park of the villa belonging to M. Edmond de Rothschild. "Forward!" cried M. René de Knyff.

The crowd streamed across the Aéro Club grounds to the boundary, where they saw M. de Rothschild's servants pouring out of the house in the opposite direction. Between them, lopsided and deflated but comparatively undamaged, *No 5* stuck firmly in the tree, with the propeller touching the ground at the stern, while Santos in the basket at the prow was high among the branches, invisible but quite unhurt. His voice was heard from time to time, giving directions for the salvage of the airship.

The commotion of rescue now spread to the next house, the home of Isabel, Comtesse d'Eu, ex-Imperial Princess Regent of the Throne of Brazil. Hearing of her gallant countryman's plight, and learning that he might be some time aloft, she gave orders for a picnic lunch to be prepared and conveyed in a hamper up the tree, where it was duly delivered to Santos, by a footman on a ladder. It was accompanied by an invitation to visit her, as soon as circumstances allowed, to tell her the story of the trip.

Accordingly, after dealing with the hamper, descending from the tree, reassuring the members of the Commission, apologising to M. de Rothschild, and giving final directions for the salvage of *No 5*, Santos resumed his coat, straightened his tie, and appeared in her salon looking his usual impeccable self.

After he had recounted his adventures, the Princess, daughter of Dom Pedro II, gave him a thousand assurances of her fervent good wishes, ending, "Your evolutions in the air make me think of the flight of our great birds of Brazil. I hope you will do as well with your propeller as they do with their wings, and that you will succeed for the glory of our common country."*

These elegant sentiments did not close the incident, for a

* *Dans l'Air*. A. Santos-Dumont.

few days later a small package from Cartier's arrived at No 9 rue Washington. It contained a parcel and a letter:

1st August, 1901

Monsieur Santos-Dumont,

Here is a medal of St. Benedict that protects against accidents.

Accept it, and wear it at your watch-chain, in your cardcase, or at your neck.

I send it to you, thinking of your good mother, and praying God to help you always and to make you work for the glory of our country.

Isabel, Comtesse d'Eu.

Though he prized this medal greatly, Santos discarded the three suggestions for wearing it. Instead he ordered a thin gold bracelet chain, to which it was fixed, and wore it round his wrist. The Paris newspapers hastened to add this latest embellishment to the descriptions of him that filled their pages. They treated the incident kindly. Nor did the dramatic end of this attempt generate any jeering or mocking in the newspapers. Unlike the Press of some other nations, notably that of the United States, most of the French journalists took the early air struggles very seriously. "This performance is above either praise or criticism!" exclaimed an eye-witness, quoted in a Paris journal. "It is a new fact in our lives!"

No 5 had suffered surprisingly little damage, and the whole incident had been more annoying than significant. Engines, even so magnificent an engine as this, were liable to lose power and even to stop, and the chief vexation had been the need for the calling out of the Commission at dawn, which had placed on Santos a moral obligation to go on with the attempt, even with a sick engine.

In two weeks the airship was repaired and ready for flight once more. Santos thought it only prudent to make some further trials, which he carried out over the grassy lawns of the Longchamp racecourse. Among other tests, he was anxious to get an estimate of the airship's speed in still air, so that he could calculate more exactly the conditions under which the Prize could come within his grasp.

As he naturally had no measurement of airspeed, he was assisted by M. Maurice Farman, who drove his automobile round the racecourse close behind the dragging guide-rope of *No 5*. M. Farman had no speedometer either, but he found that he could just keep up while using second gear on his car, and so estimated that the airship was doing about 17 miles per hour with the guide-rope dragging, and without this restraint the speed could be expected to rise to about 19 miles per hour. The sight of *No 5* circling the racecourse, with the ponderous automobile roaring and lumbering behind it, drew large crowds of sightseers, brought the stewards of the Jockey Club close to apoplexy, and anticipation to a new intensity. Everyone was waiting for the next attempt.

It came on the 8th of August. Once more the preparations were made, once more Santos conveniently forgot his self-imposed embargo on dawn flights, and the Scientific Commission assembled, having risen bleary-eyed from their beds and dressed by gaslight, to be at St. Cloud by 6 a.m. The Paris correspondent of the *Daily Express* took up station at the Eiffel Tower in a big Mors racing car, having agreed to pace Santos-Dumont back to St. Cloud after he had rounded the half-way mark.

As the chronometers clicked, Santos recorded a normal departure from St. Cloud, at 6.30 a.m. The *Express* correspondent was watching through field-glasses. "We saw the balloon climb high into the heavens", he wrote, "and turn its yellow prow towards the Tower. Santos-Dumont came rushing in flight as straight as a rifle-barrel, and seeming as fast as a rifle-bullet."

Though perhaps one of the great exaggerations of all time, this statement had some observation prompting it, for once more there was a breeze behind *No 5*, one that would cost the aviator dearly on the return trip. "His ship was sailing with the wind", continued the journalist, changing metaphors with practised facility, "and sailing faster than ever moved a Yankee cup defender. The rattle of the motor, heard a mile and a half away, brought people to the roofs. The workmen gazed aloft. It was an exhilarating spectacle, thrilling, enchanting. Soon he was at the Tower. He rounded the great iron stake boat with ease, gracefully slowing down, so as to convince all of his performance; and as the ship swung round there was a mighty cheering from far and near. Santos-Dumont waved his hat in pleased response." He was, in fact, wearing a straw boater on this flight, secured to his collar by a patent cord.

But all was far from well. Though *No 5* had reached the Tower in nine minutes, Santos knew already that she was losing hydrogen, due to a defect developing in the spring of one of the automatic gas valves. The old trouble was back again. The gas-bag slightly relaxed its normal taughtness. Santos looked up, and gauged the change in shape. Normally he would have landed. But once more the pressure of events banished caution. All Paris was cheering below, and in the distance the dark group of the Commission was waiting, stopwatches in hand. He knew the risk, but he kept on.

The aerostat now shrank visibly, and the wind blew in his teeth. By the time he was approaching the Bois de Boulogne, near La Muette, the envelope was slack enough to allow the girder suspension wires to sag, so that those nearest to the propeller fouled its turning. Santos saw the screw cutting and tearing at the wires, and hastily reduced the speed of the motor. The airship began to drift back before the freshening wind.

These dramatic events had been clearly observed from the ground. "Santos-Dumont soared upwards to twice the height of the Eiffel Tower," continued the *Express* man, frozen in the Mors by his starting position, the race forgotten: "Two thousand feet in the air he climbed from his basket and clambered along the dipping, swaying, gossamer-like keel to overhaul his motor. It was sublime daring."

The writer, coming to himself with a start, now commanded his driver to follow at full speed, and the Mors thundered across the Pont d'Iena and up the Quai de Passy for about half a mile. "Men below turned away their eyes," he went on, with more drama than accuracy, "Santos-Dumont stood well outside the basket on two slender sticks, not so large as broom handles and three feet apart. He held on by the third strand of wood that formed the apex of the triangular keel. He worked furiously for a few seconds, and then went back to his car."

Santos had not in fact been working on the motor, but had attempted to clear the wires. The shift in his weight caused *No 5* to climb. With the reduction in the engine's speed the air-pump that kept the inner ballonet inflated slowed down also, and the gas-bag grew even limper. The horrified watcher on the

Quai de Passy had a perfect view. "The ship was plunging and seemed a quarter deflated. The motor worked feebly. When the bow rose up the gas swelled it full, and the stern crumpled, and doubled over empty. As the bow dipped this action was reversed, the stern filled and was buoyant, while the other end sagged like a wet towel."

The struggle continued over the hill where now stands the Palais de Chaillot. "Bravely Santos-Dumont kept the prow to the wind; magnificently he struggled to regain St. Cloud. Once the ship turned as if to run before the wind, and it did go a few yards, until Santos swung her back on to course. The ship fluttered in the air and flopped alarmingly. Santos-Dumont was being tossed on great wind swells in a wrecked airship!"

The climax was at hand. "The stem sagged, and the propeller, still slowly revolving, caught in the supporting piano wires. There was a ripping and a rush of gas. With a sickening, despairing flop the airship began falling."

Santos stopped the motor. He could have checked the fall by releasing ballast, but even in his extremity he remembered the wind and the Tower behind him. It sprang like a sword from the far bank, enormous, pitiless. Far better to fall into the river than strike the monster and drop like a plummet down its steel side. He therefore let No 5 sink at her own speed, with her prow in the air and her empty stern waving feebly below.

"It was now half a mile distant from the right bank of the Seine. One could hear screams from every housetop. But Santos appeared in no degree alarmed. He slipped the heavy guide-rope down by the stern in order to lower that end—as he was in the bow it was better for him to have the stern hit the ground first. He fastened his belt to a hook in the basket. The wind was blowing the ship so that it slanted down a long incline, whose end appeared to be the Seine. The last thousand feet were covered with a rush like that of a lift falling down its well. At the last moment, when almost on the roof of the Trocadero Hotel, Santos-Dumont flung out ballast. Falling at that velocity it is amazing how he did it, but, when only a few feet above the roof, he threw out sand in showers."

Santos had been attempting to adjust his descent so as to fall into the Seine, or at least on to the embankment. A boat had already put out ready to pick him up. He nearly succeeded. The under-structure with its engine, girder, and basket, passed just above the roof of the Trocadero,* but the drooping envelope caught the roof.

"The keel carrying Santos-Dumont had skimmed over the high roof, but the silk lagging behind caught at the extreme end on a chimney-pot just as the last part was going over. The gas-bag exploded with a roar. The balloon itself tore right in two, but the wires running from the prow to the keel caught also, and they held. With a mighty jerk Santos stopped his flight in mid-air, suspended forty feet from the ground against a blank wall eighty feet high. The keel hung by the wires with half the balloon draped about it. The other half hung to the chimney pot. Santos-Dumont lay horizontally on his back in the car, his head and shoulders clear outside."

This was a very different proposition to M. de Rothschild's chestnut tree. Pandemonium broke loose. Crowds surged up to the hotel, and the Mors forced its way with difficulty to a vantage point where the aviator could be seen, precariously hanging amid the tangle of *No 5*. Among those thronging towards the Trocadero were, most fortunately, the Fire Brigade from the Passy station. For now there was a new danger.

The wires and the keel structure that so far had saved his life by holding to the roof, began to give way, and the keel dropped jerkily, a few feet down the wall. Santos was a good forty feet from the ground. But he was still in command. By swaying his body he swung the lower end of the keel on to a ledge, where it lodged. The crowd held its breath. Now the keel was on end, with Santos at the top. It tottered horribly. Hanging on by his belt to the basket he wrapped his gloved hands round the wire bracing, and pulled on the suspension wires until the keel was upright. Then he gave a quick jerk, the top fell slightly into a corner of the building, and the danger was over.

Amid a tumult of cheering the firemen appeared on the roof, followed by anyone who could reach it. The Seine embankment and the neighbouring roads were jammed solidly with people, but the *Express* correspondent managed to force a way through and gain the roof with the others. He peered over and down to where Santos still perched in his tiny basket. He was joking

* Since demolished to make way for the surroundings of the Palais de Chaillot.

with the firemen, and since all gas and petrol had dispersed he had lighted a cigarette which someone had dropped to him.

Five minutes later he was rescued by a looped rope, and drawn upwards to the roof. Thanks to the patent cord, he had not even lost his straw hat. "He was laughing like a boy, unworried and enthusiastic," wrote the breathless correspondent. For the purposes of a newspaper despatch this may have been true enough. Or perhaps the journalist could not recognise nervous reaction after intense danger?

The events of the 8th of August had ended in a peculiarly unpleasant accident. The leak in the gas and the gradual collapse of the airship above the aviator; the tearing airscrew biting into the bracing wires; the nightmare of the dark tower looming behind him; the long slide on to the rooftop; and finally the delicate juggling against the cliff-face of the Trocadero; each separate phase had been close and nasty.

The finale, with *No 5* draped over the chimney-pots like a broken umbrella, and the pilot hauled to safety by the firemen, had affronted Alberto's dignity before a huge crowd, and had sharpened the malicious weapons of his few detractors. In spite of the cheering, and the enthusiasm and sympathy, Santos felt the incident keenly, and he reacted at once.

His automobile and a driver rescued him from the crowds still surrounding the Trocadero, now cordoned by police. The wreckage of *No 5*, beyond repair, was being dismantled under the supervision of the tearful Chapin. Santos returned to his house in rue Washington, where he bathed and changed. For the rest of the day he remained alone. But the same evening he gave two signs that Santos-Dumont remained unaffected by the blows of fate. He issued orders for the immediate building of a new airship, *No 6*. And that night he appeared at his usual table at Maxim's. His entry, resplendent in evening dress, with a carnation in his buttonhole, was the signal for another ovation. Diners rose to their feet and clapped. The *maître d'hôtel* congratulated him on his escape. His table filled with admirers. The conversation, as a lady pettishly remarked, became wholly technical.

The directions which Santos gave M. Lachambre and his engineers for the building of *No 6* contained no new principles or revolutionary ideas. He wanted the Deutsch Prize, and there was little time to spare. In fact he stipulated a building time of only three weeks, with delivery by 1st September. He could only concentrate on correcting the known defects, and particularly on what had thrice put him into so much danger— the deflation of the envelope distorting the whole structure, with inevitable disaster as a consequence.

"In all my constructions", he wrote, "except the big-bellied balloon of the No 3, I had depended much on the interior compensating air balloon fed by airpump or rotary ventilator. Sewed like a closed patch pocket to the inside bottom of the great balloon, this compensating air balloon would remain flat and empty so long as the great balloon remained distended with its gas. Then, as hydrogen might be condensed by changes of altitude and temperature, the airpump worked by the motor would begin to fill the compensating air balloon, make it take up more room inside the great balloon, and so keep the latter distended."

Looking at the wreckage after the Trocadero accident, it was hard to say what had gone wrong first, but he suspected that the varnish on the internal ballonet had never properly dried, causing it to stick to the inside of the envelope, and impeding its action.

This problem was given great attention in No 6. The new airship was very slightly larger than No 5—33 metres long, with a displacement of 622 cubic metres. The form was an elongated ellipsoid. Santos and his assistants threw themselves into the details of construction, and work went on night and day to prepare the airship for new attempts on the Deutsch Prize.

Strangely enough, the spectacular failure of No 5 had crystallised a growing alarm among the more nationalistic "sportsmen" of Paris, and these influences now communicated themselves to the Aéro Club and the Scientific Commission. In Santos-Dumont's latest accident, and much more in his renewed activity, they saw the signs of ultimate triumph, and suddenly found them distasteful. France was the home of scientific experiment and progress! England was soporific; Count Zeppelin was doing something in Germany, but no results had come to light. France was the active and vital explorer of the air, and a Frenchman had offered an air prize for a flight over Paris! It was unthinkable that a Brazilian should walk off with this great honour, particularly when his efforts were based on French genius and invention!

A little delaying campaign might bring the native-born competitors (and the whisperers did not stop to think out who they might be) once more to the fore. Did the Scientific Commission not think——?

The result of these grubby tactics was an alteration in the rules for the Deutsch Prize, which made the test more difficult. The competing airship now had to finish the trip in thirty minutes, measured from the time at which the mooring rope was released at the starting-point, to the time at which it was caught again. This meant that the actual distance must be covered in less.

Among the choruses of praise there were also some discordant voices. Commandant Renard, now Director of the War Office Balloon Establishment, had been a half of the team that built the electric Renard/Krebs airship in 1884. He maintained that the rules of the Deutsch Prize were too easy. If he had not been a Government servant and debarred from entering private competitions (he declared), he could have won the Prize with his *France*, even as she was in 1884. The validity of this sour claim is very doubtful. He criticised Santos-Dumont's airship as "very imperfect".

"It is lacking in all the secondary qualities necessary", he continued mysteriously. "It is not stable, and cannot be steered scientifically." For good measure he also criticised the airship of a M. Roze, who was claimed by his few supporters to be in the running, as "too complicated".

Santos emerged from his workshop for long enough to protest to the Aéro Club about the new mooring-rope regulations. Horseraces did not begin when the jockey was handed the reins, he complained, nor end when the mount was led in. The Commission was evasive, and shrugging his shoulders Santos returned to his work. One way or another, the Deutsch Prize would be his.

Chapter 11

☆☆☆☆☆☆☆☆☆☆☆☆☆☆☆☆☆☆☆☆☆☆☆☆☆☆☆☆☆☆

The Deutsch Prize

There now approaches one of the two great climaxes of Santos-Dumont's life. The Deutsch Prize transfixed his attention. Since we know, and his later actions proved, that he was not after the money, and since it is undeniable that the conditions for the prize had something of the flavour of a stunt, we cannot acquit Santos of a certain degree of pot-hunting. It may even be argued that the well-meaning Monsieur Deutsch, in setting his conditions and offering so much money and fame, diverted both Santos and others from more seriously pursuing the problems of flight, and so had the opposite effect to that which he intended.

The Wright brothers, making good and steady progress, had no such stimulant; in fact nobody was taking the least notice of them even in their own country, and far less outside it. Santos himself was a great believer in prizes. He said they helped to encourage an increasing number of experimenters to take up research, and he cordially supported and sometimes initiated, as with the first Santos-Dumont prize, any scheme to promote them.

No 5 had been completely destroyed. *No 6* was designed, built and inflated in twenty-two days. That was the measure of his resilience, industry, confidence, and absolute determination to win. During this frantic three weeks, when he had little sleep and no spare time, while Lachambre's workshops and his own toiled day and night, he can be excused if he missed some of the finer nuances of his effect on the world outside his workshop. For while his popularity with the Press and public grew, there were distinct signs of an anti-Santos faction among the cognoscenti of the Aéro Club, and even in wider circles.

The melancholy fact is that the chief reason was chauvinism, but there were other causes. A man is popular among his fellows if he is a good trier. It is much harder to maintain his popularity when he succeeds. Santos, in spite of some of his statements, was essentially a modest man in a complicated sort of way; certainly at this time of his life. But he was not constantly on the watch, as an Englishman would be, to nourish and preserve a reputation for modesty, as if it were some rare and delicate plant. Even in a city where modesty was scarcely rated as a virtue, he appeared rather ostentatious to those who did not know him well. The newspapers had played up his dandyism and his wealth.

It may also seem curious to envy the success of a man who has just been publicly dragged from the wreckage of his own invention, but Santos was so obviously hell-bent for eventual triumph that jealousy was only a matter of intelligent anticipation. He had stolen all the aeronautical limelight at the Exposition.

The Commission would not give way over the changed rule. The thirty minutes must be timed from "release" to when the airship was tethered once more. There is nothing in the records of the Club to show who was pushing this line, and there is no reason for it except, by making the test harder, to postpone a decision until someone else should have a chance. Santos gritted his teeth. There was no question about it; he would have to find a little more speed yet.

His new water-cooled engine gave 20 horsepower, and would produce a pull of 145 lbs. He reckoned this worth the additional weight, and he hoped that with liquid cooling the engine would be less liable to over-heating. The airpump to inflate the ballonet was an integral part of the engine. Rigidity, he thought; stiffness of the envelope; that is the great problem. If *No 6* can keep her shape we will win; if she does not, then the next time may not be so fortunate.

By the end of August 1901, *Santos-Dumont No 6* was ready for trials. The whole construction team, from Santos downwards, was exhausted with intense and continual effort, and Chapin and the mechanics watched, red-eyed, as it rose at last from the aerodrome at St. Cloud. They had some cause for satisfaction. They had built a handsome airship, with a shape that was probably the best compromise of any of the Santos-Dumont fleet, past or future. The launching preparations had been so hurried that all ceremony had been omitted, and there was no quaffing of champagne, or mutual congratulations. The designer himself had showed signs of strain, as the days went by and the winter approached, and he was flying in a dangerous state of nervous tension.

It was probably because of this, and because the idyllic summer mornings of soft mist and pearly calm were no more than a memory, that the trials were beset with troubles. There were constant adjustments to the girder keel and rigging, and the engine was capricious. Santos took *No 6* up at least once every day, and each time he came down there was a new list of adjustments to be made by his hard-driven team. On the 6th of September there was a heart-breaking accident, when the stern bumped the roof of a house. This was due to the guide-rope catching in telegraph wires while the airship was rising, ripping the envelope and damaging the rudder. Nine precious days were lost before it was repaired and reinflated, and then on the 15th of September Santos cut some trees too closely while turning, hitting them and doing more damage.

Between these two accidents, on the 9th of September, Henri de Toulouse-Lautrec died in the Château of Malromé. The newspapers hardly noticed it. Santos may have seen a paragraph, and given it scant attention. But the bright genius of the little painter, swamped at last by drink, illness, and accumulated debauchery, evoked incomparably, then and forever, the Paris that made the background to the best years of Santos-Dumont. It may not have been the part of the world that he knew best, but it was the essence. When that flame guttered out, the twentieth century had come indeed.

On the 18th of September Santos was up again, with *No 6* held captive on its guide-rope while he tried evolutions in all directions, using a new rudder of double size. When he was satisfied he sent for the Commission once more, though their zeal was beginning to flag, and set out for the Eiffel Tower in ideal weather. "Amid cheers the aerostat mounted skyward," wrote a Paris newspaper, "but the drag-rope had hardly left the ground when it was seen that the new rudder refused to work, and a moment later the undaunted Brazilian brought his ship to earth. 'What's wrong?' cried a multitude of voices. But Senhor Santos-Dumont himself did not know. Soon afterwards he discovered that one of the bamboo rods supporting the guide-wires had broken. The airship was taken into the shed, and an hour later emerged with the rod replaced, and shot up into the air pointing at the Eiffel Tower.

"It travelled at tremendous speed, and everyone shouted 'He'll do it'. Over the Bois de Boulogne the airship was seen to descend rapidly. It was clear that something again was wrong. It landed on the Longchamp racecourse, where investigation showed tangled guide-ropes and other obstacles to progress. The remainder of the afternoon was spent making repairs." The Commission dispersed, muttering.

This very trying time was forgotten later, but it put a great strain on him. In the light of final triumph he could dismiss the torments of September. "Such accidents I have always taken philosophically, looking on them as a kind of insurance against more terrible ones. Were I to give a single word of caution to all dirigible balloonists, it would be 'Keep close to earth'. The place of an airship is not in high altitudes, and it is better to catch in the tops of trees, as I used to do in the Bois de Boulogne, than to risk the perils of the upper air without the slightest practical advantage."*

Notwithstanding these calm words of wisdom, written some time after the events, the middle of October found the *équipage* Santos-Dumont ready to try again, but with nerves stretched to breaking-point, over-stressed and over-tired. On the 14th of October he made his 25th ascent in *No 6*, flying a French flag for the first time. It is not known who had passed him this useful hint, or whether he thought of it himself. Probably M. Aimé was the diplomat. Henceforth he flew the French and Brazilian flags together.

This time *No 6* was docile. The Paris correspondent of *The Times* wrote: "The balloon, like a bird trained to obey the human voice, executed all movements with wonderful precision,

* *Dans l'Air*. A. Santos-Dumont.

turning round, advancing rapidly—in short, acting like an intelligent being . . ." It was not docile enough, however, to induce the Paris insurance companies to take it on as a risk. They had staunchly refused when Santos tried it on them, and judging from the record they can hardly be blamed.

On the 18th the weather was wretched, but Santos had received a promising report for next day from the meteorological station at the top of the Eiffel Tower. Even so it was with great misgiving that he sent out telegrams to the Scientific Commission, convening them for attendance at St. Cloud on the following afternoon. He had a feeling, not entirely unjustified, that their sympathy for him was a good deal less whole-hearted than it had been at first.

He spent the night of the 18th-19th at St. Cloud, and slept little. The weather improved towards morning, and he was up early to look at the sky and receive the latest reports. Would the wind drop? He had installed a telephone at the "aerodrome", and rang the Meteorological Office hourly for reports. At midday they gave a wind of 11 miles per hour at the summit of the Eiffel Tower, approximately the same as the best speed of his first airship. He did not like it. If only it was not so late in the year; if he had not thrice before convened a Commission showing signs of impatience—he was an anxious man as he supervised the final preparations.

The Scientific Commission was obviously thinking on the same lines. Prince Roland Bonaparte failed to turn up, and of the twenty-four other members only five made their appearance —Monsieur Deutsch himself, with MM. de Dion, Fonvielle, Besançon, and the faithful Aimé. All of them were friends of the competitor, in some degree, and the last was acting in a distinctly dubious dual capacity. They were sufficient for a quorum, but Santos, already in his basket, noted their number and set his teeth. Their faces reflected little optimism. They came over to the airship, shook hands and wished him luck, and then M. Deutsch asked if he was ready. The Marquis de Dion was acting as timekeeper, his watch already in his hand, his hand resting on his ample waistcoat.

Santos consulted his check list, an innovation of his own which is now an essential part of the equipment of all aircraft captains. Envelope, rigging, controls, ballast, engine, fuel; the important items of a pre-flight inspection were noted by sections. At this last moment he refused to be hurried. The Commission fidgeted, but he took no notice. At 2.30 p.m. he ordered everyone to stand away from the plane of the propeller while the engine was started. He had done this ever since a blade had flown off the propeller of *No 3*, narrowly missing the bystanders. After a couple of swings it started, and he spent another ten minutes warming it up, until he was completely satisfied.

He waved his gloved hands to show he was ready. The Commission shook walking sticks and umbrellas in acknowledgement. The timekeeper's watch was out. The moment had come. "Let go all!" shouted Santos. It was 2.42 p.m.

No 6 climbed crab-wise, with the south-east wind on her beam. Three and a half miles away the Eiffel Tower could be clearly seen, against a background of clouds threatening rain. The *Daily News* correspondent took up the story. "The machine flew across the Seine, keeping as straight as an arrow . . . It gradually rose, keeping in line, however, with the goal. As it came abreast of the Tower it seemed a little speck."

Santos was doing well. He had taken the airship up in a long steady climb, for while the wind was behind him he could afford to gain altitude. By the time he reached the Tower he was 150 feet above the top of it. This may have been rather high, but at least he was in no danger of hitting it.

He passed the lightning-conductor on the summit nine minutes after take-off, and immediately swung the airship into a turn, so that he rounded it on a radius of about fifty yards. There was a roar of cheering from below, and handkerchiefs fluttered and hats were waved, both from the ground and from every gallery of the Tower. Santos had a glimpse of the meteorologists in their tiny box at the very top. He was around. "Just then the balloon was seen to swerve, as if buffeted by the wind against which it was now struggling."

Santos had twenty minutes in which to regain St. Cloud, against the wind. He had the airship fairly on her homeward course, and five hundred yards past the tower, when his engine began to misfire, and slow down. Once again! Santos looked back anxiously, and forward to St. Cloud, still more than three miles away. He was more than a thousand feet up. He would have to see to the motor, though it would mean abandoning the steering.

It was a fearful risk, but he could not afford another failure.

He settled his cap more firmly on his head, and climbed out of the basket. Once again he had to clamber, foot by foot, and hand over hand, along the slender spars of the girder keel, with a sickening void of air beneath him. The engine was now barely turning over, and if once it stopped he could not restart it. Above him he could sense the ballonet relaxing, as the efforts of the airpump grew feebler.

On the embankments of the river, a thousand feet below, there was pandemonium. After the spectacular crash on to the Trocadero the citizens of Paris realised what perils *Le Petit Santos* was enduring. The first sound of his airship brought traffic to a standstill, and people poured from houses, shops, and offices. The reverent peace of the luncheon period was shattered. The streets were black with a motionless throng, looking up. They could see that he was slowly drifting back towards the Tower. A shout went up as he was seen to leave the basket. Ladies bit their handkerchiefs, and men clutched their walking-sticks. The tension became unbearable.

When he reached the engine he held on with one hand, while with the other he re-set the ignition and fuel mixture controls, which had probably shifted because of engine vibration, moving them back and forth until the motor picked up. Unbalanced by his change of position, *No 6* pointed her nose up. With the engine running faster he scrambled back towards his basket, before she should stand on her tail. He was breathing fast, and his heart was pounding. He shifted ballast weights, and got her on to an even keel.

The airship gathered way once more, and turned back towards St. Cloud. Down below hats were thrown into the air, men clambered up on to any prominence to wave, and a baker named Giri fell off the parapet of the Pont de Grenelle into the river, where he was rescued by a barge, and immediately afterwards arrested by the police. He was lucky to be rescued at all. Every eye was still on the airship, now struggling over the Boulevard Lannes, on the very edge of the Bois, with only five minutes of the half-hour left.

It was back in full sight of the *Daily News* man. "The motor was all right again. But not a minute too soon. The airship had drifted off course, and had begun to fall. M. Santos-Dumont threw out a few handfuls of sand. A slight pitching movement was observable, and gave rise to anxiety. Suddenly a roar of cheering was heard from the Auteuil racecourse. A horse-race was being run, but the crowd were looking at the airship over their heads. Cries of delight went up on all sides.'' But not, most probably, from the long-suffering stewards of the Jockey Club.

As *No 6* sank in the cool air above the trees, the engine slowed again. Santos shifted guide-ropes and balance weights to point her nose up. He had scarcely done so when the engine roared back to full revolutions, and the applause of the race crowds changed to shouts of alarm as she drove upwards at a steep angle. Her pilot was almost past caring. He was over the Bois, and the trees made a soft fall, if the worst were to happen. To those below it seemed as if the airship, in the last few moments of the measured half-hour, was staggering towards the finishing line like a marathon runner whose strength is all but spent.

He fought her back level again, at a height of 400 feet. This was much higher than he meant to be at the finishing line, for he had to secure her before the time ran out. He fixed his eyes on the black patch that marked the crowd at the line. The Commission were running and jumping like schoolboys, the Marquis de Dion striving to keep his attention on his watch. *No 6* bore down on them, losing height, and crossed the finishing line 29 minutes and 31 seconds after her starting time, the guide-rope swishing through the air above their heads.

Santos gave her full rudder, and she came round sharply, while at the same time he brought all his balance weights forward. Her rope thumped on the grass, and it was seized by M. Jerome, one of his crew. The Marquis de Dion snapped his stopwatch. The airship came to rest with a jar, held by a dozen strong men, and the engine stopped. This was just in time, for the rush of enthusiasts towards the aerostat threatened to hurl somebody into the propeller sails. A tumult of shouting and cheering rose, in which the Santos-Dumont supporters could be heard bellowing "Victory! Victory!"

Santos stared wildly round the circle of excited faces. His features were drawn with strain, but his eyes lighted up at the shouted words. "Have I really won?" he asked. "Tell me!

Tell me!'' Three hundred voices shouted back, ''Yes!!''
Behind the crowd the Scientific Commission were in anxious
consultation with the Marquis de Dion. At last Monsieur
Deutsch broke away from them and pushed through to where
Santos was climbing down from the basket. He embraced and
hugged him, while the aviator went on repeating ''Have I won?''

Monsieur Deutsch, with much emotion, said, ''My own view
is that you have won the prize, but you are a few seconds over
the time.'' He waved his hand apologetically towards the
Marquis de Dion, who came up at that moment. Santos looked
grim, and, a bystander noticed, suddenly very old. The Marquis
de Dion, watch in hand, addressed him. ''My friend, you have
missed the prize by 40 seconds.''

There was uproar.* Shouts of dissent mingled with cries of
''Give him the prize!'', ''Long live Santos!'', and even ''Down
with the Commission!'' For a few moments nobody could be
heard, and top hats wobbled on their owner's heads as the
demonstrators swayed to and fro.

Finally the Marquis de Dion shouted at the top of his voice,
''We must abide by the regulations!'' A dozen other voices
shouted ''Why?'' followed by groans. Monsieur Deutsch called
for silence, and gradually the hubbub died down. When he
could be heard he glanced nervously at his fellow Members, and
apologetically at Santos. ''We have to go by the regulations,'' he
repeated.

Santos-Dumont replied, ''I know I have won the prize, and if
I do not get it I will not try for it again. Not I, but the poor of
Paris, will be the losers.'' There was another storm of expostulation after this tactless speech, with its mysterious reference to
the poor of Paris. In the stress of the moment he had revealed
that he had already planned what to do with the money. It
must be excused to a man who had just gone through such an
ordeal, after weeks of disappointment. When he could make
himself heard, M. Deutsch said, ''I offer you ten thousand
francs for the poor''. Santos scornfully rejected this offer, and
deaf to the fury of argument and congratulations that once more
swamped all discussion, he gave orders to Chapin to put the
airship away.

He left in his buggy, brooding. The Commission dispersed,

* ''Alors c'est dans la foule des curieux un joli tintamarre!'' L'Illustration.

shaking their heads and arguing in undertones, except for M. Aimé, who stood by looking miserable. The crowd stayed until the airship was put away, and a fine rain began to fall.

Next day the Paris newspapers exploded with indignation, eye-witness accounts, and comment. The majority roundly declared that he had won the prize, since he had left the given spot, circled the Eiffel Tower, and returned within thirty minutes. Not all took this line, some pointed out the minority view that the Prize had included certain conditions, which had not been satisfied. The opposite camp instantly replied that the conditions quoted had been inserted long after the main rules had been stated. As there was little else at this time to fix the public attention, and certainly nothing which they had seen so dramatically with their own eyes, the row blazed on merrily for days. For most of this time Santos kept to his house, but on the few occasions that he went out he was plied with congratulations on his exploit, and vilifications of the Commission.

The Members were lying low, and it is hard not to suspect that they were testing public reaction, before making a final pronouncement. If they were, they could soon estimate that opinion was strongly in favour of Santos. A number of meetings were held behind locked doors, of which no note has survived. On the one hand was the letter of the rules; on the other the general outcry of public opinion, and the moral victory Santos had gained by crossing the line inside the time.

The arguments went on for two weeks, with the Press and public becoming more and more discontented. At last the Commission decided. "In the end", wrote Santos primly, "common-sense prevailed." On the contrary, emotion prevailed. On the 4th of November a full committee meeting of the Aéro Club was held, under the Chairmanship of Prince Roland Bonaparte, at which the Scientific Commission's secret ruling was ratified. Santos was declared the winner of the Deutsch Prize.

He immediately announced that he was dividing the money into two parts. 75,000 francs he handed over to M. Lepine, Prefect of the Paris Police, to be distributed to the deserving poor. The balance of the prize he portioned amongst his workmen. If there was perhaps too strong a flavour of drama in the first action, there was real affection and generosity in the second.

And despite the drama, we have already remarked his feeling for the poor and destitute. It would be the sourest of mistaken judgements to assume that he thought of this gesture with any self-interest, or wish for self-glorification. Santos was rarely studied. When he was flamboyant, it came naturally. His appearance, his interests or dedications, above all his everyday actions, were wholly spontaneous. His eccentricities were innocent of design, and nobody can remember anything he said which showed that he ever used more than the most superficial introspection or self-examination.

In fact M. Lepine, baffled by the unexpected gift, had to ask for detailed instructions as to how the money was to be spent. After some thought Santos ordered that every tool put in pledge by a workman was to be redeemed from the pawnbrokers and restored to its owner. Any money left over after this was to be spent on the poor, at the Prefect's discretion. M. Lepine, loaded with this monster task, probably wished he had not spoken.

The news of the Santos-Dumont victory was scarcely flashed across the headlines of the Paris newspapers when he received another, and less expected gift. Brazil, bursting to acclaim her absent son, who was trailing her colours across the skies of Europe, voted him a special prize of 100 contos, no less than 125,000 francs. Santos, who was already over-spent, quite rightly decided that he should keep this windfall for himself.

With the money from Brazil came a massive gold medal, deeply set with the words: "Being President of the Republic of the United States of Brazil, the Doctor Manoel Ferraz de Campos Salles has given order to engrave and strike this medal in homage to Alberto Santos-Dumont, 19th October, 1901." On the reverse side, inspired perhaps by the Exposition, the cloaked figure of the aeronaut was displayed, led by Victory, and invested with laurels by Renown, while Aeronautics hovered dangerously close to the Eiffel Tower.

His fame now reached its zenith. He was a household word. It is important to stress his public acclaim, for whether he desired it or not, it became an extremely important factor in his life, both at the time and afterwards. There is some slight parallel in this immense publicity and its aftermath, with the case of Charles Lindbergh twenty six years later. Probably no airman received so great an ovation between these two dates, and to both even the more important and valuable service they gave later appeared as an anticlimax by comparison.

Paris went mad over Santos. He was idolised and glorified. Postcards, photographs, souvenirs, ornaments; all manner of vendors and publicists used the Brazilian and his airship as the inspiration for their doubtful arts. He was mobbed wherever he went.

"His hangar, workshop, house, books, inventions and motor-cars were all photographed. The reporters diligently inquired into his habits, fancies, preferences and ideals. The whole Press talked about his life."*

Among the thousands of letters he received he treasured one particularly. It was from an old boyhood friend of the plantation days.

". . . Do you remember the time, my dear Alberto, when we played together, 'Pigeon flies!'? It came back to me suddenly the day when the news of your success reached Rio. 'Man flies!' old fellow! You were right to raise your finger, and you have just proved it by flying round the Eiffel Tower. You were right not to pay the forfeit; it is M. Deutsch who has paid it in your stead. Bravo! you well deserve the 100,000 franc prize.

"They play the old game now more than ever at home, but the name has been changed and the rules modified—since 19 October, 1901. They call it now 'Man flies!' and he who does not raise his finger at the word pays his forfeit. Your friend, Pedro."

Nor was the sensation caused by his feat confined to the vulgar or the simple. Articles appeared in all leading magazines with a serious or scientific turn, appraising the value of his flight. Monsieur Aimé, admittedly a partisan, wrote in *L'Illustration*:

"Of all the projects of dirigible balloons, studied in broad daylight or secretly for several years, Santos-Dumont's is the only one in a condition to effect its trials in the air. Whatever may be said, there are not two airships in the world, there is only one, and it is necessary to come to Paris to see it." And there was far more on the same lines.

* *Vida de Santos-Dumont*. Fontes.

He was swamped with social invitations, appeals, requests for lectures, and all the exhausting accompaniments that hang around the fringe of celebrity. He was not reluctant. He had put his airship away for the winter, the strain was relaxed, and he entered happily into the whirl of celebration. He appeared at plays, concerts, balls; he dined at Maxim's in a limelight scarcely enjoyed by royalty. New messages of encouragement kept coming in. Thomas Edison sent a letter of congratulation, together with his "photo-likeness", suitably inscribed. Professor Langley did likewise, and another letter and photograph came from Signor Marconi. The world was at his feet.

Thus it was a man with many preoccupations who received an invitation to visit England, and it is remarkable that he accepted. It had come about in this way.

It has been shown that England had displayed no signs of interest in controlled flying since Pilcher, who might have anticipated the Wrights, died in his own glider in 1899. The rich industrialists, and particularly shipbuilders, who might have sponsored work, and had every facility to do so, remained comatose. However, ballooning had become a fashionable sport, and quite the thing. About a dozen balloons were regularly flown over England, mostly in private ownership. Mrs. Assheton-Harboard and Mrs. John Dunville both owned balloons, and flew them regularly.

One of these sporting aeronauts was Mr. Hedges-Butler, a wealthy wine-merchant and an experienced balloonist. In September of 1901 he arranged to take his daughter Vera, Mr. Percival Spender, and the Hon. C. S. Rolls (who had not yet joined Henry Royce) on a motor trip to Scotland. Unfortunately their genial host had a slight accident with his car on the previous day, causing it to disintegrate, and doubtless to inspire the Hon. Rolls with the idea of building a better one.

The disappointed party was consoled by the suggestion that instead they should all go to the Crystal Palace and make a flight in Hedges-Butler's balloon, *City of York*. This was voted a splendid idea. Hedges-Butler was a good host, and a character. On one occasion he had made a night flight over Kent in his balloon *Dolce far Niente*, and had heard in the stillness the sound of wood-chopping in the trees below. He leant over the basket with a megaphone and shouted "Hello, down there!", where-upon there was a horrified silence, which he was too keen a wit to break.

On the 24th of September they rose from the Crystal Palace, equipped with a hamper bulging with lobsters and game pie, and drifted slowly over London in the light wind. Their conversation turned to the flights of Santos-Dumont, then working up for his final attempt, and Rolls said how much the Brazilian was helped by having the support of the Aéro Club of France. Hedges-Butler said why should there not be an Aero Club in England? All in the basket thought this an excellent notion, and before the champagne was finished they had worked out the details. The *City of York* landed at Sidcup, when the three men hurried off at once to register the name of the new Club.

While Hedges-Butler was whipping up enthusiasm, the great event of 19th October took place. This clinched it. The Club must be launched at once, and M. Santos-Dumont must be the first guest of honour. In this way he was invited, to be the earliest inspiration of organised British aviation.

Accordingly, on the 26th of November, 1901, Santos came to London, and attended the inaugural banquet given by the new Aero Club of the United Kingdom. Lord Dundonald was in the chair, and among the many guests were the Brazilian Minister, the Hon. C. S. Rolls, Col. Templer, Superintendent of the Farnborough Balloon Factory, and many other celebrities of science and technology.

After the preliminary speeches, Mr. R. W. Wallace, K.C., President of the Royal Automobile Club, proposed "The Naval and Military Forces of the Empire", remarking that ballooning was peculiarly adaptable to military service, as a means of observation. He believed that the contrivance Mr. Santos-Dumont had invented would be of the greatest use in war. (Hear, Hear.) The time would probably come when we should have, not only our Foot Guards and our Horse Guards, but our aerial guards as well. (Cheers.)

After the Chairman had proposed the health of the guest of honour, Santos rose, inwardly quaking, to a tumultuous reception. He began by thanking the Aero Club for electing him as a founder and a first honorary member. He hoped, he said, that he would soon be able to return to England, in more clement weather, to fly his airships over London. He concluded: "I drink to the health and prosperity of the members of the Club present, to those who are absent, and also to the great British nation, which, after gaining the empire of the seas, already aspires, thanks to your initiative, to the empire of the air." (Loud cheers.)* He spoke in English, and at what cost of resolution only he knew.

He sat down among wreaths of cigar smoke, and an atmosphere of general bonhomie. The last part of his speech, which had certainly been far more courteous than factual, had put him on the best of terms with his hosts, who all voted him a jolly good fellow.

Finally Lord Dundonald lulled the drowsy diners with an address incorporating practically every platitude in the language, ending with the words . . . "When the names of many of those who had occupied prominent positions in the world should have been long relegated to oblivion there would be one name that would at all events be remembered, and that was the name of Senhor Santos-Dumont." It was an ironic prophecy.

The Brazilian Ambassador gave him another banquet two nights later, and then he went back to Paris. He had been a success in England, somewhat to the surprise of many who had invited him. There were some who dissented from this opinion. "The voice of Anglo-Saxon civilisation, pragmatical and cold", wrote one of his own countrymen, himself sounding far from cordial, "greeted the inventor of the new dirigibles of the twentieth century."

* *The Times*. 26th November, 1901.

Chapter 12

☆☆☆☆☆☆☆☆☆☆☆☆☆☆☆☆☆☆☆☆☆☆☆☆☆☆☆☆

Adventures in Monaco

By the end of 1901 Santos was exhausted with acclaim, triumphal visits, dinners and speeches. The winter weather of Paris would give him little scope for flying an airship which was at its best in dead calm, while the inventor's Brazilian blood was chilled by the grey skies and biting rains of the capital. He was suffering from anticlimax, and began to go again to his workshop.

He was speculating vaguely on returning to Nice for the winter, when his acquaintance the Duc de Dino, doyen of French society in the Principality of Monaco, wrote to tell him of Royal interest in his projects. Santos pricked up his ears.

His Serene Highness Prince Albert I of Monaco, grandfather of the present Prince Rainier, was a well-known patron of the sciences, with a weakness for personal experiment, and for close observation of the work of others. He created the famous oceanographic museum in Monaco. He had followed Santos's exploits even before his success in the Deutsch Prize, and the inventor's work at Nice had been reported to him. He now let it be known through the Duc de Dino that if Santos-Dumont would come to Monaco and continue his tests there, the Principality would finance and build an airship hangar to serve as a base for voyages over the Mediterranean.

The advantages were obvious, and Santos had always wanted to try his hand over the sea. He notified his friend that he would accept the Prince's offer, and after long consideration of a large-scale map of the area he picked the position for the balloon house by the seafront at La Condamine, on the west side of the Bay of Monaco, facing across the water to Monte Carlo. Here, sheltered from the North by the mountains, from the East by the heights of Monte Carlo itself, and from the West by the promontory of the Royal Palace, he could rely on ideal conditions for the delicate launching and recovery operations so essential to the flying of airships.

He also made haste to work out and despatch to Monaco the main dimensions of the hangar, which was scaled to accept *No 6* with plenty of room to spare. He added some advice on the construction, since the Côte d'Azur could produce a formidable storm at short notice, and the French Maritime Ballooning Station at Toulon, a creation of Commandant Renard (already noted to be an unsympathetic critic), had twice been wrecked and once lifted bodily from its foundations.

As Parisian families gathered for Christmas, Santos, the unattached, put the final touches to his plans. *No 6*, still in excellent order, was dismantled, overhauled, and packed for transport by train. Spare parts and tools were assembled, and the technical team of mechanics, carpenter, and fabric-worker were chosen. His new car, a Mercedes, was to go, with its chauffeur. His own not inconsiderable wardrobe was packed. Finally all was ready.

The airship with Chapin and its attendants went on ahead, the car took the dusty road to the South, and finally Santos with his luggage followed in the sleeping-car express. The devoted M. Aimé travelled with him. The *Journal de Monaco* records his arrival on the 2nd of January, 1902. He was met at the station by the Duc de Dino and conducted to his sponsor's home at the Villa Perigord, where a suite of rooms was placed at his disposal. Prince Albert was away from the Principality, explained his gratified host, visiting the President of the French Republic.

In quitting Paris, Santos had sacrificed very little of the glitter of society. Monaco and Monte Carlo had already, by this time, reached fabulous heights of wealth and fashion, whose scale and sheer weight of money might be outdone later, but whose style and grandeur have never been surpassed to this day. In the Casino, the Theatre, the palatial hotels, and the concert-halls, the native Monagasques, despite their enviable freedom from taxation, had already yielded the struggle to keep up with the Princes and Archdukes of Imperial Russia, the immensely wealthy industrialists from Germany and France, the Greek and Levantine millionaires, the English noblemen in their yachts; and even the occasional American tycoon from New England, exclaiming in amazement at the lavish display, and nervously herding his bewildered wife and daughters through the splendid throng. The resident society, of which the Duc de Dino made an impressive leader, was no less formal than the highest circles in Paris, but blessed with that germ of inquisitive experiment which always welcomed something new or strange.

The enchanted visitors were regaled with the splendours of the sun and the sea and the mountains. Bands played in the formal gardens under the flags of a dozen nations; the throng of elegant open carriages seemed endless; the Casino never closed; and the consumption of champagne was staggering. The arts were not neglected, for when Santos arrived a concert of Beethoven and Wagner was advertised for the afternoon, the programme ending, rather ominously, with the Funeral March from *Götterdämmerung*.

At the theatre the standards were less severe, for the Archdukes had not come all this way to be improved. The play being offered, straight from Paris, was *M'Amour*, a production which the local critic primly remarked "was not of an irreproachable morality"; being concerned with the subject of adultery: however it was elevated by the spiritual gaiety with which it was interpreted by Mlles. Miramon and Gentes, and *la mignonne Yahne*. Finally, for those who found even the theatre heavy going, there was the famous Tir aux Pigeons (now no more), where hundreds of Spanish birds, their wing-feathers nicked to make them fly erratically, were released before the guns of the rich sportsmen. This contemptible sport sickened Santos, and he was notably uninterested in the Casino, also.

The King of the Belgians was installed (incognito) on a short visit. Almost any week in the Monaco season could produce some thinly-disguised Royalty. At the other end of the scale, during the seven days after Santos's arrival, five men were sentenced to an average of ten days' imprisonment for begging.

To all these wonders could now be added the aerodrome at La Condamine. Only the esplanade and the tracks of the newly-installed electric tramways (fortunately without overhead wires) separated it from the sea-wall. Crowds of onlookers watched the final days of the construction of this long, tall shed, and pressed nearer when Santos arrived by car from the Villa Perigord, on one of his many inspections.

On the 18th of January it was declared finished, and there was a ceremonial visit by all the notables of the Principality. Santos-Dumont and the Duc de Dino did the honours, with M. Aimé in the background; Prince Albert was represented by Monsieur Olivier Ritt, the Governor-General of Monaco; and savants, diplomats, and foreign guests mingled with the aristocracy of the Côte d'Azur, to gaze with admiration at the great airship hangar. It had been built in less than a month.

They inspected the stout iron framework of the skeleton, with its outer skin of wood and canvas. Its chief wonder was the two great sliding doors, fifty feet high and seventeen feet wide, each weighing half a ton. These were the largest doors known to have been made, yet they were easily run on their rails by the Princes Ruspoli, the small grandsons of the Duc de Dino. In the next building to the aerodrome the visitors were privileged to see the hydrogen generating plant that provided gas for the airship. Here some eight tons of sulphuric acid, shipped from Marseilles, and a proportional weight of iron filings, were held ready for mixing in a vat, from whence the hydrogen could be drawn off, washed by water, sawdust, and lime, and piped straight to the airship's gas-bag, in the adjacent hangar. Mr. Gordon Bennett, the famous balloon enthusiast, and M. Eiffel, the engineer, were among the few who showed any great partiality for this section of the display.

Santos personally conducted the Governor-General around the installation, explaining everything, including of course a detailed discourse on the centre of all this attention, No 6 shining with bright yellow varnish, newly assembled and suspended from the ceiling of the aerodrome. On each fine day, he said, while the crowds pressed nearer to hear, the airship, previously balanced in the aerodrome, would be conducted by hand to the sea-wall, where the weight would again be trimmed in the open air, ready for flight over the bay. Monsieur Olivier Ritt was transported with admiration.

"It was by introducing the scales into the vague operations of ancient alchemy that Levoisier produced modern chemistry," he observed, "and it is by introducing the scales in aerostatics, which remained for so long a time in an experimental state, that you will arrive at perfecting aeronautics." This statement was very well received by the visitors, and acknowledged by Santos with a polite bow, but unfortunately M. Ritt then passed on to an eulogy of the Monagasque engineers who had built the hangar, a subject he dwelt on for some time.

After the opening of the aerodrome Monaco became tense with excitement. All hotels were crammed to bursting, hotel-keepers pressed continually on Santos's heels, asking him when flying would begin, and visitors flocked in from Nice and Cannes. Unknown to them, their hero had a new preoccupation. Staring out to sea from the Villa Perigord, to where the purplish clouds piled like islands low on the horizon, Santos conceived the ambition to make a crossing by air from the French coast to Corsica. He was also struck, at this time, with the notion of using an airship as a scout for a man-of-war. M. Aimé, returning from a busy day at the new installation, often surprised him, during the time of waiting, staring mesmerised at the blue Mediterranean, brooding over the great and incalculable possibilities opened up by the flight around the Eiffel Tower.

His Corsican project became known to his intimates, and thereafter a shade too rapidly to the rest of the world. "On the day when it shall be established that a man can make his airship travel in a given direction during the hours which the young Santos demands to go from Monaco to Calvi," wrote the journalist Henri Rochefort, "there will remain little more for the nations to do but to throw down their arms. I am astonished that the capital importance of this matter has not yet been grasped by the professors of aerostation. To mount in a balloon which one has not constructed, and which one is not in a state to guide, constitutes the easiest of performances. A little cat has done it at the Folies-Bergère."*

* An early master of the "inspired revelation", Rochefort was described by an envious rival as: "A snake charmer who trains snakes to slip into the pockets, snuff-boxes, nostrils, pipes and wallets of Ministers."

On the 29th of January *No 6* was brought out of her hangar for the first flight at Monaco. The aeronaut stood in the basket, snugly dressed in a warm dark suit, with a very high stiff white collar, and wearing his motoring cap. The first cheers rose around the bay as the airship, exactly ballasted to a little above neutral weight, was walked carefully across the tramlines to the water's edge. But here a snag arose. The sea-wall was only waist-high on the roadward side, but on the harbour side the waves washed upon pebbles fifteen feet below. The stern of the airship dropped awkwardly over this wall, the handlers on the sea-front were helpless and shouted excitedly to one another, and a second handling party rushed down the sea-wall stairs to the beach, to bear up the airship from below. Santos was almost tipped from his basket into the surf, but remained as unruffled as usual.

With great labour, amid choruses of anxiety from the crowd and shouted directions from Aimé, the airship was handled down on to the beach and held uneasily against the wall while the engine was started. Finally Santos gave the order to let go, and threw out ballast. *No 6* rose into the air, her propeller blades twinkling in the sun, and moved slowly out over the harbour. A great cheer went round the sea-wall.

For half an hour she manoeuvred slowly over the water, while Santos felt out the controls. When he was satisfied he turned again for La Condamine, and headed straight for the aerodrome. There was not a breath of wind. The chief of Monaco's police, with a picked squad, had kept a road clear between the hangar and the sea-wall, though only by gigantic efforts. The handling party, now reinforced and split into two, was half on the beach and half astride the sea-wall, arms reaching out to catch the mooring-rope. Santos aimed for the hangar. The crowd held its breath.

Throttling back his motor as he came near the shore, Santos brought *No 6* down to walking pace. Just above the sea-wall he stopped the engine. The airship glided gracefully over the heads of the handling parties, across the road, and on towards the hangar. One mechanic was able to catch the guide-rope and use its last impetus to walk it into the aerodrome, "as the trainer grasps the bridle of a race-horse to lead it in after a victory". It was a small but convincing demonstration of skill and confidence.

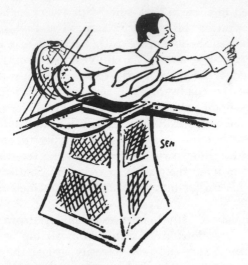

SANTOS-DUMONT BY SEM SKETCHED IN 1900

*Dirigivel, Biplano
a monoplano — minha familia*

Santos-Dumont .

Rio, 8·1·1919

SANTOS-DUMONT'S AUTOGRAPH, SKETCHED BY HIM
IN A FRIEND'S ALBUM

Amidst all the excitement and congratulations after this flight, in which many of those present had seen their first glimpse of a powered flying-machine, Santos brought up the difficulty caused by the sea-wall. While he was praised for the brilliant way in which he had piloted *No 6* back to her hangar, he pointed out that he could not be expected, every time, as it were, to thread a needle when regaining the aerodrome. A side gust of wind might catch him at any time and dash him against a lamp-post or telegraph pole.

The same afternoon he made another successful flight, with even greater difficulty in launching and recovering the airship. But by now the Governor-General had arrived at La Condamine and was offering to tear down the sea-wall opposite the hangar, exclaiming that nothing must be allowed to stand in the way of the aeronaut.

"I will not ask you to do so much," replied Santos, who was watching the securing of the airship in the shed. "It will be enough to build a landing-stage on the sea side of the wall at the level of the boulevard." This suggestion was accepted at once. Monaco was at Santos-Dumont's feet, and he could have anything for the asking.

Work on the landing-stage began immediately, in the persistent rain of an ugly spell of weather. Further flying was postponed, and Santos entered into the stately social round of the highest Monagasque society. He was the guest of honour at a number of balls, *soirées*, and dinner-parties. Though he did not visit the international chess championship then being held in the city (his mind was the antithesis of the chess player's), he graced a performance of *La Bohême*, given at the Theatre of Monte Carlo, as the guest of the Duc de Dino. Animated and cheerful between the acts, he could be seen during the performance looking down impassively from his box, starched and polished like a wooden toy figure, his melancholy eyes watching the scenes of artistic poverty, of a side of Paris life that he would never know.

On the 31st of January Prince Albert returned to Monaco. He had come as far as Marseilles by train, and then embarked on the royal yacht *Princesse Alice* to complete the journey to the harbour. At two in the afternoon he came ashore to a great reception. Cannons fired, all the bells were rung, the army presented arms, and the national anthem was played by a combined band. He had not been very long away, but he was a popular Prince, and Monaco loved to rejoice. Graciously acknowledging the uproar with smiles and waves of his hat, he climbed directly into an open landau and was driven to the Palais des Beaux-Arts, where he opened an exhibition of painting. After being introduced to the artists he stood through one more rendering of the Hymne Monagasque, and then seated himself to hear a "short but delicious concert which he warmly applauded".

Santos made haste to wait on his benefactor and invite him to the aerodrome. Prince Albert was only too anxious to come, and in fact he inspected everything on the day after his return. When he visited La Condamine, Santos was able to thank him personally for all his kindness and help; His Serene Highness's interest in the sciences was well known, and it was a privilege to be able to take advantage of such royal encouragement. Some British and American commercial interests had also offered him backing, Santos went on, but he had refused them when he had discovered that they wanted him, as a condition of their assistance, to paint advertising slogans for their products along the sides of his airship.

His Highness agreed that such an idea was unthinkable. He listened spellbound while Santos explained the details of the airship and installations to him, and left reluctantly, after wishing the aeronaut good luck and safe returns from his audacious experiments.

There were many more distinguished visitors while the airship party were waiting for the landing-stage to be finished, and one in particular is worth recording. Unannounced, wreathed in black, and escorted in a closed carriage, the ex-Empress Eugénie appeared at the door of the aerodrome, inquiring for M. Santos-Dumont. Now seventy-six years old, the widow of Napoleon III, last Emperor of the French, still showed some signs of the dazzling beauty and imperious temper that had rocked Paris, when she had come from Spain as Eugénia de Montijo, Condesa de Teba, to secure the dynastic line of the Bonapartes. She now preserved a strict incognito, though indeed living on a coast where such pretences had long worn thin; at the Villa Cymos at Cap Martin. Her terror was the camera, and she abhorred journalists. In coming to Monaco she was putting her head in the lion's jaws.

Santos gravely did the honours for the old lady. He was at his best in this role, and the visit passed off well. But though she listened to the explanations and technical details she did not seem to comprehend. Why did she come? Perhaps some imaginative memory, reawakened by the thought of a man flying; a brief revival of old dreams of conquest and glory, touched off by the vision of new fields to conquer. Perhaps she was just bored. She drove away in her closed carriage, back to the Villa Cymos, where no-one came any more.

On the 10th of February the landing-stage was ready, and *No 6* was brought out again. This time all was simple. The airship was manhandled across the boulevard and over the sea-wall on to the landing-stage. There the last balancing and weighing was done in comfort, with *No 6* riding like a ship alongside its pier.

The engine was started, and the pilot took his place. M. Aimé supervised the final adjustments, while Santos trimmed water-ballast and guide-rope for a climb.

A troupe of Italian minstrels nearby sang topical songs, in which the aeronaut's name figured prominently, but soon their voices were drowned in the spitting and rumbling of the engine. When Santos called "Let go all!" the yellow airship slanted gracefully upwards, and curved proudly out into the harbour. As she made for the open sea a scarlet pennant fluttered behind the rudder, bearing the letters P.M.N.D'A.N. They stood for the first line of the Portuguese poet Camões' epic, *Lusiad*:

*"Por mares nunca d'antes navegados!"**

No 6 flew straight as an arrow between the twin light-towers of Monaco Harbour and out into the bay. Santos was tasting the ultimate of happiness. His guide-rope dragged in the water and kept him at a steady height of fifty metres, for if he rose it became heavier, and if he descended, lighter. It provided automatic fine adjustment of ballast.

"So, with my hand upon the rudder and my eyes fixed on the

* "O'er seas hereto unsailed!" The medal sent Santos from Brazil carried the words *"Por ceos* (skies) *nunca d'antes navegados!"*

far-off point of Cap Martin, I gave myself up to the pleasure of this voyaging above the waves. Here in these azure solitudes there were no chimney-pots of Paris, no cruel, threatening roof-corners, no tree-tops of the Bois de Boulogne. My propeller was showing its power, and I was free to let it go. I had only to hold my course in the teeth of the breeze, and watch the far-off Mediterranean shore flit past me." Santos, poet and dreamer, was at the helm.

The watchers on every vantage-point at Monaco saw him dwindle and vanish over the immensity of the sea. There was some anxiety, for this was not in the programme. But after an hour he reappeared, the tiny dot growing larger, changing from black to gold, and wheeling into the harbour entrance. As he stopped his motor to glide to the aerodrome the thunders of cheering rolled up around the hills. Once more he made a perfect approach, and the handlers, reinforced by Prince Albert's bodyguard, had only to walk him into the hangar. He sprang down from the basket, laughing and excited, to tell Aimé of a perfect trip.

On the next suitable day, 12th February, he planned a longer and more daring voyage over the sea. His admirers begged him not to set out again without the guardian boats, which the wealthy yachtsmen of the Côte d'Azur jostled to place at his disposal. Mr. Gordon Bennett's *Lysistrata*, Mr. Eugene Higgins' *Varuna*, and M. Eiffel's steam yacht; all were standing by. Santos decided to fly down the coast towards Italy, and a number of launches were pre-positioned on his course. The powerful Mors automobile of Mr. Dinsmore, and the giant Panhard of M. Isidore Kahenstein, were prepared to follow and pace him along the coast road.

Last but most impressive of all, the steam *chaloupe* of His Highness the Prince, carrying the Prince himself in yachting attire, the Governor-General in morning-coat and top-hat, and the captain of the *Princesse Alice*, set course for the open sea to join the fleet of guard-boats.

As soon as he left the Bay of Monaco Santos turned *No 6* straight down the coast to the East, and put on full speed. Along the winding corniche he could see the two racing-cars thundering round the bends in clouds of dust, as they strove to keep up. "It was all we could do to follow the airship along the curves of the coast road," declared Mr. Dinsmore later. "In less than five minutes it had arrived opposite the Villa Camille Blanc, about a kilometre from Cap Martin. At this moment the airship was absolutely alone. Beneath it I saw a single row-boat, while far behind was visible the black smoke from the Prince's *chaloupe*. It was really no commonplace sight to see the airship thus hovering isolated over the immense sea."

But Santos saw the signs of bad weather, and turned once more for Monaco. Homing on the wings of the freshening wind, he seemed (to the overwrought editor of the *Journal de Monaco*) like an eagle bearing down upon him. When he wheeled into the harbour he could see line upon line of waving hats and handkerchiefs, and the shouts of encouragement came to him through the rumble of his engine. When he stopped it, some way out in the harbour because of the wind, the full clamour of the spectators rose to his basket.

As *No 6* glided towards the shore Santos signalled for the picket-boat to take his guide-rope. But the Prince's *chaloupe* had regained the harbour, piloted by the captain of the Royal Yacht, and now it surged forward under the airship. The little steamboat spat a fierce blast of smoke and sparks into the air perilously close beneath the basket, making Santos unhappily conscious of the great bag of hydrogen above him. His indulgent patron risked, unwittingly, blowing both himself and his protégé to smithereens.

His Highness had decided to seize the guide-rope himself. In spite of the anxious remonstrances of the Governor-General he boldly went forward in the *chaloupe* and reached for the heavy rope. The launch darted forward, the rope swept across its deck and struck the Prince, and he was knocked head over heels into the bottom of the boat. The water boiled with manoeuvring vessels centring on the *chaloupe*, where the crew were raising the Prince, and in the confusion Santos somehow got *No 6* securely warped in to the shore.

This drama had been played before tens of thousands of eyes. As soon as their ruler was seen to be safe the more ribald elements in the crowds seemed to think it all part of the fun, though His Highness, who suffered severe contusions, could hardly be expected to see the joke, and the incident was not reported in the *Journal de Monaco*.

Santos was now fairly launched into those technical researches so dear to him, with unlimited scope for experiment as progress required. He had fitted a simple windmill anemometer to *No 6*, to try to work out her exact speed, but the instrument was inaccurate and the airship too slow to eliminate the effect of wind gusts. Speed meant survival and practical flying in any wind, so speed he must have.

Bright-eyed, busy and happy, he spent hours with Aimé and his crew; discussing, adjusting, testing. The ultimate speed problem, as he foresaw, was that of keeping the shape of the non-rigid airship, whose form is maintained only by internal pressure, when the speed rose high enough to impose heavy forces on the nose. With a fair comprehension of aerodynamics he further noted that the suction at the stern would be even more dangerous than the push on the nose, inducing the airship to blow out its rear even before it pushed in its prow.

On the afternoon of the 14th of February, *No 6* was brought out for another flight, and this turned out to be her last. The disaster was caused by faulty preparation, a sad end for his most famous airship. It was a still and beautiful afternoon, with a warm sun. Before the *aérostat* left the hangar the steam *chaloupe* of Prince Albert was in position in the harbour, with the amiable Prince on board and not one whit discouraged, and a launch from the yacht *Varuna* carried Mr. Eugene Higgins with a party of ladies, all standing by to render help if necessary.

At 2.40 the airship was handled into the launching position and the engine started. Santos was looking pleased and contented, and waved to the crowds as usual. But no sooner had he ordered the release and put the airship into a climb, than it became clear that something was wrong.

In fact the envelope was not completely inflated with hydrogen, and the maximum expansion of the ballonet was not sufficient to take up the slack. The form of the airship was "soft", and cries of dismay broke from the crowds as it pitched alarmingly. The uneven inflation of the envelope unbalanced the aerostat, and it climbed drunkenly until its dripping guide-rope hung high above the water. Santos was experiencing yet again the unpleasantness of a ship that had lost its rigidity. The diagonal bracing wires, and those holding the rudder assembly, were caught up in the propeller, and he quickly stopped the motor before it could churn *No 6* into pieces.

The *New York Herald* correspondent noted: "The balloon seemed to stand on its head and looked as if it would turn over backwards, for a great gust of wind, blown high up from the ugly *'Tête de Chien'*, struck the frail vessel with overpowering force. Then it was seen that the rudder, presumably caught in the dragging envelope, was smashed to pieces. Slowly the balloon drifted towards the pigeon-shooting grounds. The excitement was intense. Phlegmatic Englishmen wiped the perspiration from their foreheads, and emotional Southerners wrung their hands and appealed to one another in despair."

Shattered and drifting, *No 6* was bearing down on the shore, with its sharp poles and peaks and buildings. Santos did not hesitate, though his heart must have been heavy. With a swift movement he pulled the emergency gas valve, and his finest airship, winner of the Deutsch Prize, subsided on the waters of the harbour and began to sink. The rescue launches foamed towards him, lassoed the frame with ropes, and attempted to tow the control car, with the aeronaut still in it, towards shallow water. He was going down with his ship, and seemed disinclined to abandon it.

"Leave the balloon!" "Never mind the airship!" shouted the excited sportsmen who had crowded to the edge of the shooting ground and were hanging over the rails. But Santos, now up to his armpits, would not budge, and with violent gesticulations he shouted his directions to the men in the boats, who were still trying to tow the shapeless mass of *No 6*.

Then the remains of the envelope burst, in a flutter of tattered silk. It was the end. "Save him! Save him!" shouted the frenzied spectators. The keel and control basket had disappeared, and Santos was up to his neck in water, when the Prince's *chaloupe* ran alongside him, in among the cables and debris, and he was hauled to safety. "Like a wounded bird," commented M. Aimé gloomily, "the ravished aerostat sank beneath the waves."

A roar of cheering burst from the terraces when he stood up safe in the launch, but instead of making for the shore and a dry suit of clothes he continued energetically to direct salvage operations for the now vanished airship. The reaction after danger was upon him, and a not over-acute witness in the launch reported him as radiant, self-possessed, almost elated. His ruined clothes dripping water, he remained for two hours in the *chaloupe*, until some sort of grapple had hauled the remains of *No 6* to the beach. Only then did he give up, and when he came ashore, "to say that M. Santos-Dumont had a magnificent welcome is to convey a very inadequate idea of what happened".

The buoyant Principality was in no mood to let the young Brazilian relapse into gloom. The Prince sent at once an encouraging message and condolences. To this Santos bravely replied that it was "only one more accident", and assured His Highness that as soon as he had got over his temporary misfortune he would recommence his experiments. The same night a banquet was given in his honour, at which the Duc de Dino offered to open a fund to defray his very considerable expenses. Santos replied with warm thanks, but said that before accepting he would like to give the Brazilian Government the first chance in this field.

The succeeding days brought no signs of a response to this patriotic suggestion, the Brazilian Government possibly feeling that it had shot its bolt in the previous October. The Duc de Dino accordingly opened the list with a donation of 3,000 francs, which was followed by a further gratifying response from others. The sad remains of *No 6* were parcelled up for transport by the technical crew, who were now somewhat under a cloud for their failure to ensure the airship's proper inflation. So with these melancholy bundles, the rest of his supporting apparatus, his luggage, and M. Aimé, and with the cheers and goodwill of the people of Monaco to speed him on his way, Santos finally quitted La Condamine and his kind hosts, and took the train for Paris and home.

☆☆☆☆☆☆☆☆☆☆☆☆☆☆☆☆☆☆☆☆☆☆☆☆☆☆☆☆☆☆

See the Conquering Hero

Once back in Paris, he quickly shook off his depression. In the months just before his 29th birthday, during the short pause that followed the intense living of the past year, he took stock of his progress. He had some reason for satisfaction. In four years he had come from obscurity to world-wide fame. The cold eye of the historian might look on all the fuss, and pronounce it out of proportion to its value to the science of aviation, or to anything else. But nobody could deny the impetus he had given to the conquest of the air in general.

While others had been pondering, he had acted. While some had been counting the cost, he had dared. His renown had been bought at the stake of the repeated risk of his life, and if the line he was following proved, in the light of later events, to be out of the main stream of discovery, it certainly stimulated a whole wave of new experimenters. They had been shown a man flying controllable aircraft. Now they were able to declare that they could do as well or better; that his ideas were wonderful, or wholly wrong; and that they were ready to prove their opinions in the air.

The first emulator was another Brazilian, Augusto Severo. He had been interested in aerostation since 1881, but it was not until 1892 that he managed to amass enough funds to order a professionally built balloon from the admirable Monsieur Lachambre. It was christened *Bartholomeo de Gusmão*, and delivered to Brazil by M. Machuron himself. In spite of the tuition which Lachambre and Machuron supplied with their balloon, Severo appears to have been unhandy, and made little mark with his purchase. He was enthusiastic, however, and it was mainly he who persuaded the Government of Brazil to grant Santos the big money prize in 1901.

In September he left Brazil for France, with the plans of his airship *Pax*. It was intended as a mere stepping-stone to a much larger passenger-carrying airship, to be called *Jesus*, with which he intended to carry 100 people on a regular service across the South Atlantic. In the meantime he spent all his modest fortune on *Pax*, constructed by M. Lachambre, and on a large hangar to house it, which he built in ten days. Santos looked coldly on all this reckless activity, and pointed out to his fellow Brazilian that he, Severo, had too little experience for the fast pace he was setting.

The first trial of *Pax* was held on the 12th of May. M. Severo started from Vaugirard, accompanied by his *mécanicien*, Saché. The airship had one propeller at the nose and another at the stern, with the drive running back into the gas-bag. The possibilities of trouble with this system were almost endless, but in fact it never got that far. The airship had been "weighed" too light, and as soon as it was released it sprang into the air. M. Severo and his mechanic seem to have lost their heads, and instead of valving gas they threw out ballast. *Pax* shot higher into the sky, and Saché was last seen throwing out a whole bag of sand. The airship dwindled to a dot, its propellers turning slowly, and a few moments later there was a boom like a cannon from overhead, as the envelope exploded. The tangled remains, fluttering a few shreds of fabric, fell like a stone into the Avenue du Maine. "The fall took eight seconds, and the luckless experimenters were picked up broken and shapeless masses." Pieces of the fabric were cut up and sold for souvenirs, and the Brazilian flag fetched 22 francs. It was discovered afterwards that M. Severo had sealed a faulty gas relief-valve with wax.

Other competitors appeared even less promising. Monsieur Roze's giant dirigible *Aviateur* looked, on a casual glance, as if it would furnish a still more spectacular disaster, but fortunately for him, and perhaps for the citizens below, it refused to leave the ground. Not so M. Ottokar de Bradsky's aerostat, christened simply *Bradsky*. In October it too took off from Vaugirard, with its inventor and another dauntless *mécanicien*. It crossed Paris successfully before the gondola fell off, carrying both aviators to their doom.

It seemed as if *aérostation* were not so easy as Santos made it look, though even that was none too safe. He appeared to have the sole rights to aerial travel; and then the brothers Lebaudy came on the scene. They were substantial sugar refiners, who made up their minds that this aviation needed tackling properly, in a business-like way; and they had a first-class engineer in Henri Juillot. Paul and Pierre Lebaudy had their first airship ready by the end of the year. She was a large semi-rigid, with a 35 h.p. Daimler engine, and she was a success from the first. She carried passengers, made night flights, and took up photographers. With her arrival Santos ceased to have a monopoly.

He was no longer the only pebble on the beach, but nothing could take his triumph away from him. His very success, with its inevitable train of distractions and its inevitable reaction, made it more certain that his rivals would gain on him. For in spite of Monsieur Aimé, he was a one-man band. When he was away, nothing could go forward at his workshops. From 1903 onwards he was competing with organised firms; Lebaudy, French Astra (which built the *Ville de Paris* in 1904), Clement-Bayard, and Zodiac. They planned to handle sums of money quite beyond even his reach.

In the spring of 1902 he was still on the crest of the wave set off by the Deutsch Prize, but then his thirst for work began to return. His companions, Blériot, the Farman brothers, and even Aimé, were only partly convinced that the future lay with airships, being increasingly liable to argue that heavier-than-air flight might, after all, be possible. Fired by Santos's example they were now trying to think of better ways of navigating the air, and whereas once he had merely been told that what he meant to do was impossible, now he was more often told that it was wrong, and that he should follow the speaker's pet method instead.

"How often have things been proved to me impossible!"

he wrote plaintively. "Now I am used to it I expect it. But in those days it troubled me. Still I persevered."

The Monsieur Rochefort already quoted, distressingly blood-thirsty like so many non-combatants, had a new idea for his attention. "Let us suppose," he wrote, showing a sad lack of sympathy for England's South African embroilment, "that the idea enters the daring Brazilian's head of offering his services to the Boers, who at present have everybody's admiration; thanks to his new balloon, which he is now constructing, fifteen metres longer than the previous one, with the support of two 45 horse-power engines; he would be master of space. Aided by two or three companions it would be possible for him to observe and transmit to the defenders of the Transvaal details of all the movement of the English troops. Nothing would be easier than for him to drop charges of explosive in the midst of their lines, and against the devastation so caused it would be impossible to fight."

Steady, Monsieur Rochefort; be very careful what you say. You may be starting something. Reading this suggestion, Santos, after marvelling at the inspired journalist's baleful quality of knowing his construction plans almost before he did himself, pondered deeply on the idea. He was a sincere idealist and he hated war; in principle he was horrified at this possibility. But it fascinated him; he could not clarify his thoughts on the subject; he never unravelled the confusion between abstract and particular; and he was not and is not the only inventor in such a predicament.

Sometimes he declared that he would rather he had never lived than that airships should be used for war; shortly afterwards he was suggesting ways and means. He could not fly over the Mediterranean without reflecting on the application of this feat to submarine spotting and naval reconnaissance; much later, when all this happened, he declared that his inventions had been twisted to ghastly ends. His dilemma is only too familiar today.

Indeed he had a new airship coming up, to replace *No 6*, but so far it was only on paper. In the meantime he received another invitation from the Aero Club in London. Besides offering their hospitality, and a polite request for him to consider giving a lecture (which he refused with a shudder), the Aero Club asked if the remains of *No 6*, re-assembled into a recognisable shape, might be exhibited under their auspices at the Crystal Palace.

Santos consented, and the airship, sufficiently repaired to be shown indoors, was shipped to London, followed by its inventor. It was unpacked in the Crystal Palace in May, 1902, but when the reconstructed gas-bag came out of its basket it was seen to be ripped, as with a knife. When he was told Santos was furious, and at once suspected foul play, though it seems not impossible that the repaired envelope had parted while being packed, or been innocently damaged in transit.

The Crystal Palace authorities engaged detectives, who discovered nothing to account for the damage. Santos insisted that a knife had been plunged through the basket. "I never expected it here," he said. "In Paris I had fears. But not here." A reward was offered for information, but when a rumour gained ground that Santos had done the deed himself, so as to provide a reason for not flying over London (which he had never planned to do), his wrath knew no bounds. Overhearing an Englishman in the Ritz making a sneering remark about the mutilation of *No 6*, Santos stepped up to him, rose on tip-toe and tweaked his nose, and demanded satisfaction. Cards were exchanged, the Englishman's reading "James Steven Vandercook, Savage Club, London". His hosts, however, smoothed the incident down, and there was no duel; but the mystery of the damage was never solved.

When he had regained his normal good temper, the aeronaut duly visited the Crystal Palace, to see *No 6*, patched up yet again, suspended from the galleries as if in flight. He took with him his brother Henriques, who was visiting England to raise interest in a scheme for a Channel tunnel, for which he was the consulting engineer. Neither brother can have been much encouraged by his reception, and Santos made no public appearances in London.

He did, however, go down to Tavistock, where his nephews Arnaldo and Henriques Dumont-Villares, sons of his favourite sister Virgínia, were boarders at Kelly College. He stayed for several days at a nearby hotel, while his nephews happily wallowed in his reflected glory, and he showed pleasure in taking them on small outings and treats. But he seemed to feel that moderation and restraint were expected of him in England.

Fifty years later Henriques wrote, "Although jovial and expansive among his friends, before strangers he maintained a serious and reserved attitude, which some attributed to the influence of the British habits acquired during his stay at the University of Bristol. Perhaps that is where he also gained his passion for punctuality. He never kept anyone waiting, nor would he wait for anyone."

Of the two recollections the nephews have of this visit, one is normal and the other distinctly odd. He was surrounded by boys demanding his autograph, and one asked for a memento. Santos fished out his handkerchief, and suggested that it be cut to pieces so that the bits could be shared round. This was done, but as there were still many unsatisfied customers he went back to his hotel and fetched two ties, which were likewise reduced to fragments.

The second incident occurred while walking through the college gardens with his nephews. They observed that he was carefully dislodging the bees and wasps in the rhododendron flowers, using the tips of his fingers. At last the inevitable happened, he received a painful sting, and they had to run to Matron for the blue-bag. Being schoolboys, it never occurred to them to ask him why he did it; and being Santos, it never occurred to him that it needed any explanation.

Before leaving France he had received another invitation. The organisers of the Louisiana Purchase Centennial Exposition had decided on a World Fair, at St. Louis, to be held in 1904, to mark the centenary of the Louisiana Purchase. They invited Santos to come over to the United States at once, to advise them on the organisation of the airship races which were to form one of the greatest attractions of the fair. He was flattered, and if further inducement was needed, his love of novelty provided it, for he had never been to the United States.

He therefore left England by White Star liner, sailed to New York, and took the train for St. Louis. He had a splendid Press reception, which could not be said to be so many times greater than the coverage given the Wright brothers (then only sixteen months from their first aeroplane flight) since no-one had heard of the Wright brothers at all.

He met once more his distinguished acquaintance, Professor Langley, now deeply engaged in the crucial experiments with his flying machine *Aerodrome*, but he found the organisers of the fair to be showmen rather than savants. Their first idea was to have an airship race from St. Louis to Chicago—several hundred miles. Even by 1904 this might be somewhat optimistic, Santos advised, with a sidelong look at the prize fund of 200,000 dollars. He might be competing himself . . .

Instead he put forward the scheme of erecting three towers or flag-poles at the corner of the Exposition grounds, giving a closed circuit of about ten miles: this, he said, would allow the patrons to see everything, while giving a good test of manoeuvrability. His mouth must have watered as he further suggested a first prize of 100,000 dollars, to encourage the entry of European aeronauts. Since the organisers were spending a cool 45 million dollars all told, it could not be regarded as excessive.

After an exhausting programme of banquets and receptions, which he found no less formal than in Paris, but much less enjoyable, he returned to New York. There it was put to him, as indeed it had been on his way through London, that prizes might be offered for some other airship contest or feat, while waiting for the races in 1904. The suggestions were vague. Would M. Santos-Dumont consider competing, if such an idea materialised?

He replied firmly that he would compete, probably in his new racer, if the organisers would put down a cash deposit, sufficient to warrant him bringing his airship and team from France. This business-like answer seemed to surprise his hearers, and the subject was not raised again.

Before he left he had an interview with Thomas Edison. After reading a newspaper interview with Santos, in which he had stated that he was planning to install the new Marconi wireless telegraphy system in his airship, the inventor asked him to visit the Edison research station. They had a long discussion, after which Edison showed his guest round the West Grange laboratories. The talk was amiable, but no more. Edison commented drily to a reporter, who was probably hoping for some startling project to be revealed: "Dumont came to satisfy a desire, which was mutual, to meet." He added that they had discussed the use of electric power for airships, but agreed that the apparatus would always be too heavy.

On the steamship for Cherbourg the old enthusiasms welled up once more. He had been merely marking time. He must reorganise his aerodrome and start building again. The last three months had been wasted. He must get on.

His friends were glad to see him back. A tear or two ran down the broad and genial face of the loyal Chapin as he wrung his young master by the hand. On the next day after his return to rue Washington he was out into the Bois in his little electric automobile, to look things over at St. Cloud.

The fenced-off premises of the Aéro Club were becoming too crowded, he noted with some irritation. Several ordinary balloons were moored in the enclosure, new sheds of various sizes had been put up, and foundation trenches were dug here and there. "Vague outlines," he remarked acidly, "for constructions that were never finished." One of his men, running to catch his guide-rope at the dramatic finish of the Deutsch Prize trip, had actually fallen into the earliest of these trenches, costing Santos a second or two more of recorded time.

Worst of all, M. Deutsch himself was getting into the act. This was outrageous—as if Michelangelo's patron had taken up painting. Only two airship lengths in front of *No 6*'s old hangar the huge skeleton of a new shed was rising, directly opposite his sliding doors. It was the work of the Astra Airship Company, founded by M. Deutsch and largely financed by him. He intended to produce an airship of a type which Santos coldly classified as, "on the lines of my *No 6*". It was going to be awkward enough to find the room to work, and to launch the airship, with all these latecomers cluttering up the place. But there would certainly be too little space to bring her safely back, and handle her in on the ground. Better to cut the losses, thought Santos, and move somewhere else.

The late summer of 1902 therefore found him in another whirl of intensive activity. Everything had to be done at once. The detailed plans of *No 7* were drawn and discussed with the workmen, while he looked for the site on which he had decided he would build his own airship station, free of the Aéro Club, on his own land.

After a long search he found what he wanted. On the rue de Longchamp, in what was then the suburb of Neuilly St. James, two large houses flanked a fair-sized piece of vacant ground, surrounded by a high stone wall. On the rue de Long-champ side this plot gave on to the Bois de Boulogne at the Bagatelle Gate; on the other it was backed by the Boulevard de la Seine,* and then by the river itself, opposite the Ile de Puteaux. Santos made up his mind that he wanted it, but he had a struggle to get it.

The owner was very doubtful about leasing his property for such a purpose, while the owners of the flanking houses must have been none too pleased. When he had reached an understanding with them, there was another fight with the authorities of the Bois de Boulogne, who held building jurisdiction over the area. The Aéro Club de France was one thing; a private aeronaut, household word or not, quite another . . . It was one of the major triumphs of his charm and persuasive personality that he won them over to consent to the erection of what he proudly called "The First of the World's Airship Stations".

This physical withdrawal from St. Cloud was the complement of a definite, though hardly perceptible, disengagement from the Aéro Club. Nothing was said or done, but the aftermath of the hullabaloo about the Deutsch Prize was an indefinable coolness, mingled with a mental resolve on each side that it would show the other a thing or two about aviation.

The main hangar of the Airship Station was erected on the new site at Neuilly in the last months of 1902. Its framework consisted of long rows of wooden pillars, forming airship stalls, the biggest of which was 170 feet long by 32 feet wide and 45 feet high. There were seven stalls of various sizes, the whole assembly making a large square. The pillars were braced with steel cables, and the framework was covered with heavy striped canvas, to make a huge tent. Santos declared that this was as safe as wood, and a good deal cheaper. Very large doors of wood, sliding on wooden frameworks, closed the hangar at each end. It was an economical system of construction, but even so it must have swallowed up a large part of the 100 contos of the Brazilian Government's award.

No 7 was designed, and its components made, in the old workshops at St. Cloud. Santos still lived at No. 9 rue Washington. His study was littered with plans, drawings, and schedules

* Now the Boulevard du General Koenig. The airship station has been occupied by houses No. 83-87.

of parts, for he had two other airships on the drawing-board. *No 7* was designed for racing (with St. Louis at the back of his mind), and for any other competitions which would be worth his attention. It was a large airship, of thin and shark-like appearance, requiring all of 1,257 cubic metres of hydrogen to lift the four-cylinder, water-cooled, 60 horsepower Clement engine, plus its racing pilot.

Santos was discovering the inevitable fact that all improvements are more costly. *No 7* was the first of his airships to have the gas-bag compartmented internally, for safety and some added rigidity. The compartments were made of heavy unvarnished silk, so that gas could creep from one section to another, but could not escape catastrophically if the envelope was punctured. The internal ballonet and airpump still furnished the main means to keep the envelope rigid.

Before *No 7* was inflated at Neuilly, *No 9* was designed and built. There was no *No 8*, because of Santos's unexplainable superstition about the figure. (He would not even make a flight on the eighth day of the month.) *No 9* was intended as his personal runabout, to be used practically, like his electric buggy. With it he wanted to demonstrate how airships might be flown easily and conveniently, as a personal means of transport.

The first appearance of the helicopter, in later years, gave everyone, particularly the newspapers, the same sort of idea. Every man would have his own helicopter or airship, the children would leave for school from the roof, traffic lanes would be established, and so on. There is no sign of this well-worn prediction ever being realised. On the contrary, as aviation has developed, private flying has been forced further into the background.

In the spring of 1903 the new installation at Neuilly was completed. Besides the large hangar there were workshops, a hydrogen plant, and all the needs of aerostation, as proved by the experience gained at St. Cloud. *No 7* was conveyed there in pieces, erected, and inflated. The first ascent from the Airship Station was made in the Racer.

Working from his own enclosure, Santos could have some privacy at last. He was not impelled to rashness by the presence of crowds of onlookers. The trials of *No 7* therefore went smoothly, and the first that Paris knew about the latest airship was the sight of it cruising over the Seine. This was a much better arrangement. He was able to run through the trials without a hitch, and give the airship back to the care of Aimé, Gasteau, and Chapin, to be kept in its stall ready for use.

We shall not hear very much more of *No 7*. She was expensive to run, costing 3,000 francs merely to inflate her with hydrogen. She was intended to be used in competitions, which either did not materialise, or if they were held found him busy elsewhere. She had two propellers, fifteen feet in diameter, driven from the single Clement engine; one in front and one behind; and this again made her uncomfortable to fly. She was designed for a speed of no less than fifty miles per hour, and her envelope was therefore inflated to a higher pressure than any of the earlier airships, and four times that of *No 6*. Since she was obviously no pleasure-craft, and designed to carry one man only, she could be used only for competition or research. She looked like a handful, and perhaps it is as well that Santos did not take her to her limits. He certainly never flew her at full speed. For the present she lay ready in the hangar, while her owner went on with his next model.

Santos-Dumont No 9 (also known as *Baladeuse*)* can be bracketed with his later aeroplane *Demoiselle* as the most successful of his flying machines, and significantly both were designed in the tradition that he had made peculiarly his own; small, light, simple. He called it a "runabout", and built it ostensibly for his own pleasure, when it seemed that there was going to be no immediate racing challenge to *No 7*. It was short and chubby, with a gas-bag of only 220 cubic metres capacity, driven by a 3 horsepower Clement engine. It had a very large rudder for its size, and its short length made it highly manoeuvrable. A triangular-section girder keel was slung under the envelope, holding basket, engine, propeller, and all apparatus.

The first trip of *No 9*, from the new Airship Station, was absurdly simple. In a condition of calm air one man could walk her out of the hangar to the take-off position. Her "weighing" took no time at all, since she only carried 120 lbs. of ballast. Gasteau started the engine with a casual flick of his wrist. Santos took his place in the basket wearing a bowler hat, though

* A stroller (feminine, of course).

it was secured to his coat lapel by the patent safety cord. A last check according to the list system he had established (Is the balloon properly filled? Is there any possibility of a leak? Is the rigging in condition? Is the motor in condition? Do the cords commanding rudder, motor, ballast, and shifting guide-rope work freely? Is the airship properly weighed?), and then he was ready.

From force of habit he called "Let go all!", whereupon Chapin took his hand off the guide-rope, and *No 9* was away. Half an hour of buzzing about over the trees of the Bois, like a fat bumble-bee looking for honey, and he was back again. His accumulated skill brought her to a standstill in precisely the right place, and Chapin caught her rope with the utmost ease.

In contrast with the many other dangers which Santos and the early balloonists knew so well, there seemed little appreciation of the menace of static electricity. Since this provided the last and worst airship disaster of all time, when *Hindenburg* dissolved in a great eruption of flame, it is strange that Chapin, who caught many a mooring-rope, never received any electric shock which either he or Santos thought worthy of mention. The slow speed of the airships may have had something to do with it, but they must have been lucky none the less.

Santos needed to keep before the public eye, for Paris was finding new interests. On May Day, before he could put his new airship into the air, but when the avenues were ablaze with blossom and new leaf, King Edward VII paid a state visit to the capital. The Boer War was over, and Anglo-French relations were on the mend. As President Loubet and his royal guest drove through the main streets, with the tossing plumes of the *Garde Républicaine* undulating before and behind their carriage, the King must have allowed himself an occasional nostalgic glance up the side roads, leading to that more rollicking Paris he once had known.

The whole capital was anxious to do the King honour. Even M. Rochefort was mollified. "It was agreeable", he wrote, carefully, "so to see the President and the King of England receiving together the plaudits of the people." England, which had always been fashionable with the highest French circles, returned to public esteem also.

Santos watched the celebration from the balcony of his house, from which he had suspended the French, British, and Brazilian flags. He invited a small party of friends, and they drank toasts in champagne. He was in the best of spirits. His voice, which could be quiet and melancholy, rattled out clipped sentences at high pitch and top speed, like a toy Gatling gun spraying pellets of comment and opinion.

"And why," asked the sententious M. Georges, who was present and making great play with the champagne, "is our aeronaut not flying his latest creation above the heads of the procession? Paris should greet the new event with her own novelties."

"It is not, you understand, not—seemly." The inventor's eyes twinkled; his whole face creased with mischief. "In England they would think it ostentatious. And for this reception today it is the prerogative of France. I am Brazilian. I stand aside."

But as he spoke his gaze became dreamy and unfocused once more. The glass in his hand was forgotten. He looked out over the crowds, the people of Paris, those who seemed to him sharers of his dream; his support and inspiration. He believed that he was firmly in their hearts, Alberto Santos-Dumont, the one and only.

Chapter 14

☆☆☆☆☆☆☆☆☆☆☆☆☆☆☆☆☆☆☆☆☆☆☆☆☆☆☆☆☆☆

The Fairy Vehicle

In June of 1903 Paris was becoming used to the excursions of *No 9* and her pilot. On calm summer days one might expect to meet Monsieur Santos-Dumont and his little airship anywhere, at any moment. He had mastered the control of the new craft so well that he could attempt trips, and casually bring them off, which put him once more ahead of all competition. Compared to his gay cavortings around Paris, the efforts of other and possibly more serious competitors seemed remote and boring.

In the fine sunny mornings of early summer he would be off to Neuilly in his electric buggy, the bodywork bright and the wheelspokes glinting in the morning air; as polished and quiet and purposeful as the dapper owner himself. Into the Bois he sped, threading his way easily through the crush, into the patches of bright sunshine, through the cool shadows of the trees, past the lake where the nursemaids threw bread for the ducks, until he swung in to his own gate in the wall of the Airship Station, and halted beside the gay striped canvas of his hangar.

No 9 would be ready and waiting on the grass of the launching-ground, already weighed to positive lift, held easily on one rope, like a horse awaiting its master. He need pause only to exchange pleasantries with Chapin and Gasteau before vaulting into the basket. He would be dressed in the height of fashion, in tight suit, high collar, and bowler hat. A pause to pull on his gloves, and shoot his cuffs. One twist of the propeller, and *No 9* would be off on another jaunt.

He usually started pointing away from Paris, slanting up across the Boulevard de la Seine and curving round above the river, to aim the nose back towards Longchamp. The neighbours objected when he took off in the opposite direction. He passed their roof-tops dangerously close, it seemed to them, while they also got the mistaken notion that he was looking into their bedroom windows. With everything fully under control on board the airship he would then be ready for the business in hand, business which often looked as if it were promoted by a mischievous desire to shock and amaze the Parisian man in the street.

One of his first trips in *No 9* was the short run across the Bois to St. Cloud, where he landed in the Aéro Club's enclosure, in the midst of six fully inflated spherical balloons. He dismounted and stopped the engine, to pass the time of day with his wide circle of acquaintances, a number of whom were probably thinking that this demonstration was intended to make them all look somewhat old-fashioned; and was succeeding, at that.

When the time came for him to go he raised his bowler, and swung a leg into the basket. "Can we not give you some gas?" asked one of his fellow-clubmen, politely.

"You saw me coming all the way from Neuilly," replied Santos; "did I throw out any ballast?"

"You threw out no ballast," they admitted, chastened.

"Then why should I be in need of gas?" On this powerful exit line he flew off, leaving his watchers holding their hats, and probably grinding their teeth. He could be very irritating. They must have been more than human if they did not sometimes think it was high time he had another accident. Nothing serious, you understand; nobody could really wish him ill, but the way the little fellow bounces about in his balloon! He seems to be everywhere at once.

Santos was as happy as a schoolboy. His audacity began to strain even the almost inexhaustible tolerance of the Paris police and municipal authorities. M. André Fagel, of *L'Illustration*, had a curious experience on the 28th of June.

"I had just sat down at the terrace of a café on the Avenue du Bois de Boulogne," he records, "and was enjoying an iced orangeade. All of a sudden I was shaken with surprise on seeing an airship come right down in front of me. The guide-rope coiled round the legs of my chair. The airship was just above my knees, and M. Santos-Dumont got out. Whole crowds of people rushed forward and wildly acclaimed the great Brazilian aviator; they like courage and sportsmanship. M. Santos-Dumont asked me to excuse him for having startled me. He then called for an *aperitif*, drank it down, got on board his airship again, and went gliding off into space. I am glad that with my own eyes I have been able to contemplate the bird-man."

As this happened at the time of day when fashionable society was promenading, it created a traffic jam along the Avenue as far as the Arc de Triomphe.

"The next day," continued M. Fagel, "I went to the Bois de Boulogne. Just as my car was about to go through the Porte Dauphine the bird-man landed in the roadway. The policemen rushed forward, stopping the passers-by, on foot, on horseback, and in all kinds of vehicles. The trotting horses snorted, the motors loudly hummed on the cars being brought to a sudden stop, shaking up the occupants. The nurses taking children out for an airing became nervous. What was the matter? Was it a riot? Had the King of England returned to Paris? No. It was M. Santos-Dumont on another of his aerial promenades."

These tricks were distinctly risky. They looked very amusing so long as everything went well. But as Santos well knew, one unexpected spike, lamp-post, snag of a branch, or sharp corner, and he would have exploded 250 cubic metres of hydrogen among the crowds. There is some reason to suppose that the bird-man got a polite letter from the Prefect, for thereafter he chose his place and time more carefully.

But M. Fagel was haunted. "It is evening. I am walking under the trees. Suddenly I stumble against a rope. It is by no means a gossamer thread.* I hear the noise of crumpling leaves above me, and an angry voice shouts, 'I can't see a thing! I shall split my skull!' I raise my nose, I see a dark monster whose eye gleams with acetylene. It is not a gigantic owl; it is the fairy vehicle of M. Santos-Dumont!"

* "*Ce n'est pas un fil de la Vierge!*"

It is also the fairy imagination of M. Fagel, for *No 9*, though it possesses a headlamp, has not yet been let off the leash at night. But the next account is factual.

"In the small hours" (continues M. Fagel), "I regain my own neighbourhood. Supper has lasted long, and we have unwisely been sampling new drinks of American origin. My legs are like jelly, and my brain uncertain. Champs-Elysées is deserted in the light of dawn. Suddenly somebody challenges me. It is evidently an illusion, for there is no-one by. But no! I must believe my ears! It is indeed to me that a mysterious voice calls; 'Move over to the right! My guide-rope will hit you!' It is him again! Always him! Him, above all! He alights softly on his balcony, and his servants bring him breakfast."

While M. Fagel staggers home to sleep off his carousals, it is worth looking at Santos-Dumont's own version of this exploit. For some time he had been thinking again of the trip from Nice to Corsica, which had first occurred to him at Monte Carlo. A noble project, he thought, far removed from these little junketings round Paris. But it must wait for a large airship, and in the meantime he thought it would be fun to take *Baladeuse* up to his own door, at the corner of Champs-Elysées and rue Washington.

"Knowing that the feat must be accomplished at the hour when the imposing pleasure promenade of Paris would be least encumbered I instructed my men to sleep through the early part of the night in the Airship Station, so as to have *No 9* ready for an early start at dawn. I myself rose at 2 a.m., and in my handy electric automobile arrived at the station while it was yet dark. The men still slept. I climbed the wall, waked them, and succeeded in quitting the earth on my first diagonal course over the wall before the day had properly broken.

"Turning to the left, I guide-roped my way across the Bois. When I came to trees I jumped over them. So, navigating through the cool air of the delicious dawn, I reached the Porte Dauphine and the broad Avenue which leads direct to the Arc de Triomphe. 'I will guide-rope up the Avenue of the Bois,' I said to myself gleefully. At times I was lower than the roofs of the houses on either side, and I might have passed under the Arc de Triomphe, had I thought myself worthy. Instead I rounded the national monument to the right, as the law directs.

"For a moment I was confused. The avenues radiating from l'Etoile all appear alike. It was only by looking back that I could locate my own. Far down its length I saw a solitary cab. As I guide-roped along towards my own house I thought of the time, sure to come, when the owners of handy little airships will not be obliged to land in the street, but will have their ropes caught by their domestics on their own roof-gardens.

"So I reached my corner, to which I pointed my stem, and descended very gently. Two servants caught, steadied, and held the aerostat, while I mounted to my apartment for a cup of coffee. From my round bay window at the corner I looked down upon the airship. Were I to receive the municipal permission it would not be difficult to build an ornamental landing-stage out from that window."*

When it was time to go, the morning had advanced. A huge crowd had collected, and his embarkation was greeted with huzzas. By the time he had started up, and his popping motor had driven him diagonally away from his house, there was once more a traffic jam, halfway down the Champs-Elysées.

He never went so far as to take *No 9* to Maxim's, where even his popularity could hardly have survived the experiment. But the excellent restaurant in the Bois, called *Les Cascades*, was very suitable, and he and his friends were well known to the management. During the summer he formed the habit of giving small luncheon parties there, for which the guests would assemble from their different directions. When it was time for their host to appear, the punctual rattle of his motor would be heard, and the bulbous shape of *No 9* would loom through the trees. As he brought her gently down to the grass next to the restaurant two of his men sprang out of the bushes, where (for better effect) they had lain concealed, seized her mooring-rope, and secured her safely while her master briskly strode up the steps to join the table.

He took an unaffected delight in these demonstrations, and was quite unmoved by the suggestions, which sometimes came to his ears, that he was nothing but a show-off. Despite his studied air of casualness, each trip had its problems and its element of danger. Indeed, on 6th July, while setting out on one of his "aerial promenades" the engine of *No 9* caught fire, while he was still climbing up from Neuilly. The trouble was

* *Dans l'Air*. A. Santos-Dumont.

started by a backfire through the carburettor (*retour de flamme*), which set first the carburettor and then the petrol feed alight. He had little time to act. The petrol tank would be next, and after that the envelope. Fortunately the engine of *No 9* was close behind his basket. He was out on the keel girder in a moment, pulled off the panama hat he was wearing, and beat out the flames with it. The engine never even stopped running, and he immediately returned to the Airship Station. After this he wore his panama more often, and observed more rigorously his own rule, "Keep close to earth".

"I attach little importance to my crashes," he told a magazine later;* "I believe in my star—and in my lucky charms. The navigators of the air are like sailors, they have beliefs and superstitions; and every aviator carries some mascot which he would not be without."

Shortly before the engine fire his ubiquitous shadow had appeared over a French-American children's fête being held in the Bois at Bagatelle. When he landed he was instantly surrounded. He stood in the basket smilingly surveying the excited faces. "Does any little boy want to go up?" he called, in his high-pitched voice. Not any child: any little boy. While mothers paled, and nurses bit their nails, a dozen young volunteers clamoured round the airship.

Santos chose the nearest, an American seven-year-old called Clarkson Potter. His parents, quaking on the outskirts of the crowd, were members of the diplomatic community of the United States in Paris. Santos swung him into the basket, where his head barely appeared above the rim. The engine started, they were away, and Master Clarkson Potter became a strong contender, at least, for the claim to be the first genuine airship passenger. "Are you not afraid?" Santos asked him, as *No 9* rose. "Not a bit," he answered coldly. It was a very short trip, as they could barely move in the basket, and Clarkson was soon safely returned to his mother.

The balance of attention was dramatically redressed in favour of girls, by one of the strangest and most uncharacteristic incidents in Santos-Dumont's life. During early June of this fine summer of 1903 a certain Mlle. Aída D'Acosta arrived in Paris from New York, where her family was well known in

* *Lecture Pour Tous.* January 1914.

smart American society. She came of an ancient Cuban lineage, and her beauty startled even the ultra-sophisticated Parisians whose circles she joined during her brief visit. Seeing and hearing of Santos, as everyone who came to the capital was bound to do, the Cuban charmer evinced a strong desire to meet him, and she was taken to Neuilly, probably by Sylvio Alvares Penteado.

Santos was greatly impressed. Mlle. Aída was deeply interested, though whether by *aérostation* or by its chief exponent may never be known. She came a number of times with various friends, and finally confessed to an extraordinary desire to fly in the airship. She could not have found a surer way to his regard. "Would you have the courage to be taken up in the free airship?" he asked her, "with no one holding its guide-rope? Mademoiselle, I thank you for your confidence."

"Oh, no," she said, "I do not want to be taken up. I want to go up alone and navigate it freely, as you do."

This was a bombshell. Granted, his first playful suggestion was impossible, from lack of room in the basket. And it would have been unthinkable that he should take her up sitting on his shoulders, or clinging to the rigging, like a performer at a fair. But to go up alone! Not Aimé, not Chapin; no one had flown a Santos-Dumont airship but the aeronaut himself.

Fair tyrant! She must have been very persistent as well as very attractive (Santos himself referred to her as "a very beautiful Cuban lady"), or his well-known immunity to feminine wiles would have defeated her. For to everyone's utter amazement she got her way. Santos gave her three lessons, on different days, in the handling of the controls of the engine and steering machinery. The last lesson took place with *No 9* held by the guide-rope some fifty feet from the ground, with the engine running.

Finally, on the 29th of June, he sent her solo. While the apprehensive launching team stood around, while her friends wondered whether they had not taken matters too far, and the inventor himself smiled encouragement from the grass of the landing-ground, she called in a high, clear voice, "Let go all!" With the guide-rope trailing, and Santos trotting beside it, she navigated *No 9* slowly from Neuilly to Bagatelle, about half a mile distant. There she made a good landing. The crew seized the mooring-rope, panting, and she was assisted, flushed and delighted, safely back on to earth. Her relieved friends applauded vigorously, and Santos looked pleased; but not even a peck on the cheek marked the end of this memorable event.

Mlle. Aída was the talk of the town, both for her audacity and for her conquest over the young Brazilian's strictest prejudices. Tongues wagged delightedly. But although she went again to Neuilly, nothing seemed to come of it, and a few weeks later the "intrepid girl navigator" returned to New York. She was probably as baffled as everybody else, that a more conventional offer had not followed so outstanding a favour. No other woman ever received such a gift from his hands.

On the 11th July he set out from Neuilly in *No 9*, to take luncheon with friends at *Les Cascades*. It was a gusty morning for airship promenading, but he had made a wager that he would go, and he betted so seldom that once the bet was made he was inclined to over-reach himself to win it. All went well, and by 12.45 his party were regaling themselves with *fruits de mer*, *rognons flambés*, and a choice selection of wines. Outside on the grass his crew guarded the tethered aerostat.

While luncheon was in full swing, in a happy haze of good food and conversation, some Army officers appeared through the trees and gathered round the airship. When Santos emerged from the restaurant they greeted him respectfully. They had come from Longchamp, almost next to *Les Cascades*, where they had been marking out the positions for the troops in the forthcoming Grand Review, arranged to coincide with the celebrations of the 14th of July. They crowded round him while he explained the details of *No 9*, until his hat vanished among a crowd of kepis.

"Shall you come to the Review in it?" asked an officer. Santos, looking every bit the diplomat (as an observer noted), swayed to and fro on the balls of his feet, his right hand thrust into the side pocket of his tight suit. "I-er-I have not quite made up my mind," he said, in his high voice, rising almost on tip-toe; "I feel it might, it might, be of interest to His Majesty the King of Italy" (who was coming). This was something more than a strong hint that it had not been of interest, so far, to the French High Command. "I cannot really say," he went on, "how such an apparition would be viewed, and my *No 9* is not, is not, you understand, my best airship for battling with high winds. I could not be sure to keep an engagement in it, not sure, you understand.''

The staff officers persisted. ''Come and choose a place to land,'' they suggested. ''We will mark it out for you in any case.'' And while Santos continued to insist that he could not guarantee to be present, they marched back to Longchamp and marked a place for his airship, opposite the enclosure reserved for the President of the Republic.

In this agreeable fashion he found himself included. The invitation had been contrived with consummate French diplomacy. General André, Minister of War, wanted Santos on parade with *No 9* but did not want to issue an official invitation; both for fear of a fiasco, and also because the airship had nothing whatever to do with the French Government. He had therefore arranged the informal approach.

Santos in his turn now squarely faced the familiar dilemma of the inventor with something on the shelf that can be applied to war. It did not engage him long. All his sincerely-felt sentiments about the essentially peaceful purposes of the flying-machine, which had already received a twist or two over the Mediterranean, promptly evaporated in the warm light of the interest and approval of the Army. It is sad that an idealist like Santos fell so quickly, and it is only fair to remember that before 1914 there was very much more excuse for the fall.

In the early morning of *quatorze juillet* he was ready and waiting at the Airship Station, nervous, as he himself confessed, in case something should go wrong and prevent him appearing. While *No 9* was weighed he fussed anxiously round, unable to conceal from himself that this first presentation of his airship to an Army would be a great occasion. How bitterly he regretted it later!

The Grand Review of 1903 was an imposing spectacle. The stands of the racecourse at Longchamp were packed with distinguished visitors. A sea of top-hats, whose owners' formal frockcoats sagged under the weight of stars and orders, was liberally interspersed with every military uniform in the world. Stiff plumes, tossing plumes, gold helmets, silver helmets, breast-plates, cuirasses, sabretaches, dolmans, shakos, bear-skins, turbans, caftans, caps, kepis, tarbooshes, pickelhauben;

every conceivable colour and every conceivable design were all represented. France was at peace with the world.

Cavalry formed more than half of the parade. The regiments whirled, cavorted, and cantered by in the sunshine; horses' tails swishing, trappings jingling, foam flying on to the grass. From under a thousand parasols of different colours the ladies bowed and smiled to each other, and commented on the gorgeous scene below. President Loubet sat in state, surrounded by his ministers, occasionally getting to his feet and doffing his hat as the colours rode by.

Suddenly there was a raucous popping sound from the direction of Bagatelle, and the plump shape of *No 9* appeared in the distance. Everyone craned to see the airship, and the horses rolled their eyes uneasily as it puffed over the parade ground.

To be quite certain that there should be no hitch, Santos had caused it to be walked on the guide-rope, as far as Bagatelle. Thereafter he could not use the rope, without cutting a swathe through the gallant soldiery, and so appeared at 300 feet over the parade, where he proceeded to carry out evolutions to right and left above the troops. After making a circuit round the racecourse he halted in mid-air before the Presidential enclosure, where he fired a salute of twenty-one blank revolver cartridges.

President Loubet seemed to be dumbfounded, while his bodyguard automatically reached for their pistols. One or two ladies gave faint screams, hastily suppressed in view of the formal nature of the occasion, and Santos blandly flew on again, wheeling to and fro above the assembly, with all imaginable grace. He kept it up for ten minutes, enthusiastically watched by the French spectators, and minutely observed by the foreign military attachés, until he judged that he had stayed long enough (a conclusion which some of the officers in the review strongly supported); when he flew off and landed at the Polo Grounds, where he was met by his admiring friends.

The next day the newspapers were full of this exploit, coupled with all manner of conjectures, from the practical to the imbecile, for the use of airships in war. The aeronaut was warmly congratulated by his Army acquaintances, and also by the Press, on his convincing demonstration. Their eulogies quite carried him away, and he sat down at once and wrote to the Minister of War, offering to put his aerial fleet (at this time

No 7, No 9, and an embryonic *No 10*) at the disposal of France, should hostilities break out while he was resident in that country. He added, with the naiveté of the pure scientist, that this offer did not apply if the foe in question came from North or South America, while if Brazil itself was embroiled against France he would feel compelled to offer his aircraft and his own services to his mother country; like a footballer transferred, on the eve of an important match, to the opposing side.

The reply came on the day before his thirtieth birthday.

République Française
Paris, le 19 juillet, 1903

Ministère de la Guerre
Cabinet du Ministre

Monsieur—During the Review of the Fourteenth of July, I had remarked and admired the ease and security with which the balloon you were steering made its evolutions. It was impossible not to acknowledge the progress which you have given to aerial navigation. It seems that, thanks to you, such navigation must, henceforward, lend itself to practical applications, especially from the military point of view.

I consider that, in this respect, it may render very substantial services in time of war. I am very happy, therefore, to accept the offer which you make, of putting, in case of need, your aerial flotilla at the disposition of the Government of the Republic, and, in its name, I thank you for your gracious proposition, which shows your lively sympathy for France.

I have appointed Chief of Battalion Hirschauer, commanding the Battalion of Balloonists in the First Regiment of Engineers, to examine, in agreement with you, the dispositions to take for putting the intentions you have manifested into execution.

Accept, Monsieur, assurances of my most distinguished respect.

(Signed) General André.

The meaning of this gratifying letter, if it meant anything, was that the Government would be happy to accept whatever

Santos could offer gratis, and might actually lend him an adviser to suggest how best to provide the public with something for nothing. This is a well-known aspect of governmental ethics. In the name of public benefit a public body can get away with conduct which would produce scandalised comment in a thieves' kitchen. Santos, who never took out a patent, and seemed indifferent to material advantage, made an ideal customer.

Chief of Battalion Hirschauer, and his assistant Lt.-Col. Bourdeaux, called without delay. They were shown over Neuilly by the proud inventor, being able to see *No 9* and *No 7* in working order, and *No 10* nearly ready. This last airship, twice as big as anything he had built so far, was intended to carry ten people, a complete departure in principle. It was nicknamed *The Omnibus*, and although originally conceived as a peaceful passenger-carrier, it was obviously the first attraction from the soldier's point of view.

It was very expensive for an individual to build and to run, as the sorely tempted inventor pointed out. At the present time it was completed with envelope, rigging, and the passenger girder keel, but the propelling and control mechanisms, together with the pilot's basket, were intended to be borrowed from *No 7* when needed, and slung above the passenger girder, to make, as it were, an upper deck.

The military balloonists were very intrigued by what they saw, but were at something of a loss to suggest what to do about it, to fulfil the extremely vague conditions of the last paragraph of the War Minister's letter. When in doubt, in a case like this, it is usually considered sound practice to go back to the last war. They had to go quite a way back for an aviation instance —thirty years—to the Siege of Paris, and the evacuation by free balloon that formed so spectacular a part of the operations.

The very thing for a test of the usefulness of the new invention! Col. Hirschauer explained his project with enthusiasm. They would take the airship, deflated, on a railway truck, to the Franco-German frontier area, inflate it, and attempt to introduce it into Belfort or Nancy (assumed to be under siege), to show that supplies could be taken in by air, and evacuees out. Santos fully approved this scheme, and the officers left to "examine the dispositions to take for putting the intentions General André had manifested into execution".

Santos was dealing with a government department. The first moves took so long that he had half forgotten about it when he decided to go home to Brazil, on his first visit since becoming world-famous. There had been some comment on his having crossed the Atlantic in the previous year without continuing down to South America. There seemed then, and still seems, no good reason for the omission, and it produced the embarrassing and totally untrue rumour that he was adopting French citizenship. This, as we know, was far from his mind.

Before he left he committed himself fully and utterly to the conception of the airship as a war weapon. This point should not need such emphasis, being unfortunately only too normal a behaviour pattern for an inventor, were it not that he made such a case to the contrary in later years, insisting that his brain-child had been torn from his arms and perverted. Count Zeppelin was different. He listened with increasing dismay to the bright ideas of the German High Command, and only his desire to see his plans for civil airship services vindicated before he died induced him to receive Government help.

In September 1903 Santos-Dumont was on the high seas, returning home to a hero's welcome. As he leant over the rail and looked at the tumbling Atlantic, he could little have guessed that on the far shore, where the rollers crashed against the sand bars of North Carolina, the Wright brothers were arriving at Kitty Hawk, bringing with them the crated components of an aeroplane called the *Flyer*.

Chapter 15

☆☆☆☆☆☆☆☆☆☆☆☆☆☆☆☆☆☆☆☆☆☆☆☆☆☆☆☆☆☆☆☆

The Flying Arrows

It goes without saying that his reception in Brazil was a riot. No hero's homecoming could be more satisfactory. Mayoral processions, banquets with speeches (alas, poor Santos), schoolchildren given holidays to see him pass, illuminated addresses; nothing was lacking. Nothing, that is, from the viewpoint of the organisers. In Rio de Janeiro, São Paulo, Minas Gerais, wherever he went, he was received with the greatest honours and the most effusive demonstrations of affection.

What was lacking, for him, was the presence of his father. "He who had given me such good counsel, and the means to realise my dream, was no longer in this world to see that I had 'made a man of myself'." How much he would have loved to have shown his father that Henriques's puny, wool-gathering little Alberto had taken his portion and projected it into the skies; whereas his big brothers were still solid, heavy men, content with their horses, their provincial gossip, and their business!

"It is an oriental custom to attribute to the father all the merit, all the glory, that a man achieves in life. This way of looking at things may be criticised or censured, but in my case, however, it would be very just, because I owe everything to my father; advice, the examples of hard work, of confidence, of economy, of sobriety, and the wherewithal by which I was enabled to carry out my inventions. I owe him everything from these examples."*

Beneath his uncommunicative exterior, behind his attitude of habitual reserve, Santos-Dumont was in fact a sentimental person. More than once during this tour his feelings overcame his self-control. He dearly loved his native country, and angrily denied that he was becoming "Frenchified" by living abroad. He explained at some length that he worked in Paris only because it concentrated all the technical resources he needed close to his hand, and contained all available advice from the foremost experts in the world of science and technology.

The warmth of his reception did not confine itself to the authorities. Wherever he went he was acclaimed by the people, who surrounded him in the street when he was recognised. A ballad† was composed about him by Eduardo das Neves, and unknown singers would appear beneath his window and serenade him. But after a month he grew restless once more. He was tired of the whirl of tributes that filled his days in Brazil. He longed to return to Paris, to the peace of his own house, to his study and workshop; in fact to his normal life. Whenever tribute flagged, he wanted it again; and when it came, he renounced it.

Late in 1903 he embarked on the French liner *Atlantique*, taking with him his nephew Henriques Dumont-Villares (now finished with his English schooling), who was to accompany him as far as Portugal. They had a royal send-off from Rio de Janeiro, and when the ship touched at Bahiá, three hundred miles to the north, another huge reception presented him with a model of *No 6*, fashioned in gold and diamonds. The members of his family received a reproduction of the gift in silver. As the ship drew out of the harbour and set her course for Europe, whistles and sirens wailed a farewell.

As always when he turned his eyes back to France, he was full of ideas and plans for the future. He discussed these with young Henriques, as they paced the decks together, the school-

* *O Que eu Vi, O Que nós Veremos*. A. Santos-Dumont.
† *"Santos-Dumont, A glória do Brasil."*

Number 14 bis being tested   (*Collection Dazy*)

Number 14 bis on the way to Bagatelle   (*Courtesy of Charles W. Rule*)

The control position of *Number 14 bis*   (*Collection Dazy*)

The beginning of the flight of November 12, 1906
(*Courtesy of the Science Museum, London*)

Santos-Dumont with Gas-
teau at Neuilly

(Collection Dazy)

Santos-Dumont outside the
workshop at Neuilly work-
ing on *Number 18*

(Collection Harlingue)

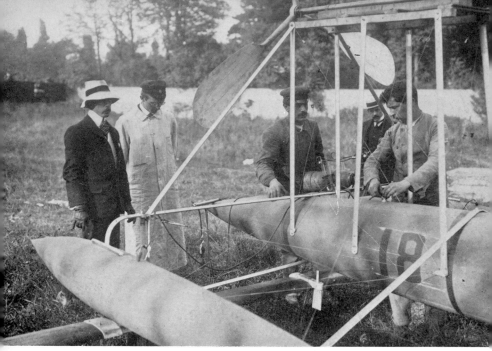

Building *Number 18* at Neuilly. Gasteau making an adjustment

(Collection Harlingue)

Santos-Dumont in his study at rue Washington. The photograph on his desk is of Mlle. D'Acosta   *(Collection Dazy)*

Number 19 ready at Neuilly   (*Radio Times Hulton*)

Number 19 on the road to St. Cyr   (*Collection Dazy*)

Santos-Dumont at the controls of the *Demoiselle* (*Collection Dazy*)

Queen Elizabeth of Rumania congratulating Santos-Dumont at a showing of the *Demoiselle* (*Collection Harlingue*)

Advertisement (*circa* 1911) for a commercially built *Demoiselle*

(*Courtesy of Charles W. Rule*)

Santos-Dumont in 1924 (*Radio Times Hulton*)

boy already as tall as his famous uncle. As his own father had unbent with him during this voyage, so Santos too found he could now talk more freely to the boy at his side.

While uncle and nephew were still on the sea, on the 17th of December, 1903, Orville Wright succeeded in launching the *Flyer* into the air at Kitty Hawk, controlling it for all of 59 seconds, and landing it without damage at a point as high as that from which it started. Five spectators, Coast Guardsmen and their friends, from one of the remotest posts in the Service, were the only witnesses of the event, and the outside world heard nothing of this memorable occasion.

In Paris, Santos began what has been referred to as a "rest period" in his life. We will see that this is hardly a just description. His first enterprise, for which M. Emanuel Aimé provided some stimulus, was to begin a book on his experiences and lessons in aerostation, so far as they had gone to that date. He wrote this book, which he called *Dans l'Air*, in his study at rue Washington, using a quill pen and his best writing-paper. (His love of new gadgets did not extend to the fountain-pen, then coming into use.) He wrote in French. It is an odd, disjointed work, wavering between the practical and the visionary, often gay and readable, but perhaps overfilled with self-justification. It has throughout a faint flavour of persecution complex, for which there is little real reason, and in spite of his practical generosity to his helpers they get very little credit in the book. (M. Aimé is never mentioned.)

Dans l'Air was published in Paris in 1904, when it aroused a great deal of interest, though this was more because of its author's fame and expertise, than for any intrinsic value in the book itself. In the same year it was translated into English and published in New York and London, under the title of *My Airships*, and into Portuguese, as *Os Meus Balões*.

Dans l'Air is a brief account of his work up to 1903. Two important points come out of it. Firstly, it is apparent that up to this time he had given very little thought to the conquest of the heavier-than-air problem, and was not sanguine of it ever being solved. He was very soon to change his mind. The second is his awareness and indeed his constructive thought towards the use of aerial vehicles in war. He devotes one whole chapter to "The Airship in War", mentioning its use for maritime reconnaissance, attack on submarines,* bombing of armies, scouting, and photography.

The slightly resentful attitude of mind shown by this book was produced partly by his own temperament, still reserved and secretive despite his ever-increasing circle of friends, and partly by the subtle change that had come over his relations with the Aéro Club after the winning of the Deutsch Prize. To his friends it seemed that he was more shy than ever, and yet quicker to resent any tendency, real or imagined, to deny him any part of the credit for what he had achieved, or to share it with others.

He had hardly seen *Dans l'Air* in print when the first rumours reached him that the Wrights had flown in the U.S.A. These stories had reached Europe by way of a number of items in American newspapers, which almost universally ridiculed the very possibility, and published the articles only to dismiss the claims as those of a pair of country crackpots. As a result, although the rumours caused him to doubt his previous conviction that heavier-than-air flight was a long way off, Santos joined with all informed European opinion in discounting the Wrights as thoroughly as their own country had done.

It is one of the major mysteries of aviation history that the birth of flight was given this reception, in America of all places. Part of the reason is found in the unfortunate Professor Langley, who had just registered two widely-publicised and resounding failures to launch his *Aerodrome* into the air: on each occasion the aircraft, piloted by Charles Manly, was catapulted from a boat, fouled the catapult on take-off, and ended at the bottom of the Potomac River.

Thus the Wrights' modest announcement that they had flown an aeroplane under control for six hundred yards, on a deserted coast in front of a handful of rustics, was dismissed out of hand as just another yarn from the corn belt, and the editors who threw it into the wastepaper basket, or wrote sardonic comments of complete disbelief, even committed the cardinal mistake of failing to send a reporter to check up. Only one magazine did so, and was consequently convinced of their

---

* "Indeed, it may be able to destroy the submarine boat by sending down to it long arrows filled with dynamite, capable of penetrating to depths under the waves impossible to gunnery from the decks of a warship."

claims, but since this was *Gleanings in Bee Culture* it carried little technical weight, and might even be supposed to have a partisan interest. As late as January 1906 the *Scientific American*, a magazine of unequalled prestige in its own field, scornfully dismissed the claims of the Wrights to have flown at all.

In Europe, though the rumours were likewise discounted, a feeling was gaining that this thing was possible. Otto Lilienthal had shown how the aerodynamic shape of an aircraft should be disposed to allow it to fly under the pull of gravity, with some control by the pilot; while the internal combustion engine was growing rapidly lighter and more powerful. One is tempted to suggest that we do not need hindsight to have predicted, at the time, that true flight was not only possible, but imminent. It is odd that more people did not think so. It is equally strange to reflect that there is no drastic reason why gliding, as the sport is known today, should not have been practised two thousand years ago or, in China, even earlier. All the materials and workmanship were available to the man ingenious enough to take advantage of them.

The most important spur to events in Europe was the visit of Octave Chanute in April 1903. An American citizen of French birth, Chanute had published, as early as 1894, his most carefully reasoned and exhaustively collated work, *Progress in Flying Machines*, a volume that had long been on Santos-Dumont's bookshelf. Although too old to launch into the air himself, Chanute had constructed gliders on the Lilienthal principles, which had been flown successfully by Herring. He had been the greatest encourager of the Wrights, and when he lectured the Aéro Club in Paris he was able to describe and illustrate their methods and progress, up to the time of the building of the *Flyer*.

The effect of this visit and lecture, with its preponderant bias towards heavier-than-air, was so great, that even while the rumours from America were dismissed, the feeling gained ground that even if the Wrights had not flown someone else would very soon. Santos was still puttering about Paris in *No 9*, making very occasional experiments with *No 7* and *No 10*, but the sight of his passage overhead was becoming sufficiently frequent to be almost commonplace. His increasing skill and experience kept at bay the ever-present possibility of an accident, which would have put him once more among the headlines.

In his design office he was as busy as ever, but his line of progress reflects his own uncertainty of mind. Visitors remarked the profusion of plans, drawings, pieces of machinery, apparatus, and models. He designed, and incorporated in his engines, improvements to the carburettors and magnetos, modifications that were later adopted by others, and even patented by the copyists. He devised a catapult to throw lifelines to ships in danger (the result of a casual conversation), experimented with gyroscopes,* and showed the general symptoms of a prolific and ingenious mind that lacks a sense of direction.

There was a pointer, however. Coming unexpectedly into his large workshop at Neuilly, Goursat surprised him with a species of fixed cross-bow, from which he was firing arrows at the far end of the room. The arrows were fitted with small vanes instead of feathers, the vanes varying in shape and thickness. When his friend questioned him Santos shrugged and changed the subject (strange conduct with his closest friend, but typical); though it was obvious enough that he was experimenting with aerodynamics. Where others had used models on rotating arms, and the Wrights had even constructed a small soap-box wind-tunnel, he had hit on this method: not, it must be feared, a very promising one.

The thought of the aeroplane was pulling strongly at him. Even while he packed up *No 7* and arranged its transport by sea to New York, for the St. Louis races, he was beginning to turn his back on the airship, though, as we will see, it took him some time to break free. Even in 1904 he could still write: "And now that I have, not only my racing airship, but also my airship for pleasure trips, with which I amuse myself flying over the city's trees, it is in Paris, as fair recompense, that I wish to enjoy the keen pleasure of being what they once censured me for being: 'A sportsman of the air'."

---

* He showed remarkable foresight over his experiments with the gyroscope, writing: "Another difficulty which is present in aerial navigation is that of determining the position of the aircraft at a given moment. The use of the sextant in the air is not now possible. I believe that an artificial horizon, produced by a mirror, held in a horizontal position by a gyroscope, will solve this problem." As indeed, many years later, it did.

But when he sailed for America he left no designs behind for pure airships. *No 11* was on his drawing-board. She was a monoplane.

Before he left Paris, Santos was informed that he had been made a Chevalier of the Legion of Honour. This distinction was considerably more impressive when given to a foreigner, but even so it was no great sensation, for like many honours the brightness had been rubbed off it by its award to a host of non-entities. A more exhilarating experience awaited him in New York: an invitation to the White House to meet President Theodore Roosevelt.

The President, who was interested in anything new, or in fact in anything, had been particularly struck with the articles on the possible use of the airship in war at sea. He received the inventor with his usual bluff hospitality, and chaired a meeting at which the American Admirals Dewey, Mahan, and Chester were also present. Next day the President thanked him for his help, and turned him over to the Admirals, who took him on to the Naval Academy at Annapolis. There the discussions continued, with other high-ranking officers of the U.S. Army and Navy. Once more, the prophet was doing considerably better outside his own country.

The results of these conversations were not divulged, and Santos himself remained the soul of discretion on the subject. But it is significant that the United States was the only country thereafter to make extensive and regular use, until very recent times, of semi-rigid airships. The Goodyear "Blimps", used for spotting by the U.S. Navy and the Coast Guard, were nearer to Santos-Dumonts than any other practical aircraft that flew, and for many years they gave good and reliable service.

After this excursion into high strategy he went on to St. Louis, where his crew were waiting with *No 7*. It was still packed in the three large boxes in which it had arrived by freight train on the 27th of June. Declaring that he would unpack the crates on the following day the aeronaut went to his hotel, whereupon they were moved to the Exposition grounds by the transport authorities, and the nails drawn, so that they could be opened quickly on the morrow.

The contest was to take place on the 4th of July, and time was short. Santos and his mechanics were early on the scene,

ready to assemble the airship. But when the envelope was
drawn out of its crate they were horrified to discover that it
had been slashed and ripped with a knife, to such a degree that
there was no hope of repairing it in time for the race. Santos
was beside himself with grief and rage. Again this had happened!
And again the occurrence seemed a complete mystery.

The crates had been watched during the night by Exposition
guards. At first they swore that no-one could have come near
their charge. One of them then admitted that he had twice left
his post to fetch sandwiches, and it was apparent that the deed
had been done while his back was turned. "There is absolutely
no explanation to be advanced," Santos told the newspapers.
"It must have been done by some enemy, although I cannot
imagine who would be the guilty person. . . . The balloon
cannot possibly be repaired here. It will have to be returned
to Paris."*

The Exposition officials, furious, disappointed, and highly
embarrassed, placed the case in the hands of the local police,
and offered a reward of 1,000 dollars for the arrest of the guilty
party. Colonel Kingsbury of the Jefferson Guard plunged into
an immediate investigation, and interrogated everyone who
could even remotely be suspected. He began by grilling Santos-
Dumont's own crew, which did nothing to improve the aeronaut's sorely-tried temper, and in twenty-four hours he had
sacked the erring guard, but was hinting that Santos himself
was chiefly to blame, for failing to look after his own property.

This brazen excuse, from the man responsible for the security
of the wrecked airship, caused an explosion indeed. Hard words
were exchanged on all sides. Santos angrily demanded the
withdrawal of the Colonel's suggestions. The Chief of Police,
unrepentant, went on to state that one of the Brazilian's own
men possessed a large knife, while the surviving guard now
claimed to have seen a suspicious stranger lurking round the
crates, whose description could conceivably have fitted three
of the five French mechanics.

Pausing only to point out scornfully that any airship rigger
would have a knife in his toolbox, Santos declared that he
would leave St. Louis at once. Torn between injured local
pride and hospitable concern for the visitor, the wretched

* St. Louis Daily Globe-Democrat. June 30th, 1904.

Exposition Committee members did what they could to smooth everyone's outraged feelings. But both deeds and words had gone too far. On the 1st of July Santos left for New York, a picture of tightly-buttoned fury, taking the hacked envelope with him. While the committee were still biting their lips over this unhappy incident, the maladroit Colonel Kingsbury, alert to keep the party going, closed down the French pavilion in the Palace of Electricity, claiming that the staff were illegally selling their displayed goods. International good feeling seemed to make little headway in this Exposition.

The St. Louis mystery, like the London one, was never solved. Gossip suggested that one of Santos-Dumont's own mechanics was the saboteur in both cases, or even, once more, that he had done it himself, for some strange reason. Neither solution was backed by a shred of evidence. It is certain that Santos himself was as mystified as anyone, and that he sailed from New York with very black and bitter feelings.

He arrived back in Paris disgusted, and disappeared once more into the retreat of his *atelier*. Through the winter of 1904-1905 he resumed his normal life in Paris, often appearing at parties and dinners, lunching at the best restaurants, and dining at Maxim's with his friends. Usually he was gay and even high-spirited, but occasionally an acquaintance would have cause to remark that he seemed to have grown more touchy, more secretive still; and sometimes he showed more than a trace of pomposity.

His Airship Station at Neuilly, with its airships, required a staff that varied around a figure of about fifteen men. His carefulness with money was needed in real earnest, for his expenses, even after all possible economies, were still slightly above his income. The trials of *No 11* were not therefore taken very far. She was completed as a glider, equipped with floats, and towed on the Seine behind the fast motor-boat *Rapière*, first unmanned, then with the inventor at the controls. Once or twice she lifted off the water, but the control was not good, and the experiments stopped. As he became more and more interested in heavier-than-air flight, it absorbed an increasing share of his time and energy; but he could not devote much money to it.

Because of this his new efforts appeared rather half-hearted. He made some designs for a helicopter, starting with the construction of small models worked by rubber bands. His friends, driving by his flying ground at Neuilly, were surprised to see him manipulating a large kite, a box design with multiple cells. Like a thousand dreamers before him, he studied bird flight; and like them, lacking the help of high-speed cinematography, he drew a great many wrong conclusions.

At the beginning of 1905 he wrote a long article on the possibilities of aviation for the Paris journal *Je Sais Tout*. This covered, in his jerky, unscientific style, the main fruits of his experience with airships, coupled with predictions of their future, which very fairly match the realisation of the large Zeppelin type of later years. ("We dine. We watch the stars come out. We are suspended between the stars and the earth. . . . And day follows day. We cross over frontiers. Here we are flying over Russia—in a little while we are over Hungary and Austria. Look at Vienna!", etc.)

In this article also, he harked back to a project that had intrigued him ever since he had read about the Andrée Expedition, and which finally displaced his idea for a trip from Nice to Corsica. This was a voyage by airship to the North Pole. He never made much progress with this idea, which had to wait many more years for Amundsen and the airship *Norge*, but for some time it was included in the schemes and plans which littered his office.

The important point he stated in *Je Sais Tout*, for the first time in public, was his belief that the aeroplane could be developed to a successful conclusion, as well as the dirigible airship.* That he was so late in admitting this is certainly curious, particularly when it is remembered that his original inspiration, Jules Verne, had a partiality for heavier-than-air craft as vehicles for his heroes' aerial adventures.

But it is not for others to carp at Santos's slowness, least of all the gentlemen in England, who if not abed, were certainly half asleep. The most outstanding aerial event in the official British scene, during 1904, was a visit to Malta by the British Army Balloon School, where a team deployed and flew their tethered balloons, to the amazement of the locals. They found

* In *Dans l'Air* he quoted the holding of this theory as a satirical stroke against those whose line of scientific development lay in copying Nature. (In this case, birds.) It has been repeated by Napoleão as an inspired prophecy!

conditions difficult however, and when they got back to England one of the balloons, called *Trusty*, was found when unpacked, to have "formed sustenance for mice or insects".*

During this "rest" period of 1904-1905 Santos found time for the more active recreations which had always attracted him. He still hated all forms of hunting and shooting, but he loved to walk, to climb, or to row and sail on the river. He made his first attempts to play tennis, and liked it, though announcing in his solemn way that he was taking to it because it developed the quickness of eye and fitness of muscle so necessary to the aeronaut. His quickness and agility made him a natural sportsman of this athletic type, and his inclination and adaptability served him well, for truth to say, without these open-air relaxations he might have led a very unhealthy life, either bent over a desk or bench, or fighting the French battles of the table, in dining-room or restaurant.

His design work went on; and the construction of test models, structural assemblies, installations, and adaptations; but nothing came out of the Airship Station besides the little *Baladeuse*, on one of its rambles round Paris, or very occasionally the short test flights by *No 7* and *No 10*. The monoplane glider *No 11* had later been re-designed as an aeroplane with two engines, but it was never completed, and the design itself was lost. *No 12* was next on the drawing-board, a helicopter with two contra-rotating propellers, but it was years ahead of its time, and there was no hope of an engine light enough to give it any chance of success. The designer made a full-scale model of it, such as now would be called a mock-up, but never attempted anything further.

His next project, *No 13*, was designed as a large semi-rigid airship, on the familiar lines that he had made his own. It was intended as an "aerial yacht", with a very long range. He meant to keep it flying by replacing lost hydrogen in the envelope with hot air supplied from a petrol burner below. Even his most faithful friends were open-mouthed at this suggestion, and his critics pounced on it with joy, for Santos had rashly written in an article that he hoped to have such a monstrosity flying shortly, and "cruise over Europe for a whole week". The main structure of *No 13* was actually completed, having a normal airship envelope with a sinister-looking bulge attached to its belly,

* *Per Ardua*. Saunders.

which contained the hot-air cell and heating plant. M. Lachambre was no longer there to protest, or this latest outrage would have broken his spirit.* The danger was so obvious that, although Santos obstinately brought her out of his hangar, there is no record that he ever flew her.

But *No 14* was built, and flew. She too, was a conventional "Santos-Dumont", semi-rigid, of a good lifting capacity, with the propeller in front again, and the load-carrying girder slung farther below the envelope. It might be thought that Santos was reversing his trend of design, and making negative progress, and certainly the appearance of this latest product of the Airship Station caused some patronising remarks. But *No 14* was built for a purpose, different from anything that had gone before. She was not an airship in her own right. She was a test vehicle.

He combined the first flights of the new aerostat with a holiday for himself and his men. During August, 1905, they took the craft to Trouville, near Deauville on the Channel coast, where it was assembled and flew happily over the water, Santos using his maritime guide-rope technique to allow him easy control and constant height. As ever, it was immensely popular with the holiday crowds, and he even had the gratification of seeing, below him on the beach, the words "*Vive Santos-Dumont!*" spelled out in white boulders. His Panama hat or straw boater could often be seen waving back from the basket. The trials went off without incident, and in a week or two the team was back in Paris, and *No 14* was added to the "flotilla" at the Airship Station.

It is somewhere about this time that Monsieur Aimé, his "faithful collaborator", fades from the scene. It may be uncharitable to assume a coldness between them which cannot be proved, but in the course of the many cross-currents of partisanship and intrigue that distinguished the intensification of aviation research in France at the time, and in view of Santos-Dumont's own shift in character, it seems reasonable to assume that they became estranged. And perhaps he never completely acquitted Aimé for the débâcle at Monaco. It is significant that in the whole course of the book written in the preceding year Santos does not mention him once.

In his place, during this summer, he met Gabriel Voisin.

* He died on the 12th of January, 1904.

Chapter 16

☆☆☆☆☆☆☆☆☆☆☆☆☆☆☆☆☆☆☆☆☆☆☆☆☆☆☆☆

Sixty Metres

The forerunners of the aeroplane, as opposed to the "professors of aerostation", are easily traced through da Vinci, Cayley, Pocock, Stringfellow, Pénaud, Ader, Lilienthal, Langley, Hargrave, Pilcher and Chanute. By the end of the nineteenth century, Pilcher and Lilienthal had shown that a heavier-than-air machine could be controlled in the air, using gravity as the motive force and body balance to preserve equilibrium; and Chanute had collated their results.

But with Pilcher and Lilienthal both dead, and the threshold of powered flight still to be crossed, there was a natural hesitation. Far away in Australia, Lawrence Hargrave was working on the aerodynamics of box-kites, and in America Chanute was digesting and publicising his results. The Wright brothers had managed to bring all this research to the point of a first flight, but they might almost have been working in Tibet, for all that the rest of the world knew of them. The key to the eventual solution in France was the legacy of Lilienthal, the stimulus of Chanute with his collation of Hargrave and others, the support of wealthy Frenchmen who were not afraid to subsidise what some people thought lunacy, and the persistence of Captain Ferber.

The interweaving of these influences is a complicated story,

admissible here only in so far as it affects Santos-Dumont.* But
we must follow Captain Ferber, who kept contact with the world
outside France, and Ernest Archdeacon, who provided the
impetus inside. Ferber, whom we last saw gliding, with modest
success, among the French Alps, had continued his experiments,
and hearing of Chanute's work, and through him of the early
gliders of the Wrights, changed his designs to the Chanute-
Wright-type biplanes, made tentative glides with them, and
even designed a power-driven model. He tested this machine
on a swinging arm, but it never flew.

By 1904 Ferber heard about the latest Wright experiments.
For some time he had been in correspondence with Octave
Chanute. The news, which trickled through as a very much
unconfirmed rumour, that the Wright brothers had actually
flown a powered machine, was greeted in France, as in America,
with frank disbelief. It would be wrong to say that Ferber
believed when all others doubted, but he certainly thought
that there must be something in the story, and he redoubled his
efforts to get at the truth, and awaken France to the need for
urgent action.

Immediately after Chanute's historic address to the Aéro
Club, in 1903, Monsieur Ernest Archdeacon, the new President,
took a hand. He was a substantial Paris lawyer, prominent for
some time in the Club, and of course a friend of Santos. He
was well known already as a sporting balloonist and a pioneer
motorist, and like M. Deutsch and the Marquis de Dion he had
the money to indulge his enthusiasms. He decided to award a
prize for the first heavier-than-air flight, as a supplement to that
already offered by the Club.

In 1904 Captain Ferber gave a lecture at Lyon on his gliding
experiments, and afterwards a young man named Gabriel
Voisin, just finishing his architectural studies, came to him
and asked for advice on how he could break into aviation. He
wanted, he said, to "consecrate his life" to flying. Ferber suggested that he contact Archdeacon. Voisin did so, to find that
the lawyer had already produced a glider, copied from the
Wright No 3 design (via Chanute) and built for him by M.
Dargent, a model-maker of Chalais-Meudon. Archdeacon

* The reader is recommended to *The Aeroplane: An Historical Survey*, C. H.
Gibbs-Smith, for the analysis of this period.

engaged Voisin to fly this glider, for if the young man had no experience, neither had anyone else. After some tuition by Ferber he flew it successfully from the sandhills at Berck. Voisin and Archdeacon, aided by Ferber, thus launched the real beginnings of practical French (and European) aviation.

Meanwhile, Ferber persistently went on trying to gain experience from the New World. In 1905 the rumours from America grew stronger that the Wrights were making long, sustained flights, and to Ferber at least these stories now had the ring of authenticity. But to most people the continued disbelief of the U.S.A. itself was proof enough that there was nothing in them. The extraordinary thing is that by 1904 the brothers had given up Kitty Hawk as too remote and awkward, and started a programme of tests, with a new machine, at a field some eight miles from Dayton, next to a main road. They could then be seen flying by anybody who took the trouble to look. Amos Stauffer, the farmer who owned the next field, used to watch them while he cut the corn. "Well, the boys are at it again," he would remark to his hired man, as the white biplane left its launching track and took to the air. He would go on with his reaping, keeping one eye on the machine sailing round the big field. "I would just keep on shocking corn," he stated later, "until I got down to the fence; and the durned thing was still going round. I thought it would never stop."*

Against this factual background, the efforts of Ferber to discover whether anyone had yet flown in America seem incredible. No-one in authority would endorse the Wrights' claims. But by May 1905 he was sufficiently convinced to persuade his military superiors to allow him to get in touch with the brothers. Accordingly he wrote to them to tell them of the interest of the French Army, and to open up negotiations, with the object of the purchase of a Wright flying machine. Busy with their tests, the brothers did not reply until October. Then they wrote to say that they would consider delivering such a machine for a fee of $250,000, this sum to be paid after they had demonstrated their aeroplane before representatives of the French Government.

At once Ferber found himself in the well-known position of a prophet who has to extract money from Government in order

* *The Wright Brothers.* F. C. Kelly.

to see his prophecies fulfilled. More letters were written and considered by Service chiefs and ministers. Commissions were appointed, and one actually visited Dayton. The Government, offered an invention worth untold millions for $250,000, wanted to get it for less (thus running drearily true to bureaucratic form). The arguments dragged on for months and years.

We must leave the unfortunate Ferber involved in this dismal process, and return to Archdeacon. He was much encouraged by his Wright-type design, and impressed with the skill and imagination of young Gabriel Voisin. Throughout 1904 and 1905 they were busily experimenting with gliders, and projects for powering them with various internal combustion engines. Together they designed and built a glider using the Hargrave box-kite principle and, like the No 11 of Santos, they fitted it with floats and towed it behind a motor-boat on the Seine. Voisin constructed a similar machine to the order of Louis Blériot, which was tested in the same way. Voisin piloted both machines, until they were damaged and the tests were stopped, the Blériot machine ending its career by ducking its test pilot in the river.

This was not by any means all of the effort being put into aviation, during the closing months of 1905. Two years had passed since the Wrights had first flown. In Europe pioneers were pressing forward everywhere, and the Voisin-Archdeacon combination might achieve the great goal at almost any moment. Archdeacon himself decided that his prize should be three thousand francs, for the first aircraft to fly for 25 metres. This would give a keener edge to the Aéro Club's already standing offer of 1,500 francs for the first to do 100 metres (with, they hastily added, a maximum drop of 10 per cent.).

And where was Santos, while all this was going on? His intimates had so fixed him in their minds as the "aerial sportsman" of Paris, devoted to his little airship, that it came as something of a shock when a letter arrived from his workshop addressed to the Aéro Club, entering M. Alberto Santos-Dumont for both these prizes. So the little Brazilian had turned his genius to aeroplanes! What was hidden in his workshop now?

He met Voisin in the last months of 1905. Gabriel had decided to go seriously into the aircraft building business with his brother Charles, and was available for orders; as yet he lacked the money to build for himself. Santos picked him as an enthusiastic and dedicated engineer, who already knew more about aeroplane structures than his own crew, who were all airship men. Many conversations took place behind locked doors at the Airship Station, when the possibilities and probabilities of design were discussed, and ideas put forward and discarded.

Santos once said to a journalist: "I have never sat down to work seriously on abstract data: I have perfected my inventions through a series of tests, fortified by common sense and experience."* When he came to tackle heavier-than-air aerodynamics he needed to handle abstract data, and it was probably Voisin who took the place of his former mathematical adviser, Emmanuel Aimé.

Santos had heard of the Wrights, naturally, but he could not bring himself to believe that they had really flown, while like many others he confused the reports of their launching track, to the effect that they probably used some kind of catapult, which could fling any sort of apparatus into the air for a few yards. Thus they had no direct influence on him, now or hereafter.

From his conversations with Voisin a design emerged, which Gabriel undertook to build. How much of it was his work and how much belonged to Santos is not known. Santos was not accustomed to taking suggestions from others, and must have found it hard to do so from this inexperienced young man; while Voisin was later torn between the desire for his fair share of the conception of an historical aircraft, and his aversion from what is generally agreed to be one of the most horrifying pieces of apparatus ever to leave the ground. He guardedly says, in his autobiography, that his contribution was small.

The wings of the Santos-Dumont/Voisin aeroplane were based on the Hargrave box-kite, and therefore probably came from Voisin. There was a pronounced dihedral angle between the main planes, for lateral stability. The engine was placed between the wings, with the propeller behind, and the fuselage extended forward, ending in a small box-kite cell which could be swivelled left and right, and up and down. This was the only flying control. Whereas the first Wright biplane, the *Flyer*, had the main recognisable characteristics and arrangement of later

* *Lectures pour Tous.* 1914.

conventional aeroplanes, the new Santos-Dumont was almost as different as it is possible to be. In most of its characteristics it was Santos personified, a monument to his individuality, obstinacy, and flair for success in the teeth of odds.

Once more he had a tangible prize in front of him: two, in fact: the Aéro Club and Archdeacon prizes. Once more they provided the stimulus that spurred him to those special efforts which had astonished Paris in previous years. The accumulating weight of evidence showed him clearly that true aerodynamic flight was possible, after all, in the near future. Very well then; Santos would be first.

During the early months of 1906 he and Voisin worked on the new machine. The young constructor was caught up in the maelstrom of Alberto's enthusiasm. Night after night they sat late at rue Washington, or in the design office at Neuilly, sketching, arguing; discussing power-weight ratio, camber, stability, control, centre of gravity and lift, details of engineering, and again stability. Would the machine control in the air? If they managed to leave the ground, could they get it down again in one piece? Together they pored over the writings of Chanute and Lilienthal, and every scrap of information they could glean from Langley, Hargrave, Ferber, and the new French glider expert, Robert Esnault-Pelterie.

In case it should be thought that they were making heavy going of what seems in retrospect a fairly simple problem, it might be appropriate to quote a well-informed English opinion of the time. On the 24th of January, 1906, the engineering supplement of *The Times* contained a letter from Mr. Alliott Verdon-Roe (later founder of Avro Aircraft Co.) stating the writer's absolute belief in the claim made by the Wright brothers to have flown twenty miles, and adding that if he were able to construct a full-size machine on the lines of models he had made and flown, it would be possible for him to perform the same feat.

"It is not to be supposed," wrote the Editor acidly, "that we can in any way adopt the writer's estimate of his undertaking, being of the opinion, indeed, that all attempts at artificial aviation on the basis he describes, are not only dangerous to ·life, but foredoomed to failure from an engineering standpoint."

This crushing statement from the foremost engineering nation

in the world, coupled with others no less definite,* show clearly
enough how great the problem must have seemed to the little
Brazilian and his young assistant. Once more Santos was under a
continual mental strain. Gabriel Voisin must have found his
employer difficult, and at times impossible. He still showed
flashes of jollity and high spirits, but his buoyant twenties were
behind him, he had become a responsible man of the world,
and he was aware of that other penalty of achievement—the
knowledge that further success is expected as a matter of course,
and that the generosity extended to a gallant tryer will be denied
to someone who has already received the acclaim of the world.

The new activity inside the Airship Station gave little sign
outside. *No 7*, *No 9*, and *No 10* hung neglected in their stalls.
No 13 was put aside (though this was just as well). The "aerial
sportsman" was seen no more, for a while, rattling about the
clear skies over Paris. His life became more austere. In his
discussions with Voisin his own self-confidence hardened into
obstinacy, flavoured with a dangerous tendency to believe that
he knew all the answers.

The actual work on the aeroplane was done partly at Neuilly
and partly in Voisin's own workshop, where his brother Charles
was just beginning to assist him. Here Gabriel must have taken
on something of the mantle of Lachambre, torn between doubts
that what he was doing was wrong (he never built another aircraft like it) and complete confidence in the project, inspired by
the bland self-assurance, which ignored all criticism as if it were
non-existent, of his world-famous employer.

The new aeroplane was 33 feet from wing-tip to wing-tip,
and 40 feet long. It was a large machine by comparison with the
gliders of the day. A 24 horse-power Levavasseur Antoinette
engine drove a pusher airscrew. The main structure was a series
of boxes made of pine struts panelled with fabric, and lavishly
braced with piano wire, on the lines of the airship keel girder.

In the late spring it emerged from the Airship Station where
the final assembly had taken place, and Santos was ready to
begin his first tests. Once again he showed how careful and
methodical he could be, when the occasion demanded, and how
utterly deaf to criticism or ridicule. He began with a series of

* e.g. "I have not the smallest molecule of faith in aerial navigation other
than ballooning." Lord Kelvin.

trials to determine the balance and centre of gravity of the machine. For this he erected two high poles, with a wire hawser stretched tightly between them. From this tightrope he suspended his aeroplane, attaching the lower end of the suspension cable at the supposed centre of lift. He then mounted to the control position, wearing a straw boater to shield himself from the sun, and carefully measured the balance of the structure, and tested the movement of the controls.

Those of his friends who returned to watch progress next day found that he and Voisin had arranged a carrier pulley on the tightrope, and hung the aircraft from this. It could now be moved through the air along the rope, and a donkey had been pressed into service to provide the pull. The sight of this astonishing rig gave rise to a choice variety of witticisms from the spectators, but although they were all his friends, Santos for once was not amused, and huffily ignored them. He climbed into the aeroplane with a distant dignity, and gave the signal to go. The idea was to test the response of the controls to movement through the air, but although the donkey gave of its best it was unable to move the suspended aeroplane faster than a brisk walking pace, at which speed the controls naturally gave no response whatever. It was very vexing.

Undismayed, the inventor went straight on to his next series of tests. These involved the use of the new airship, *No 14*, projected for the very purpose, and kept in good condition against this moment. The aeroplane was attached to the envelope of *No 14*, slung like the keel of a normal airship. Santos intended to use the aeroplane engine as motive power, and the aeroplane control for manoeuvre, while at the same time he operated the gas valves, ballast, and the other devices of the airship part of the combination.

In this ingenious arrangement, besides producing a monstrous hybrid that made the spectators blanch, Santos succeeded in providing a control problem which must have made his first real flight simplicity itself by comparison. It is doubtful whether any aeronaut, before or since, has attempted to control such a horror single-handed, or any other way, and the first efforts to launch the combination into the air were chaotic. It was brought out, weighed in the traditional manner, and the pilot climbed on board. Chapin started the engine, which was more powerful than anything installed in an airship up to that time, and the aeroplane showed an immediate tendency to leap forward and leave the airship envelope behind it. Santos tried it a number of times on the guide-rope alone, calling "Let go!" to the moorers, while Dozon and three of his most agile mechanics ran forward with the guide-rope, trying to keep the combination "on the lead".

It spoke volumes for his extraordinary dexterity and courage that he was actually able to master this contraption sufficiently to win some results out of his tests. None the less, the trials were extremely difficult, dangerous, and undignified. He found that he could not let the apparatus fly free, for fear that he would not be able to get it back again, and the tests became a shambles of shouted orders, roaring engine, crowds of scampering handlers; and in the middle the envelope of *No 14* bobbing and lurching on its guide-rope, with the swaying shape of the aeroplane straining ahead of it, and the small figure of the inventor yelling at the top of his voice from the control position.

But he persisted. Nothing would put him off. He has been pictured, by official Brazilian historians, as moving with calm assuredness towards the solution of flight, his carefully reasoned theories justified, step by step, through a series of deliberately-planned trials. The truth shows him in a more human light, and as a greater rather than a lesser man. In the face of appalling difficulties, if necessary by the most incongruous means, he somehow wrung out sufficient results from his experiments to give him a working idea of what he would face if his aeroplane was to fly.

When he separated it once more from the envelope of the airship, he christened the aeroplane *No 14 bis*,* since it had first left the ground attached to *No 14*. He decided, on second thoughts, to fit the more powerful 50 horse-power Antoinette engine. His tests gave him some idea of the difficulties of control inherent in the design, though he was not to know the full story until later.

The arrangement of *No 14 bis* was what is now known as a "canard", that is, an aeroplane with the elevators ahead of the main plane. Although the Wrights had the same arrangement (but with a much sounder balance of the machine) the idea

* *"Bis"* = "again, encore". The English equivalent would be "14a".

afterwards went out of favour, and the tail plane and elevators were banished to the rear for many years to come. But with the canard configuration, and the centre of gravity alarmingly behind the centre of lift, No 14 bis was sufficiently unstable to be, by modern standards, uncontrollable. There is nothing against putting the tail in front when the centre of gravity is properly positioned. On the earliest aircraft the tail was far safer placed behind.

There were two reasons why Santos and the Wrights, as well as others of the early pioneers, hit on such an apparently unsuitable system. The first was undoubtedly due to the death of Lilienthal, universally revered by the early aviators. His glider dived into the ground after stalling. His tailplane was behind, and the reasoning was that had it been in front it would have positively lifted his nose and borne him up and clear. Every glider and aeronaut dreaded the uncontrollable nose-dive.

The second and sounder reason was that when the elevators are behind, and the aeroplane steers like a boat, a down-load is imposed on the tail to bring the nose up and make the aeroplane climb. This opposes the increased lift from the wing, and, at a time when aeroplanes were barely expected to fly at all, it could tip the narrow balance between thrust and drag, and put the aircraft back on the ground.

The box-kite cell on the front of No 14 bis was modified during the tests, so as to give only elevator control. There was now no lateral or directional control, and the nose was pointed up or down by tilting the whole cell, with the natural result that a small movement gave a violent alteration of trim. It would not be too unkind to call the machine a freak, and a most dangerous one at that.* But Santos had eyes solely for the two prizes, and for the honour of being the first man to fly. He was, after all, risking only his own neck.

It is indisputable that with the engine power then available the required flights of 25 and 100 metres were very short.

---

* In spite of the hard things said about the aerodynamics of No 14 bis it should be noted that a reproduction of this machine was constructed in Brazil in 1956, and flown 500 yards at a height of 20 feet. (It was reported by Le Figaro as "repeating the historic experience of the French pioneer of aviation".) But it is possible that some minor alterations had been made, if only for the sake of the pilot who demonstrated it.

Almost anything, of any shape remotely aerodynamic, might possibly be projected through the air for that distance, since it would not have to turn, and scarcely to climb or glide. But Santos must get the credit, as before, of acting while others considered. His concentration was absolute. For the first half of 1906 he dropped out of the social scene. Hostesses sighed for him in vain. What he set out to do he eventually did, and on the 13th of September his aircraft was tenderly conveyed from Neuilly to the open space of Bagatelle, in the Bois de Boulogne, where once the kite-flyers had saved his life.*

Besides his own crew he was accompanied by the Voisin brothers, Monsieur Archdeacon, a delegation from the Aéro Club, and a large crowd of sightseers, including his young nephews from Kelly College. All these enthusiasts had risen early, for the same principle was observed as with airships, that the best test condition was a dead calm. The dew was still damp on the grass when the aeroplane was lined up at the north side of the clearing, where it rested uneasily on its two bicycle wheels and three skids.

At a quarter to eight the engine was started and warmed up. Santos took his place standing in the wicker basket that formed the pilot's position. He looked pale but determined. The ordeal he faced would be shorter but far more critical than anything in his airship experience.

At exactly 7.50 he gave the order to stand back, and opened up the motor to full throttle. No 14 bis began to trundle towards the belt of trees forming the southern border of the clearing. It gathered speed very slowly, and as it passed the officials of the Aéro Club they threw themselves prone on the wet grass, in a gallant attempt to see whether the wheels would leave the ground. They didn't; and Santos had to stop, and have the machine towed back again. He was not getting full power from the engine.

Feverishly Chapin worked on the motor. At 8.40 all was ready for another run. Again the engine was opened up to full

---

* The flying-field at Bagatelle was called after the house of that name, built in sixty days by the Comte d'Artois for a wager. It was later the property of Louis-Philippe, who sold it to the Paris-domiciled Marquis of Hertford. This celebrated miser and art connoisseur used it to house the accumulated treasures that eventually became the Wallace Collection.

power, and the ungainly machine rolled lurching forward, trailing a rich cloud of castor-oil behind it. It was going faster. At about 25 m.p.h. it seemed lighter on its undercarriage. Santos, his face set, wound back the wheel that operated the elevator box-cell, and the front of the aircraft rose. The spectators were transfixed. Slowly the main wheels left the ground and spun idly on their axles. It was clear, and flying! For a second or two the aeroplane hung on the empty air.

But Santos had not managed to reverse his control fast enough, and the tiny climb was too much. *No 14 bis* staggered, stalled, and a moment later subsided heavily on the turf. The undercarriage collapsed, and the machine slid to a standstill in a shower of fragments from the shattered propeller. Santos stopped the engine and sprang out, quivering with excitement. The onlookers, who had been frozen to their places, burst into wild cries. Monsieur Archdeacon threw up his hands to heaven, and Voisin rushed up and embraced Santos. Everybody began pacing out the length of the flight on the ground, but before all marks were obliterated it was clear that the machine had only covered a few metres.

Neither this nor the damage to the aeroplane could detract from the triumph of the occasion. Santos led Chapin aside, to tell him at once what must be done. The machine was to be repaired immediately, and the response of the elevator made to follow the pilot's movement more quickly. The fore-and-aft control was very sensitive, he told Voisin. He talked to everyone at once. He was completely his old self again, delighted by the day's work, optimistic, sparkling, and volatile.

The damaged aeroplane was tenderly removed to the new Voisin workshop at Billancourt, for repairs to be made. Santos was impatient to try again before the bad weather set in, but Voisin was not to be hurried. Fortunately for everyone's nerves there was a distraction to hand, sufficient to engage the attention of the mercurial inventor for the short while of waiting.

Some time before, he had put down his name for the first balloon race organised by Mr. Gordon Bennett, and had commissioned a large new balloon. The interest here, other than the novelty of the race and the many experienced aeronauts competing, was that Santos's new balloon was fitted with motor-driven propellers, turning in the horizontal plane, designed to propel the aerostat up or down, and so reduce or eliminate the use of ballast.

It is not clear why he persisted with this old idea of his, after he had progressed so far along the path of controlled flight, and when he was on the brink of the greatest adventure of all. It seems that he had commissioned the work and entered almost idly for the competition, actually coming to the starting line at the last minute, for want of something better to do. But the course of Santos-Dumont's genius always ran erratically.

The race began on the 30th of September; from Paris of course. Sixteen of the monsters bobbed and swayed at their moorings, to be released simultaneously on the firing of a gun by Mr. Gordon Bennett. Santos was seen to be having some trouble with the complicated mechanism of his propellers, and the flight proved an unhappy one. He received a special cheer as he left the ground, but shortly afterwards he caught the sleeve of his leather coat in the mass of levers and rods operating his new device, suffered a painful injury, and had to descend near Bernay, after covering just under 100 miles. While he was attended by a doctor, the cloud of spherical balloons sailed on and out of sight. The race was won by a French-domiciled American, Frank Lahm.

Although his arm was nastily wrenched and bruised, he was back at the workshop three days later. Only when *No 14 bis* was ready for another test did his streak of cautious thoroughness come again to the fore, and he spent many days working over every aspect of the aeroplane and engine. His few seconds in the air had shown him that there was no room for mistakes. When he was ready he planned to make an attempt with proper observation, and as it was then mid-October he had to wait for the weather.

On the 22nd of October, he again informed the Aéro Club that he would attempt, next day, to fly for 25 metres. The faithful members, including M. Archdeacon and M. Surcouf ("secretary of the mixed commission for scientific time-measurement"), who had been summoned so often to his bidding, rallied once more. At 8 a.m. on the 23rd they were in place at the Bagatelle field, together with photographers, reporters, and a good-sized crowd of both sexes. The Santos-Dumont equipage had arrived well before them, and *No 14 bis* stood ready. At

8.45 the engine was started, and Santos climbed into his basket.

There followed a series of snags, well known to inventors, but maddening in front of a large crowd. "Owing to a little flaw in the gear, the flight was postponed until the afternoon."* In fact Santos made five runs across the grass, to test the control response yet again, and at the sixth attempt one of the landing wheels fell off, fortunately without causing further damage. After it was replaced four more runs were made, but still without leaving the ground. Next, a propeller blade flew off, and was replaced. The observers from the Aéro Club looked sceptical, when the tests were suspended until after luncheon. "M. Santos-Dumont explained to us that the shaft pins of the motor and rudder† connecting gear had somehow got loose. . . . 'Everything will soon be in order,' said the inventor, 'and I have great hopes of succeeding'."‡ Brave words, from a man keeping a tight hold on his nerves.

But it was not until 4 p.m. that *No 14 bis* was declared ready to try again. Cold, damp air was rolling up from the Seine. Once more the engine was started. The crowd, now over a thousand strong, pressed forward. Santos waved them away with an imperious gloved hand. "Stand back!" he shouted. The aeroplane began to move forward faster than before, and he gave the engine full power. Suddenly everyone realised that the moment had come.

A third of the way across the field he wound back his control. The long nose lifted. "And now," said a witness, "the two wheels are no longer on the ground; now they are ten, thirty, fifty centimetres up, then a metre . . . two; and the aeroplane keeps on flying." Santos had pulled her off more gently, and at once corrected forward. "The elegant, all-white outline is seen to describe a graceful curve to the left; then it begins to descend, and comes to a stop on the ground." Santos had lost lateral balance, cut his motor as the aircraft began to rock, and came down abruptly. It was a rough landing, and the wheels collapsed again, but the aircraft stopped with little more damage.

The crowd let out its breath in a wild shout of joy. Many

---

* A. Napoleão, translated by d'Oliviera.
† A journalistic mistake. There was no rudder.
‡ *Le Petit Journal*.

could not believe their eyes, and stood in silent wonder. Men and women, prominent among whom was "an enormous Englishman", rushed across the grass, plucked their hero from his aircraft, and carried him in triumph. Jolting on the shoulders of his half-hysterical supporters, Santos called across their heads to Monsieur Archdeacon, who had come trotting up: "Did I win? Did I win the prize?" It was 1901 over again.

Pushed, jostled, and short of breath, Monsieur Archdeacon answered: "In my opinion there is no doubt about it. But why did you stop so soon?" Santos shouted back, "I lost my way!" and then all further conversation became impossible, in the laughter, cheers, and general babel of congratulations.

Such was the stupefaction of the observers that they had failed in their allotted duties, of marking the exact distance of the flight; but it was generally (and officially) agreed to be about sixty metres, at a height of two to three metres, and the Aéro Club forthwith announced that the Archdeacon prize had been won, and the first flight by a power-driven aircraft had taken place. The news was flashed round the globe, even while the ground-crew were conveying the aeroplane away, and Santos was preparing himself for a dinner of celebration. So far as public and even specialised knowledge went, it was the first true winged flight by a man. "L'Homme a Conquis L'Air!" shouted the evening headlines, "Une Minute Mémorable Dans l'Histoire de la Navigation Aérienne!"

Chapter 17

☆☆☆☆☆☆☆☆☆☆☆☆☆☆☆☆☆☆☆☆☆☆☆☆☆☆☆☆

The Steering Is Half the Battle

The uproar that followed the events of the 23rd of October was far from surprising. It would be tedious to examine here just what constitutes a valid claim to have flown. It has all been carefully analysed elsewhere. At the time, to all inhabitants of the informed world, the feat they had been awaiting for so long was that just performed by Monsieur Santos-Dumont. The balloonists, airship pilots, gliders; all were dismissed. The Wrights were still unknown. "Man has conquered the air!" Santos was the man.

The last weeks of 1906 were the crowning glory of his life, and the happiest days he was ever to know. Scientists, celebrities and savants, all crowded forward to shake his hand; his slightest word commanded silence and rapt attention. His lionisation went further and deeper than in the days of 1901, for he was now not only a public hero once more, but the only man known to have experienced that achievement of winged and powered flight, which had been the dream of mankind down the ages.

At the same time, his rivals felt a certain understandable chagrin. Some of them claimed, with justice, that they were better engineers, better aerodynamicists, and more sensible and practical than the eccentric Santos. *No 14 bis* was an enormity, scarcely meriting the name of aeroplane. It was unendurable that such a contraption should leave the ground, and one went so far as to say that the 50 horse-power of the bigger Antoinette would propel a grand piano through the air for sixty metres, under favourable conditions. But all this was fruitless. While they had thought and calculated, he had flown.*

He was often indifferent to criticism, but these remarks got through the barrage of acclamation which surrounded him. He had intended in any case to try, as soon as possible, to fly the 100 metres needed to win the Aéro Club prize; now he became determined to show that *No 14 bis* was a real flying machine, and no freak. But first he wanted to do something about lateral control. He had hated the sensation of heeling over sideways, with nothing he could do to right his aircraft, and this had been the real reason for his sudden landing on the 23rd.

He and Voisin went into details. They devised two surfaces, octagonal in shape, mounted between the outer wing struts of the aeroplane, and movable by the pilot, so as to impose a force at the ends of the wings. With this idea the "aileron" was adapted from Esnault-Pelterie's glider (constructed late in 1904) and here Santos was ahead of his chief rivals, since even the Wrights had not thought of it. His method of operation was a trifle bizarre for, since his other control arrangements left him with no hand to spare, he had the wires led to a metal T-piece sewn into the back of a special coat. Thus by movements strongly suggesting the action of a rhumba dancer, he could sway the aeroplane one way or another.

On the 10th of November the Aéro Club de France gave a banquet in his honour, and to commemorate the flight of 23rd October. Among those present were MM. Archdeacon, Surcouf, Caillelet, Deposse, Voisin, Crenod, Blériot, and Faure;

---

* Captain Ferber generously wrote: "The Brazilian inventor had proved that the flying machine could fly . . . On the 23rd October, in the presence of the Aviation Committee, at 4.45 in the afternoon, his aeroplane left the ground smoothly and without shock. The crowd watched, spellbound, as though witnessing a miracle; it remained mute with astonishment, but immediately afterwards, at the moment of landing, gave vent to a roar of enthusiasm and carried the aviator shoulder-high in triumph."—and again—"He fixed his propeller for direct action . . . in this way he lost in motive power, but gained in construction time, as complicated transmission gear is always a delicate arrangement. The whole of 1906 was spent in vain by M. Blériot and myself in trying to find out how to do this."

his old rival Commandant Renard; Captain Ferber and Don
Jaime de Bourbon.* These worthies let themselves go, and the
speeches were longer than usual; though no more deserving of
quotation. Santos replied briefly, and with his usual modesty.
But when he finished he seemed to have something on his mind,
and was seen to sit twirling the stem of his empty wineglass
reflectively, his prominent eyes unfocused in the light of the
table lamps.

He was certainly thinking of the Aéro Club prize, to be
awarded for the longer distance; and he was also not unmindful
of the critical remarks made about his sixty-metre hop. Only
the Committee of Observation had been warned, but he had
already laid plans for another flight at Bagatelle, in two days
time. He looked forward to it with mixed feelings. Launching
oneself into the air in this way, even for a short distance and a
small height, was not the same thing as airship flying. There
was no stopping or turning back, and each landing so far had
been a minor crash. He had not liked the feeling of the razor-
edge balance of control of *No 14 bis* (and probably no-one but
Santos could have flown the beast at all); and if he were to hit
something hard, the engine was just behind him.

But he put all these thoughts aside. If *No 14 bis* could clamber
into the air, he, Santos-Dumont, could keep her there long
enough to win the prize. First one must fly; and then attack the
problem which the flight revealed. It was the basis of his
philosophy.

So it was that the 12th of November found his equipage in
position once more. By good fortune it was a fine and sunny
day. Besides the usual crowd and the Aéro Club Observation
Committee, there was a brand-new sensation; the appearance
of Monsieur Blériot with an enormous biplane (also mounting
an Antoinette motor), which he had been working on, in
collaboration with Voisin also, throughout the year.

There was some fear that this incursion might disastrously
divide the attention of the public, as indeed it was dividing the
time and talent of Voisin. But Santos was confident that he had
nothing to fear. With a gesture bordering on the gallant ("Would

---

* Napoleão includes in the party a Monsieur Bouquet de la Grog. Much
as one would like to believe in this gentleman, his presence must be put down
to a misunderstanding in translation.

Monsieur care to fire first?'') he insisted that Blériot begin his trials at once, while *No 14 bis* waited her turn. The situation was satisfactorily resolved by Blériot wrecking his machine, after a number of runs, without leaving the ground; and Santos then shot his cuffs and prepared for action.

He made a few short runs, each time rising clear for a hop of a few metres. He was getting the feel of the machine once more. The wintry sun was already setting behind the trees when he told M. Archdeacon that he was ready for an observed trial. The President had decided that this time there should be no doubts over the measurement of the distance, and was firmly mounted in the back seat of a giant Mors, which the chauffeur was to drive alongside the aeroplane, as close as possible. M. Blériot deserted his battered machine, and sadly joined the spectators.

At 4.30 p.m. the word was given. The clattering of Santos's engine rose to a roar. A thousand people pressed forward, while photographers rammed home new plates and levelled their cameras. Stopwatches were held in gloved hands. The chauffeur of the Mors engaged first gear.

No 14 bis ran forward over the grass, and the big car kept pace with her. M. Archdeacon bounced in the back seat, holding on to his top-hat with his free hand. After three hundred metres the long white finger of the fuselage lifted once more, in response to the swivelling of the box-kite control. Up rose *No 14 bis*, white against the dark trees; unstable, ungainly, and vibrating from end to end, but flying.

She was fifteen feet above the ground, and the bounding Mors seemed to race beneath her. Santos stood straight in his basket, working his hands and shoulders. On the ground there was pandemonium, and the crowd rushed forward, even into the path of the aeroplane. Santos saw the green grass ahead of him vanishing under a host of black dots, as the frenzied spectators spilled on to the course. The Mors had to weave through the running figures.

He was already near to stalling when he used his ailerons to turn. The aircraft lurched from side to side. Once more he felt his control going. There was a clear patch ahead now. He closed the throttle, and as *No 14 bis* came wallowing down he franticly wound back his little wheel. At the last moment the fuselage rose, and she settled on to the ground. The wheels collapsed again, but gently. He stopped the engine, and heaved a deep sigh. Then the crowd surged up to him.

The scenes which followed were even wilder than those of 23rd of October. Someone shouted out the time and distance— $21\frac{1}{3}$ seconds; 220 metres. M. Archdeacon, purple with excitement and cold, stood up in the back of the car and roared out his congratulations. Santos was radiant as the crowd hauled him from his perch. This was a real flight! This was no bounce or hop! He had won the Aéro Club award, his aeroplane had really flown, and the world would know, beyond possibility of argument, that Santos had done it!

The field of Bagatelle made a strange picture in the waning November light, at that time of evening when the colour of the ground seems to drain into an empty sky. All the wide space of the dark green grass was empty, except where the circular black blob of the crowd surrounded the angular white shape of the flying machine. Around this target the figures ebbed and flowed, while the cheering echoed back from the trees. At the centre of the demonstration, the little Brazilian smiled and waved, his eyes bright with happiness. Somewhere, among the sea of human faces, Louis Blériot cheered with the rest.

The winter of 1906-1907 was a glorious time for Santos-Dumont. He was not only the unrivalled aviator, but apparently the only one. He had safely ventured on an experience which no other human was known to have possessed. He had entered a world still closed to the rest of mankind.

What he now experienced would have inflated the ego of a saint. To understand the effect of what he had done, we must remember that it had been repeatedly called impossible, by the most weighty judges. It is difficult to convey the impact which this had on everyone, and particularly on the Press. Even English reporters pushed forward, eager for a few words with the great man.

They all found him in excellent humour. "The steering of the machine is half the battle. That is the subject to which M. Santos-Dumont is now particularly attending," wrote one. "His airship is fitted with three rudders. Direction is given to the ship by means of a rudder in the front, operated by a steering-wheel. The aeronaut is a perfect adept with this apparatus, but the other two rudders, which are situated in the wings, are less easy to master. When the motor moves forward in the air the intrepid pilot inclines first one rudder and then the other. The wicker basket-car in which he stands is balanced on pivots, and takes up any desired angle.

"Santos-Dumont's name is on everybody's lips. . . . He is the very figure, the very type of energy. Small and wiry, he is the stuff of explorers and conquerors. It is no light test of nerves to thrust oneself into the impalpable air upon the back of one's own invention.

" 'I am serving my apprenticeship to the *métier de l'oiseau*', observed the aeronaut, very happily. 'And the descent, is it not of great difficulty?', I inquired. 'Oh no', replied M. Santos-Dumont. 'I feel no shock.* I am confident of the future of aeroplanes. Consider how inexpensive they are, and how comparatively easy to make: I constructed mine in a few months. The cost has been slight in comparison with a steerable balloon, and is much less than an automobile.'

" 'But the danger is greater?'

" 'I fail to see that. On the contrary, it seems to me that motoring on land provides a more fruitful source of accident than motoring in the air. At least, the risk of collision is less,' and the aeronaut laughed gaily."†

It could hardly be expected that this furore would fail to reach the United States, or be diminished on the way, and very shortly the Wright brothers were reading of Santos-Dumont, hailed as the first man to fly. They wrote to Ferber, asking for details, but after sending the letter they seem to have smiled sardonically, and gone their own ways. They certainly qualify as the least excitable inventors in all history. But Santos unwittingly did one thing for them. As he had galvanised France into widespread effort, so he shook America. It seemed that powered flight was possible! If Europe could do it, pondered the editors, then so could Americans. What about those strange old stories from Dayton, Ohio? . . .

---

* Since the interviewer was obviously utterly at sea, and appeared to have adopted pidgin English for the interview, Santos can be excused for replying with some disregard for truthful detail.

† *Illustrated London News*. November 24th, 1906. "From our Special Commissioner in Paris."

But now, as belief in the Wrights grew in their home country, it was once more refuted in Europe. Frank Lahm, the winner of the Gordon Bennett balloon race in which Santos had been injured, instigated another investigation into the Wrights' claims, the latest in the long train first sponsored by the indefatigable Ferber. Finally convinced, he sent a letter to the Paris *Herald*, on February 10th, 1907, stating his absolute belief that the Wrights had long been flying for considerable distances.

The paper made short shrift of this letter, in an editorial headed, "Flyers or Liars". "The Wrights have flown or they have not flown," the writer stated profoundly: "They possess a machine or they do not possess one. They are in fact either flyers or liars. . . . It is difficult to fly; it is easy to say 'we have flown'." It was an outlook typical of European opinion, and Santos received a thousand assurances, from every source that should be qualified to judge, that his feat was unique, and that he was indeed the first to fly.

On the crest of this wave he moved gaily into 1907. To be sure, he privately had no great illusions about *No 14 bis*. It had won him the prizes he had coveted, and an undying place in history, but he speedily realised its shortcomings. It made one more test outing in his hands, at Bagatelle during April, when it hopped for a distance between one and two hundred metres, and then it was put aside, and flew no more. Probably no other pioneer aeroplane owed so much to its pilot, and no-one else offered to try it out for him.

He was teeming with new ideas. The aftermath of the previous year's work was a release of nervous tension, and some reaction towards the gay and social life of the "aerial sportsman" who again was the toast of Paris. His workshop and Airship Station were once more thrown open to all comers, and every aspirant to aeronautical knowledge came respectfully to the master's feet, to inspect his aeroplane at close quarters, and to hear his theories of aerodynamics.

It must not be supposed for one moment that this reaction spelled any lessening of his activities; it was merely a change in attitude. Already in January he had dashed off the general arrangement of a design to supplant *No 14 bis*. *No 15* was a small box-kite biplane of more conventional arrangement, with the airscrew pulling instead of pushing. It mounted a 100 horse-power engine. The wings were still built up of Hargrave cells, but Santos made extensive use of plywood in the construction. It was first tested on 27th March, at St.-Cyr, but during its first run it heeled on to one wing-tip and was seriously damaged, before even leaving the ground. Santos himself was cut and bruised, rising tattered from the wreckage with his immaculate clothes stained with dust and blood. No 15 was counted out, and he made no effort to repair her.

He had hardly changed his ruined suit for another, when he called the chief designer of Lachambre and Co. to his office, to assist him in the drawings of No 16. He seems not to have been put out in the slightest by his gruelling experience with No 14 in her composite form, for this new Santos-Dumont was to be a combination aeroplane and airship, with a gas-bag lifting a fuselage, complete with wings and tail. He appears to have got the bit completely between his teeth, and the comments of Blériot, Farman, and Voisin can easily be imagined. He was not to be put off, and the ill-omened device was duly built. It is kinder not to go into details, and also unnecessary, since for once all the critics were right, and the half-breed was destroyed on the ground at its first outing in June. The best which could be said for it was that from so unlikely an idea emerged a surprisingly graceful machine. But its looks belied it, and once more he was fortunate that it did not fly.

Leaving his crew to pick up the pieces, he went straight back to his study to start again on a clean sheet of paper. This charac-teristic, which he kept for so long, of rebounding from every crash with renewed vigour, must have supplied the first instances of the hoariest of aviation gags—"Back to the old drawing-board!" which follows after some dramatic mishap. During the summer of 1907 he worked on the details of No 17 and No 18.

There is some mystery about these two designs. Brazilian records say that the first was a biplane similar to No 15, which was never built. No 18 was a wingless hydroplane, supported on the water by floats, and driven by an aero engine and propeller. This he tested on the Seine, with some intention of converting it later into a seaplane by fitting wings. But neither of these projects can be related to the straight course of his researches, mainly due to the loss of all his notebooks and records. The cause of this tragic mishap will emerge in its proper place.

If it were possible for Santos to feel discouraged (a state of mind he was just beginning to know) he had some reason, by summer's end. 1906 had seen him at the pinnacle of triumph. So far, 1907 had been a strenuous, painful, and unlucky year. But the extraordinary thing was that his feat of the previous November had still not been equalled, nor approached, by himself or anybody else, at least so far as anyone in his own world could prove. He was apparently still the first and only man to have flown; but now nothing seemed to go right. He dismissed the previous months' failures from his mind, unpacked one of the two spherical balloons that he kept at Neuilly, and took once more to the sport of ballooning for fun. He went back to Nice, and made some tentative experiments with the glider on floats. He played tennis. He planned to visit Switzerland to take up ski-ing.

This happy-go-lucky attitude was not for his rivals, now thoroughly on their mettle. At last they were in full cry. The Wright brothers, not yet rivals in any true sense, had already flown several hundred miles in the course of various tests. These veterans had actually stopped flying, since 1905, to concentrate on improving their designs. In late summer of 1907 Wilbur Wright himself came to Paris—an outcome of the latest move in the long-drawn-out attempts by Ferber to get the French to buy one of his machines. He met all the principal members of the Aéro Club, including Deutsch, and important figures in the Government and Army. He had his first trip in a balloon. He was joined by Orville, and though the negotiations were as maddeningly vague as ever, they paved the way for one of the brothers to come back, the following year, for a practical demonstration.

One man whom the "mysterious" Wrights did not meet was Santos-Dumont. After all the discussions they had with others, and after the impression of quiet and capable confidence they made on everyone they met, there should have been very little doubt in Paris, apart from professional Government doubters, that their claims were valid. Indeed, many Frenchmen were working on that assumption. Yet somehow, in spite of everything, official and private opinion managed to keep on thinking that the first flight in history had happened at Bagatelle on an October afternoon in 1906, and that the next steps in aviation might be expected shortly.

The European Santos-Dumont rivals were about to take wing. The Voisin factory had started up. The Voisin brothers built a biplane for Henri Farman, who flew it successfully in September. In October 1907 he broke the Santos distance record at last, and managed to stagger round a turn. Another Voisin was made for Delagrange, who was close behind Farman. And Louis Blériot, his great disappointment overcome, and pressing on-ward with unrelenting fervour, built three monoplanes in succession. Eventually he wrecked all three in crashes, but he managed to fly five hundred yards by November. Esnault-Pelterie built a tractor monoplane, which flew in October and November.

The pace was getting too hot, and one man, even a rich genius, could not hope to stay out in front. Santos had many misgivings as he took stock of the situation, just before Christmas of 1907. Blériot and Farman appeared as determined, as oblivious to danger, and as resourceful as even Santos himself; and they had financial backers. A cold feeling must have crept over him as he listened to those who had met the Wrights, heard of their impact on Paris, and assessed the casual assuredness with which they had related their achievements.

He seemed to feel that something drastic must be done. At a time when most families were preparing for the feasting and cheer of Christmas, he made the great decision to turn his back on his first love, the airship. Once converted, he kept back no sentimental regrets.

"To propel a dirigible balloon through the air," he remarked scornfully to a friend, "is like pushing a candle through a brick wall." This betrayal sounded like kicking *No 7*, his Racer, while she was deflated; for only a very short while before he had predicted endless possibilities both for her and for the "aerial yacht". But from now on he was to spend no further money or time on the great yellow envelopes of silk and linen, and the workshop of Lachambre, Machuron and Co., would see him no more. He pulled his note-pad towards him, and thought long and hard. As so often before, he had another ace to play, and presently he fell to work, and began the first sketches of *No 19*.

Although this is not a history of early aviation, it has been necessary to go into the details of pioneer flying at some length. For flying was Santos-Dumont's life; his life was now at its full tide, and his own destiny was swept along with the rising tempo of the new science. He had stirred up the hive, and the bees were buzzing. He had provided the great encouragement. It may be that some were spurred by the familiar principle that if he could do it, with that weird apparatus, then so could they. If that was so, it was still encouragement of a useful sort. But most took his feats at their face value. He had showed the impossible to be just possible. Now, in sheds and workshops all over Europe, oil-stained and determined men were preparing to go one better.

By the close of 1907 eight aviators had flown in Europe, in heavier-than-air machines. They were Santos-Dumont, Vuia, Voisin, Blériot, Farman, Esnault-Pelterie, Delagrange and Pischoff. So fast had the wave of invention rolled on in the wake of *Le Petit Santos*. The best and longest of these short, staggering hops had been made by Henri Farman. So the pre-eminence of Santos had lasted less than a year, and had now been surpassed. It is wonderful enough that it lasted so long.

But it was exceedingly galling to someone of his temperament to be overtaken by sheer weight of numbers. Though he had worked and dreamed towards the realisation of practical aviation, it had never quite dawned on him that when the great moment came there would be others, as bold and imaginative as himself. At the close of the year he felt increasingly that the situation was slipping out of his control.

But there was one more prize he must have. M. Deutsch had combined with M. Archdeacon—the two patrons of the first real airship and the first aeroplane flights—to offer an award for the first aeroplane to fly one kilometre in a closed circuit. It was called the *Grand Prix d'Aviation*, and *No 19* was the vehicle chosen by Santos to bring home this crowning trophy. As he put down his neat little sketches on the squared paper he always used, he must have cleared his mind of all that had gone before, and returned to the principle of lightness and simplicity that had been his first and greatest contribution to aviation.

He drew a small monoplane, simple and graceful, with a strong bamboo pole carrying a wing and engine in front, and a tail with rudder and elevators at the back, with the pilot sitting on the centre of lift, and with three landing wheels. In its essentials, it was the shape of most aeroplanes for decades to come. It had ailerons, dihedral, and all the requirements of stability. It was so unlike *No 14 bis* that it is hardly believable that both came from the same inventor. Admittedly, the petrol tank was placed precariously above the pilot's head. His nephew drew attention to this, receiving the disconcerting, and rather inconsequential reply, "Only turkeys die before the day!"

Once more Santos had a winner. But not immediately, for the design did not come out right in the first model, and when he tested it on the 21st of November there was another mishap during the early hops, and it was badly damaged. This time he was seriously discouraged, stopped work on the aeroplane, and spent a week in gloomy contemplation in his study, wondering what had gone wrong.

This hitch was fatal to his latest hopes. The year 1908 heralded the great leap forward in flying, when suddenly everyone would seem to be in the air. On the 13th of January, Henri Farman won the Deutsch-Archdeacon *Grand Prix d'Aviation*. Aeroplane engines were starting up everywhere. And in a warehouse at Le Havre, unopened in its crate, lay a Wright biplane which the incredibly casual brothers had brought to France during their visit of the previous year, and had never unpacked. Soon it would fly, and transform the scene.

Chapter 18

☆☆☆☆☆☆☆☆☆☆☆☆☆☆☆☆☆☆☆☆☆☆☆☆☆☆☆☆☆

The *Demoiselle*

Everybody flew; or so it seemed. But in reality only Farman, Blériot, Delagrange and the Voisins were making much progress, and at first their flights were a series of short staggers, during moments of dead calm, with a hair's-breadth only between rising into the air or flopping back on the ground. Although landings usually took place to an abandoned chorus of snapping spars and struts, they made swift progress, and by the summer Delagrange had flown for over ten miles (in Italy), while in July, Henri Farman covered more than twelve miles. (On May 29th he had taken up the indefatigable M. Archdeacon as a passenger.)

On the same date Wilbur Wright arrived at Le Havre, as the culmination of the long campaign by Ferber, and proceeded to unpack the Wright biplane that had lain there since the previous year. He assembled the machine at the Leon Bollée factory close by Le Mans, and prepared to give a demonstration which he hoped would bring him orders to build aircraft in France. At the same time, in America, Orville was preparing another *Flyer* to show to the U.S. Army.

During the long preparations at Le Mans, methodically conducted by Wilbur with his usual disregard for outside opinion, a new wave of scepticism rolled over the French aviation world. Now that her own aviators were following so well in the wake of *Le Petit Santos* (himself almost, as they repeatedly assured themselves, a Frenchman), it seemed easier to doubt the claims of the laconic brothers, to a feat so remote in time and place.*

The shock was all the greater when it came. On the 8th of August Wilbur made his first flight at Le Mans, before a crowd which included M. Archdeacon. He took off easily, and though he was in the air for only just under two minutes, he showed such mastery of control that the onlookers were stunned. He continued in the same way with further trips, apparently doing what he wished with his aircraft, and when he moved to the Camp d'Auvours manoeuvre ground, where there was more space, he set about the business in earnest, and in two months handsomely broke every flying record in existence.

Public opinion swung violently from one extreme to the other. No-one had seen flying like this before. The sensation caused by the displays at Auvours was as extravagant as the previous disbelief had been adamant. "Blériot and Delagrange were so excited they could hardly speak," Wilbur wrote, "and Kapferer could only gasp, and could not speak at all." The main cause of this most unusual speechlessness was not the distance achieved, but the pilot's easy mastery of the apparently docile machine. Instead of a daring but pale-faced aeronaut, sweating and fumbling at the clumsy controls of a lurching machine obviously intent on dumping him at the first opportunity, they saw the calm, terse, and humorous Mr. Wright; climbing, turning, gliding and landing an aeroplane that seemed to want to do his bidding.

So great was the astonishment at these displays that the Press and experts went so far as to publicly repent and beat their breasts. *Le Figaro* wrote: "It was not merely a success but a triumph; a conclusive trial and a decisive victory for aviation, the news of which will revolutionise scientific circles throughout the world." And Blériot said, when he recovered his voice, "The Wright machine is indeed superior to our aeroplanes."

There is no mention of Santos attending with the rest of the worshippers at Auvours. It is impossible to believe, knowing his

* In July one Paris newspaper carried the headline "*Le bluff continue*".

devouring enthusiasm, that he did not go at some time during the autumn of 1908. It soon became fashionable for parties to take the train from Paris to see Mr. Wright flying at Le Mans, and by December Wilbur had obliged his admirers by remaining over two hours in the air on a single trip. Santos was in Paris, and had the spare time. He could hardly have kept away. But he must have gone very inconspicuously, and he does not figure among the many aeronauts who met and talked with Wilbur, during the time when he was the man of the hour.

Indeed, following the crash of *No 19*, Santos was in a fretting state of melancholy. His friends noted his low spirits. He did not seem to have responded to the previous year's holidays and sports. He was back in his study, working, and he seldom came out to play. Though he had quite recently suffered from too much idolisation, he sometimes affected to think himself a failure. Over lunch with Ferber, he even brought up again the subject of his small size, bewailing his shortness of stature. A man should be reconciled to his physical failings at 35 years of age. To console him the burly soldier said: "But my friend, Bonaparte stood only 1.65 metres, and moreover he was pale and sickly." "Yes," replied Santos sadly, "but he was a great man."

If there was something unbalanced about his present state of mind, the attitude of his friends did little to settle it. French opinion was torn between stupefaction at the present feats of Wilbur Wright, and a determination not to believe, just because of them, that the brothers had really stolen a march of nearly three years on the rest of the world. Frenchmen were showing an increasing tendency to set up Ader, Voisin, Blériot or Farman as their champions for the claim to be first. Somehow Santos would get left out of the argument. The reason for this was certainly because the Wrights' claims were only worth contesting if the contestants were French; but the whole complex of motives was muddling, even to contemporary observers.

Out of this confusion, in the last months of 1908, while Wilbur flew again and again in front of cheering crowds and Santos stayed alone in his workshop, the great Wright Brothers versus Santos-Dumont Controversy was born. To this day the whole South American continent, and particularly of course Brazil, believes as an article of faith that Santos was first. Weighty volumes have been written to prove it; harsh words have been exchanged, delegations have withdrawn, Press attacks have been launched to sustain it. Briefly, the argument rests entirely on whether or not the Wrights flew before October 23rd, 1906. For there is no doubt whatever that Santos did so on that date, in front of a large crowd, an official committee of observers, and a battery of newspaper cameras.

But the mysterious brothers, far off at Kitty Hawk, performing in front of five people and their own camera—did they really fly? And supposing they did leave the ground, was it true flight, or were they catapulted through the air, as any light-weight contraption might be projected for a few yards? The Latin-American world has answered these questions, firmly and apparently for ever, in a sense favourable to its champion. "From all the facts which we have examined, the conclusion is drawn that, on the one hand there is luminous, dazzling proof, and on the other, indications, doubts, incredulity, and the presumption that there really occurred the facts alleged in 1908 by the Wright Brothers, five years after the Kitty Hawk flight about which so much has been said, and three years after they had abandoned their aeroplane experiments. . . . Having to choose between said alleged flights and the Bagatelle flight, we prefer the last-named one."* And again, "Why did the Wright Brothers not enter the (Archdeacon) competition, and why, knowing afterwards, through the world wide comments, about the aeronautical feats of Santos-Dumont, and the victories achieved by our Countryman, did they not tender a claim, or lodge a protest against the granting of said prize to Santos-Dumont, vindicating for themselves priority of flight, when the Press conferred same on Santos-Dumont?"*

The same sentiments were repeated with variations, many times over. The Brazilian argument rested on the strangely obscure conduct of the Americans, the obstinate disbelief of their own countrymen in the United States, the paucity of their evidence, and their (by most standards) unnaturally laconic behaviour. They are all good points, except perhaps the last. The Wrights just happened to be like that.

Unfortunately for this doctrine, and tragically for Santos-Dumont, there is no historical doubt whatever about the true

* A. Napoleão, translated by d'Oliviera.

facts and the true happenings, at the birth of aviation. The Wrights were first. It is indisputable.

It is no part of this chronicle to take the reader through all the arguments which lead to that conclusion. Our concern is with Santos, and the effect that this verdict had on his life. The verdict itself is set out in great detail by historians who have considered every scrap of evidence.

Santos flew in October 1906. There is no question of that. The first field of inquiry therefore lies in the claim of the Wrights to have flown at Kitty Hawk in December 1903. Though the legal evidence is scanty it is enough. The claim has been acknowledged, and December 17th, 1903, is accepted by nine-tenths of the world as the occasion on which the first true powered flight by a man took place. But if anyone doubts this there are the Dayton flights of 1905. And here there can be no doubt at all.

If we are not to sift all the evidence, we must accept the opinion of the overwhelming majority. But there should be no mistake about the partisanship, and the vehemence of the supporters of Santos-Dumont, both then and now. It is highly probable that he himself, for the rest of his life, was never sufficiently detached from their influence to think objectively about this question, nor allowed to examine any aspect of it which did not favour his own case.

While the arguments in Paris, during 1908 and 1909, grew more bitter and acrimonious, it is pleasant to record that neither of the principals took any part in them. To Santos especially, whose life's dreams and aspirations were being publicly dismantled, belongs the greater credit of saying and doing nothing whatever at this period in defence of his own claim. Though he did not speak, his sensitive nature quailed under the impact of the furious arguments around him.

The times were in step with his mood of bitterness. *La Belle Epoque* was passing away, into the unease of the years that led all too soon to the Great War. Already Clemenceau was Premier, and the changing temper of the country was expressing itself in widespread strikes and civil unrest. The nation was restless, and her self-confidence receded from the lofty peak achieved during the Great Exposition. Santos withdrew further into the solitude of his study and workshop, where happiness of a sort could always be found, in the increasingly eccentric course of his pursuit of knowledge and invention.

Ignoring the side-issues (and he was always liable to take time off to design something fantastic, which never saw the light of day), his efforts were now concentrated on *No 20*, the natural development of *No 19*. This aeroplane, soon christened the *Demoiselle*, was the last and perhaps the most satisfying realisation of his genius. All the faults of *No 19* were corrected, but he kept the general shape and arrangement. The machine was very small—only eight metres long by five and a half metres wing-span, with a wooden propeller of no more than one metre diameter. The fuselage was built up of bamboo spars, with metal joints. The wings were covered with Japanese silk. Like all Santos-Dumont's aircraft, it was beautifully made and finished, and the effect of simplicity and transparent elegance gave rise to its nickname.*

The engine, mounted on the front of the main plane above the pilot, was a special creation of his own. It was a flat twin-cylinder design, based on a Dutheil-Chalmers motor-cycle engine, but extensively modified to give 35 horse-power. When he had it nearly finished he took it to the Darracq motor-car factory, for final machining and assembly, and contracted with them for the manufacture of spare parts and engines. He followed his standard practice of taking out no patents. In this case there was an unfortunate sequel.

The eventual and considerable success of the *Demoiselle* brought Santos many offers from the new aircraft factories, for the rights to produce his machine commercially. He told them that any firm was at liberty to copy it without fee. This attitude was inspired by a genuine wish to see aviation advanced without the handicap of patent rights. To his surprise and annoyance he discovered that the Darracq firm was trying to patent his engine, on the grounds that it had been built in their works. This roused him to fight, and he immediately briefed counsel and brought Darracq's to court. His opponents may or may not have sincerely

---

* "*Demoiselle*": Young girl, or dragonfly. *No 20* was named in the latter sense. "Santos-Dumont was somewhat fastidious, and always insisted on a perfect finish to all the parts of his machines. The elegance, both of his diri gibles and his aeroplanes, was remarkable and bore the impress of his own artistic sense." (Dumont-Villares.)

believed in their case, but Santos won, and the engine, like all
the rest of his inventions, reverted to the status of public
property.

In March of 1909 he began trials of the *Demoiselle* at St-Cyr,
between Paris and Versailles, and made rapid progress. The new
control system was workable at last, with rudder and elevator
at the rear, and lateral control (abandoning his pioneer work in
ailerons) by wing warping. He kept his individual eccentricity
by controlling the wing-warping through cables, which ended
in metal rings which he slipped over his arms, so that swaying
the body still remained his method of correcting any tendency
for a wing to drop.

Except for the business with the engine, there was no collaboration in the design of the *Demoiselle*. Voisin was not involved,
and one suspects that the short partnership was dissolved with
relief on both sides. It must have been an added satisfaction to
Santos that the new aeroplane, flying better every day, was
entirely his. In later years he declared that he bracketed her
with his cherished *No 9* as his favourite flying machine.

The abandonment of the airships brought him an important
economy, at a time when he had been running well over his
financial limit. Though his investments continued to increase in
value, his spending had gone up enormously, and the airship
fleet had been very expensive to keep in commission. The airships were still stored at Neuilly, but were not maintained, and
most of his old staff were paid off. Chapin, originally an engine
man, still kept watch over the motors of his master's new
creations. But the change to aeroplanes came in the nick of time,
to allow him to draw back within his means.

Thus the encouragement provided by the first flights of the
Demoiselle was able to transform him again into the carefree,
concentrated man that his friends knew best. Almost at once
he realised he had a winner, and the ground was cleared for him
to exploit it. His temperament whisked him back to the heights
of exuberance. The continued triumphs of Wilbur Wright, and
the tiresome arguments about who was first, could all be ignored.
For his little aeroplane could fly: easily, safely, and neatly: he
could take it anywhere he wished to go, and once again he
could be the aerial sportsman, pioneering a new world in his
own machine.

His old Brazilian friend Antônio Prado now became his unofficial assistant, helping him with the programme of flights and adjustments that filled his days during the summer of 1909. The *Demoiselle* was fulfilling his fondest hopes. She was stable fore and aft, in very marked contrast to *No 14 bis*, and so steady laterally that he was able to demonstrate her ability by flying past his observers with a handkerchief in each hand and his arms outstretched (though still prudently through the rings of the controls). When he released the handkerchiefs they fluttered to the ground, where they shared the fate of his tie at Tavistock, being cut into pieces as souvenirs; one piece was kept by his old admirer, the Comtesse d'Eu, who was present. He progressed quickly from straight flights of a few hundred yards, to turns which permitted him to stay longer in the air. Within a month he could cover several miles in a single flight.

In the golden light of the drowsy weeks of mid-summer the graceful *Demoiselle* took almost daily to the air. Her tiny transparent wings and slender spars were seen buzzing and flashing around the leafy woods and deep green fields of the Ile de France, carrying her diminutive pilot about the busy little visits, technical or social, that he delighted in. For after an incredibly short time he had her so well tuned and adjusted to his satisfaction that he could use her, as he did *No 9*, for a practical means of transport. She could land and take off in less than a hundred metres of grass, even in still air, and this allowed him to visit his friends with country houses near to Paris, and alight in their grounds. At a time when very few people had seen an aeroplane at all, such an appearance was the sensation of sensations, and once more he took a naïve delight in his ability to astonish and intrigue.

He became so casual that he caused what was possibly one of the first "overdue" searches. Early in September he took off from St-Cyr on a rainy day, without saying where he was going. He vanished into the dark clouds, and after a couple of hours his crew gave the alarm. The newspapers were told, and *Le Matin* speedily had its best man on the job.

"What was one to think? What could one believe? We telephoned everywhere, in all directions. He was not at St-Cyr, not at Versailles. We telephoned his home; he had not returned. At half-past one in the morning M. Chapin got word at last that his aeroplane had made an eighteen kilometre flight in sixteen minutes, and descended at the Château d'Aion, owned by the Comte de Galard. The landing had been effected without accident, and when the information was received, Santos-Dumont was sleeping the sleep of the just in one of the Château bedrooms, as the guest of the Comte de Galard. Well, we have had enough sensations!''

The warm, happy glow of achievement, like the summer sun ripening the cornfields below him, brought him out of his dark moods, and he became the Santos of old. He recovered all his panache. He was eager again to see and applaud the deeds of others. (Except that he still did not visit the Wrights, who had moved to Pau.) On the 25th of July, Blériot electrified the world by flying across the Channel in his newest monoplane, a feat that even brought some twinges of disquiet to the comfortable English. Santos was genuinely pleased with his old rival's success. He wrote Blériot a warm letter, ending: ''This transformation of geography is a victory for the air over the sea. One day, thanks to you, aviation will cross the Atlantic.''

Blériot wrote back: ''I only followed and imitated you. For us aviators your name is a banner. You are our pathfinder.'' The phraseology of both letters, which in translation sounds as if it were intended for publication (as it probably was), expresses none the less the sincere sentiments of two generous souls.

As another instance of his gayer mood, Maurice Percheron relates how Charles Voisin landed one of his own aeroplanes after a test of controls, which Santos had been watching. ''When the propeller stopped he rushed up to Voisin, and standing on his toes—he was very short in stature—heartily congratulated him in the Brazilian fashion by tapping him on the shoulders. 'I believe that you have found the solution of the problem! Hurry! You have only to put enough gasoline in your tank and you will be able to fly for an hour, as easily as if you were playing!' ''

On through the summer and autumn the little Dragonfly danced and darted through the clear mornings and hazy evenings. Whenever the weather was calm it would be up and about. In quick succession he designed and built two improved versions— No 21 and No 22. The first had a new Darracq engine, based on his first design, while the second was strengthened, and carried a powerful water-cooled Bayard engine. But each was a *Demoiselle*. The last version, and the last aircraft he was ever to build, was very fast by the standards of the time, and it was in this machine that he claimed a flying speed (not officially timed) of close on 70 m.p.h.

But he was no longer out for prizes. The great Week of Aviation, held at Rheims in August, drew an entry of no less than thirty aeroplanes. Henri Farman covered 112 miles in one flight on this occasion. Santos was not there. He was busily experimenting with his latest *Demoiselle*, but it would have been as natural for him to have appeared at Rheims as at Le Mans. He gave no explanation for either absence. And six weeks later the first pilot to be killed in an accident, Eugène Lefebvre, crashed his Wright biplane. The second death occurred shortly after-wards. It was Captain Ferber, in a Voisin. He grieved for both.

However, the *Demoiselle*, and Santos, were on show at the Grand Palais, when the Hall of Aeronautics was inaugurated in October. The model he showed was actually *No 19*, which he had modified considerably since its crash. It made a great impression on all the notables who crowded to see the new machines, by its grace, simplicity, and lightness. "Alongside the Wright, Farman, Voisin and Blériot machines," wrote *L'Illustration*, "near the *Antoinette* and the tiny *Demoiselle*, one saw machines hitherto unknown: some more or less inspired by previous machines, others of a great originality, but in which their inventors, who were hovering around, full of their own importance, had not had time to risk their necks."

Santos was much in evidence at this exhibition. He was in the thick of every conversation and discussion, his little figure often on tip-toe, his high, insistent voice dominating the circle around him. His old friend "Sem", Georges Goursat, welcome as his companion wherever Santos went, sketched him again in this most natural situation, with the influential figures of French aviation bending to hear his opinions. Enthusiasm for flying broke out like an epidemic. A number of would-be aviators wanted to build *Demoiselles*. Santos agreed to show them the designs, and encouraged them to construct their own aircraft. Anyone was free to copy his plans, everyone should get into the air, and now it was no longer necessary to invent and build your own machine.

The exact number of *Demoiselles* built by others is not known.
It was probably between ten and fifteen. By the middle of 1910
they were flying in several parts of France. The first aeroplane
built in Germany was based on a *Demoiselle*, and one was made in
Argentina. Their designer had recently been granted his monoplane pilot's licence by the Aéro Club de France, and added it
to those he already held for biplanes, airships, and balloons. In
early 1910 he was the only aeronaut to hold all four. "Therefore,"
he somewhat immodestly wrote later, "I was the only man
who really had the right to the title of Aeronaut, for I had
flown every type of flying machine."*

This then is the picture of the man at the start of the year
1910, 36 years old, in the heyday of success at the work to
which he had dedicated his life; great triumphs behind him, busy
and engrossed, and still in the forefront of a vast new movement.

Suddenly all is transformed, and we have come to the climactic
moment of his life, as dramatic as it is mysterious. The last
occasion of which there is record of him flying was in November,
1909. In March, 1910, he was fit and well. A day or two later,
without warning, the news was passed round Paris that Santos-
Dumont had suffered a nervous breakdown. He was ill, and
confined to his house. No-one was to see him. Next, an announcement was made that the Airship Station would be sold, and the
remains of his fleet disposed of. His workmen were to be paid
off. Even Chapin was to be pensioned.

This was extraordinary, inexplicable. That Santos, of all
men, could contemplate such a thing! Did it mean, his friends
asked one another, that he could intend to give up?

They were not left long in doubt. The invalid sent word,
through Antônio Prado, that he was abandoning aviation, and
meant to retire. He was overworked. His doctor had ordered
him to rest. He must have a long holiday.

Of a surety, declared his circle, *Le Petit Santos* has driven
himself very hard for some long time. Evidently, he needs a
holiday. Piloting is a strain, and he should employ a test pilot for
his experiments. But to give up everything. . . . The rumours
and theories buzzed and circulated. It was a seven-day wonder,
and a major mystery. But the centre of it all remained closeted
in his house, and no-one was admitted.

* "*O Que eu Vi, O Que nós Veremos*". A. Santos-Dumont.

It is still a mystery, maintained all his life, and the lack of personal papers or close confidants makes it impossible to offer a certain solution. But research coupled with careful surmise leads to a strong probability, which must now be examined.

The overt reasons given by himself and his Brazilian biographers should first be set down. Napoleão writes: "Santos-Dumont, who had passed through all the vicissitudes of aerostation and aviation, resolved to bring his aeronautical career to a close. He had already given generously, with all his inventive genius, enthusiastic efforts and realisations, towards the conquest of the air. He could, and should, stop. Just like his aeroplanes, after flying for ten years, he needed a rest."*

And Henriques Dumont-Villares: "The constant cerebral effort, required by this work, may readily be imagined. . . . He had, nevertheless, to yield to the insistence of his body. He had always been very careful of his health, and concerned to keep himself physically fit, not for reasons of vanity, but because he realised that on this the success of his experiments essentially depended. When he recognised, therefore, that he was not so fit as he had been in his youth, he decided to retire and rest."†

Santos himself writes: "To obtain these results it was necessary for me not only to invent but also to experiment, and in these experiments over ten years I have had the most terrible shocks; I felt that my nerves were worn out. I told my friends of my intention to end my career as an aeronaut—and I had the approval of all of them."‡

It is probably true that when first he consulted his doctor, in that crucial spring, Santos had the superficial symptoms of a nervous breakdown. But no previous trouble, physical or mental, had kept him away from his life's work for longer than the minimum time needed to get well. And his latest flying experiences with the *Demoiselle* had been glorious. There must have been something else. We know, however, that eight years later he was a fully-diagnosed and admitted case of the disease now known as disseminated sclerosis, and herein lies the vital clue.

The medical profession, in 1910, knew this nervous disorder as multiple sclerosis. Its cause, then as now, was unknown. Some factors which appear to precipitate it are fatigue from

* Translated by d'Oliviera. | Translated by Bradley and West.
‡ Translated by Bradley.

overwork, injury, infections, and allergies. Its onset is most common between the ages of 35 and 45. The most usual early symptoms are faulty vision, weakness and unsteadiness, dizziness, and inability to control the urine. The symptoms come and go, but usually the general condition, despite apparent recoveries, becomes steadily worse. There is no known cure.

Santos was extremely reticent and fastidious about all personal matters, and certainly required from his doctor the highest degree of discretion. Even if his symptoms had in fact been merely those of nervous exhaustion, he would not have broadcast them. But a Parisian doctor of this period may easily have made a correct diagnosis, even in the earliest stages of the disease, for it was not uncommon. And an aeronaut who was almost a teetotaller would certainly take very seriously any slightest symptoms of blurred and double vision, or trembling of the limbs. Finally, the victim's normal expectation of life is some twenty years after the first signs appear. Santos in fact died twenty-two years later.

The conclusion is that since he certainly had sclerosis later, it is more than probable that its first symptoms appeared, and were recognised, in 1910. This alone would account for the way in which he reacted. He would never have thrown away his life's work, his heart's desire, and his greatest pleasure, only for a passing illness. Why he would not admit to it then, though he had to later; why he persisted years afterwards in declaring that he gave up semi-voluntarily; why his own supporters pretended much later, that he merely wanted to rest: the answers to all this must be sought in his own character. The most likely theory is that he could not bear to be pitied.

It is certain beyond reasonable doubt that in his high room above the traffic of the Champs-Elysées, with the soft air of spring gently blowing the curtains inwards, the doctor, after some days of careful consideration, told Santos his worst fears. While the Dragonfly waited, silent in the hangar at St-Cyr, its owner heard a sentence passed on him, which would spell their final parting.

His delicacy shrank from the coarse details. He would tell no one. He instructed his valet to give Prado the message for his friends.

Then black despair came down, and he let everything go.

Chapter 19

☆☆☆☆☆☆☆☆☆☆☆☆☆☆☆☆☆☆☆☆☆☆☆☆☆☆☆☆☆☆

The Wandering Melancholic

Santos-Dumont said to Pierre Paquier, "Never allow yourself to be discouraged, even at your worst moments. Always use a check to begin again." So far he had faithfully held to this precept: at last, in early 1910, it could not avail him. The worst moment of all had come.

This chapter will span nearly twenty years, and whether or not this obeys the rules of biography, is for the reader to judge. Henceforward his life was one long postscript, sometimes happy, far more often sad, and nearly always sterile. This is not to say that it was dull. By comparison with most men he was still a figure of envy; rich, famous, revered; travelling where he willed, doing whatever he wanted, and meeting the great and famous whenever he wished.

But in spite of this it was a collapse. He never flew an aircraft again. He never built another after the *Demoiselle*. He who had lived for flying, as much for the sheer pleasure of it as for the delight of pioneering, never took another machine into the air, and went only twice as a passenger. Once the wave of development had rolled by him, knowing him as we do, it might be understandable if he gave up designing and building his own aircraft. He would not want to be second best. But for the aerial sportsman to stay on the ground—that was no passing convulsion due to normal illness, staleness, or mental fatigue, but the action of a man whose world had crumbled. Nothing else fits the facts but his knowledge that he had an incurable disease, with no prospect but the slow gaining of its handicaps upon him, and no hope but increasing humiliation and final death.

He would not expect to go steadily downhill, as the tiny lesions gained on his spinal cord and central nervous system. There would be periods of apparent recovery, before the symptoms returned more strongly than before. We must remember these ups and downs in the course of his condition, to understand his varying periods of seeming normality, alternating with those of darkest wretchedness.

As soon as his doctor allowed him to leave the house he fled to Nice, from where he issued the instructions which dispersed the remainder of his aviation property. There he faced his fate, looking out again on that blue sea which once had been the highway he would follow to fly to Corsica. There also he had to recognise, at the least, that the Wright brothers had established a powerful claim to have forestalled him in his greatest triumph, and that they had a large and vocal following.* French support for his claim was dropping away.

Nobody knew his thoughts during that time. He closed up completely, as might be expected of him, and gave no further explanations. Later, when challenged on the subject of his retirement, he would either snub the speaker with calculated rudeness, or obstinately insist that he had stopped because he thought he had done enough, and needed to rest. He maintained this attitude even when, sixteen years later, he was obliged to enter a sanatorium for treatment.

---

* In the 1910 revue En Avion! Marche!, appeared the song Dans Mon Aéroplane.

> La p'tit' Suzann' dernièrement
> Disait à son amant:
> "A! que j' m'embête
> Je n'aime plus l'auto
> J' veux que'qu' chose de nouveau."
> Il lui répond: "Mon amour
> J'ai pour toi l'autre jour,
> Fait une emplette
> C'est quelque chose de vraiment chouette
> Que j'ai acheté à Monsieur Wright."

In December of 1910 the Aéro Club de France voted for the erection of a granite column on the field of Bagatelle, inscribed with the words: "Here, on the 12th November, 1906, under the control of the Aéro Club de France, Santos-Dumont established the first aviation records in the world. Duration of flight—21.2 seconds. Distance—220 metres."

This simple monument, though the meaning of its inscription might seem ambiguous to a lawyer, left no doubt in his mind that the Aéro Club supported his claim. In fact, the Committee was mentally confused to a high degree, but quite unable to give the palm of victory, finally and unequivocally, to the Wright brothers. Santos had to be content with this small satisfaction, together with the fervent and loyal assurances of his friends, when he cautiously returned to his old circles in Paris.

He was a completely changed man. After his absence of some months, he was at first reluctant to meet his acquaintances again, and though he attended a number of aviation meetings, he was painfully diffident and withdrawn. He must have made even these cautious contacts with a great effort. Only his superb courage, which has been emphasised again and again, could have driven him back to be a mere spectator, since now he could be nothing else.

After these few appearances he began slowly extending his radius of action, as if he were meeting people for the first time, to include quiet visits to a few old friends, such as Antônio Prado, Sylvio Penteado, and Georges Goursat. It has been remarked that one of the burdens of his life was the lack of a wife or a really intimate friend to confide in, and there is no trace of his taking any of his hosts into his full confidence. They found him melancholy, quiet, despondent, and sometimes bitter about the Wright controversy. Sometimes his black moods were more pronounced, and sometimes so much less as to be almost normal.

He already had the feeling that people were forgetting him. After his death some papers were found in a locked drawer, one note referring to this time. He had written: "It was—I may say so now—rather painful for me to note, after all my work on dirigibles and heavier-than-air machines—the in-gratitude of those who a few years ago covered me in praise."

There was now nothing special holding him to Paris. He had

always been restless, but the pursuit of aviation had kept him in the Capital. That was gone, and now his suitcases were always being packed and unpacked. He went to Portugal to see his sisters; back to the French Riviera again; and then when he returned to Paris he found he could not bear to stay. After some inquiries he rented a small house at Bénerville, near Deauville, a square villa with a flat roof, in the latest style of architecture. The house, called *La Boîte*, commanded a view of the sea, and its roof made a good situation for a small observatory. For Santos had found a new interest in astronomy, and at once equipped himself with a quantity of expensive telescopes and instruments.

He spent a large part of the summer of 1911 at *La Boîte*. He had also become intrigued by the study of meteorology as a science, so that he could if he wished spend the day in observations and calculations of the weather, and every fine night turn his telescope on the stars. The Paris newspapers had not entirely forgotten him. "He has temporarily deserted flying for astronomy," wrote one, "but those who know him best say it will not be long before he designs another machine that will command universal attention."

This reporter was guessing. There was nothing temporary about his condition, and there were no new designs in his study. But he was finding sufficient peace of mind at Bénerville to change the habitué of Maxim's almost into a provincial. Indeed, the municipality of Deauville, thirty-two years later, named a small street after him. And to his housekeeper he was a kind and polite, though somewhat eccentric gentleman, whose constant air of gentle sadness aroused all her best instincts.

For months he pottered and peered, apparently content, noting down his results on his favourite paper squared in millimetres, while the European scene slowly darkened around him, and the forces marshalled that were to sweep away the France he knew. Occasionally he would leave the villa to make another visit, in each of which, as time went by, it became more and more obvious to his hosts that the motive force had gone for ever.

Three years after his collapse, the Aéro Club de France, seeing that he was serious about retiring, bestirred itself to sponsor him for some more worthwhile distinction. Through the usual channels it was suggested, and approved, that he should be promoted to Commander of the Legion of Honour, and a more imposing monument was commissioned, to commemorate the flights of 1901 and 1906. The Club members suggested that another granite plinth, this time surmounted by a figure of Icarus, should be placed at a small crossroads at St. Cloud, on the edge of the Bois de Boulogne. The crossing would be re-named Place Santos-Dumont. The sculptor Colin, an exponent of the rugged-realism school, was engaged for the figure.

On the 19th of October, 1913, Santos attended the unveiling ceremony. He looked better than he had for some months, and seemed even to have gained a little weight. A good crowd of officials, public, and Press were gathered, and flags fluttered bravely in the fresh autumn breeze. The proceedings were opened by M. Léon Barthou, representing the Président du Conseil, who after a "spiritual and moving address", placed the ribbon of Commander round the inventor's neck, and saluted him on both cheeks. Cries of "Vive Santos!" echoed back once more from the houses and streets, as the crowd cheered again and again.

Monsieur Soreau, vice-president of the Aéro Club, came next with a speech recalling the early triumphs. Santos-Dumont, he said, commanded, for his unforgettable feats, the admiration, not only of the Aéro Club, but of all France. He then read a telegram from M. Deutsch, regretting he could not be present; while in fact there is no mention of the attendance, which would hardly go unremarked, of any celebrated aviators, such as Blériot or Farman.

At the end of this discourse, to the strains of the *Marseillaise* and the Brazilian national anthem, the statue was unveiled. It must be admitted that it did little credit to its subject, or to M. Colin; Icarus wore a ferocious expression and was heavily muscled; but Santos liked realism in art, and he was perfectly satisfied.* His voice trembled, and his hands shook, as he rose to reply. He spoke haltingly, but from the heart, and though the words he used were trite, they were charged with emotion. He spoke of his airships, of the great days that were past, of his

* "This superb being, of athletic shape and grave profile, from whose powerful arms extend two great wings like shields, nobly symbolises the great work of Santos-Dumont." *L'Illustration*, 25th October, 1913.

gratitude to the Aéro Club, both now and formerly, and above all of his love for the people of Paris, who had cheered and encouraged him through every reverse, and upheld him to the point of final victory.

When he sat down there was a most moving ovation. Crowds pressed forward to shake his hand, and many shed tears. At the lunch which followed there was one more moment of truly generous feeling, when Monsieur Albert Chapin was called forward, and presented by the Club with *les palmes d'officier d'Académie*. (Given to technicians, writers, artists, scientists, educators, etc.) Santos handed the mayor of St. Cloud a lavish donation for the poor people of the community. As a final stroke, a cluster of spherical balloons, piloted by his friends, rose from the Aéro Club grounds nearby, and the day ended with a display of fireworks.

Once more his charm had conquered everyone present. He had been the man whom engineers had told, again and again: "That will be difficult . . . but we will try it just the same . . . to please you, M. Santos." Such occasions would get fewer and fewer. Before he left Paris he gave a long interview to the influential magazine *Lectures pour Tous*, in which he mixed sober, modest, and sensible advice and prophecy with the most wildly inaccurate recollections of his life and adventures. He had some technical conversations with the aeroplane firm of Morane and Saulnier, who were building an improved *Demoiselle*. Then he went back to Deauville, packed his bags, and departed for the Côte d'Azur, where he spent the winter like any invalid, who grumbles and mopes along the Promenade des Anglais.

A sign of recovery was given, during the winter, by his sudden decision to go back to Brazil. He had not been home for over ten years. Four years were needed after his collapse, before he could bring himself to see his relatives and friends in South America, and even when he had finally made up his mind, he decided to travel incognito, and arrive unannounced.

The rather half-hearted ruse failed, for the Press got to hear of his journey, and cabled the news to Brazil. Both public and friends instantly forgave him his neglect, and prepared a mammoth welcome. When his ship arrived at Rio there was an official reception; speeches, bands, salutes, and huzzas; followed by a ceremonious procession to escort him to the house of his brother Henriques. The past years, both of his absence from Brazil, and of his retreat from public life, were as nothing. The hero was home again. There were gala performances at the theatres; receptions, banquets, and general rejoicing. The newspapers welcomed him back to their front pages.

In Rio it was mid-summer, and the heat oppressed him. He escaped as soon as he could, going first to Petrópolis, and then to São Paulo to stay with his family, and to Minas to see again the house where he was born. He loitered for a while in the deep countryside, whose serenity never failed to lull him. Then back to Rio, where he stood before his parents' tomb.

All over; he must have thought. You sleep there together, and I have run my course, done what I tried to do, and come already in sight of the end.

The restlessness in his bones seized him again, and in July he returned to France. He arrived just in time to see the last days played out, before the war came that would change the face of Europe for ever. He had never cared for exaggerated patriotism, and Paris seemed like a madhouse to him. As the reservists marched through the streets, singing and blowing kisses to the girls they left behind them, he fled to his villa at Bénerville.

There, anxiously scanning every edition as it came from the presses, he read of the German drive into France, and suffered the agony of watching the country he loved invaded, while he looked helplessly on. He conjured up scheme after scheme to serve France in her extremity. But what could he do? His airship flotilla was no more. He was forty years old, an invalid, and a citizen of Brazil. As the first crisis passed and the Western Front became stabilised, he moodily returned to his telescopes.

Then occurred a choice stroke of irony. The spy-fever which produced so many acid jokes in England was even more virulent in France. Sooner or later, as the unworldly Santos might have guessed, a foreigner living by himself within sight of the sea, constantly out on the roof of his house with a German Zeiss telescope by day and night, would certainly be suspected. Zealous residents of Bénerville concluded that he was doing something inexplicable with enemy U-boats, and an information was laid against him as a likely spy. An unimaginative police chief ordered a search of his house.

Santos was first horrified, then outraged, and finally consumed with a corroding bitterness. The incident was hastily concluded, with apologies from the authorities. But it was the last straw. He was already shaken to his soul by the events of the war. And now this! He, who had offered his aerial fleet to the French Government—it was too much. Trembling with anger, hurt, bewildered, slighted; and overcome by self-pity for the past four years of supposed neglect, he determined to shake the dust of France from his feet. He offered the villa for sale, and packed his bags for South America.

This was the moment when the tragedy happened, which has plagued his memory ever since. In *La Boîte* he had concentrated all his papers: letters, notes, designs, files, scientific and experimental data; private records of every sort, and even, it was suspected, a diary. In a fury he burned it all. He made a clean sweep. He had arrived in France with next to nothing but his money and his hopes. He left equally empty-handed.

It is because of this paroxysm, sparked off by a clumsy policeman, that his real personality is so hard to fathom. He was never a great man for putting his thoughts on paper, but such priceless clues to his character as might have been gleaned from a lifetime's jottings, went up in smoke during his last days at the villa.

He landed at Rio in a mood of the blackest despondency. A new nightmare visited him, which would remain with him for the rest of his life. The first Zeppelin raids had begun; and aeroplanes were dropping bombs, and fighting each other above the fronts of the armies. When the news reached him, he shook as if in a fever. He was gripped by a terrible remorse, none the less fearful because it was, pathetically, a type of *folie de grandeur*. He was responsible for this! His inventions were being used for frightful ends, killing women and children! Aviators, the new race of which he had been the first archetype, were burning and slaying each other in mid-air!

It was unbearable, and it was all due to him. *Mea culpa!* He was like a man possessed. Though now surrounded by his own people he was inconsolable, and, unfortunately, to suggest that anyone besides himself might share the guilt of inventing aviation, brought wrath on top of remorse. The idea became an obsession. "He now believes that he is more infamous than the devil," wrote Martin du Gard, "A feeling of repentance invades him, and leaves him in a flood of tears."

He aged rapidly during the war years. He spoke hesitantly, his hair thinned to baldness, and his eyes became deeper-set and full of pain. He carried with him an air of tragedy that made an immediate impression even on strangers. He returned again and again to his obsession. Every evil that aircraft could commit was his doing. He was like an atomic physicist contemplating the ruins of Hiroshima. His family feared for his reason.

Much of this could be laid to his nervous illness. Such symptoms agree with a modern diagnosis of sclerosis, with its severe depressions and introversions. Typical, also, are the periodic recoveries and long periods of normality. For early in 1915, when he received an invitation from the Aero Club of the United States to take part in the second Pan-American Scientific Congress, he accepted with alacrity. The Congress wished to found a "Pan-American Aeronautical Federation", and put forward his name as the first President. He was delighted with this vague but sonorous appointment coming, as it were, from the stronghold of the enemy, and he carefully prepared an inaugural address, to be given before the Congress.

This speech was delivered in Washington, before a most distinguished audience. The United States was still, of course, a neutral. Not having heard of his overpowering guilt complex, the Congress was not surprised to hear him emphasise the part that the aircraft could play in war, remind them of his own past predictions of its military possibilities, and enlarge on the scope for further development. But those friends who had known him recently, reading the transcript of his speech that was later published in the papers, were very surprised indeed.

During the remainder of his stay he caused even his hosts a good deal of bewilderment, for during visits and tours, to aircraft firms and public meetings, he gave several more addresses, most of which were strongly pacifist in nature, while some contained vehement and detailed advice for waging war from the air. His early confusion over this question had become chaotic. Even in 1905 he had written: "As for myself, I have never made it any secret that, to my mind, the first practical use of the airship will be found in war." Now, his attitude changed from day to day.

But the general tone of his speeches during this visit (he seemed, for a while, to conquer his fear of public speaking) was pacific, and stressed the future hopes of air lines, air commerce, and the peaceful use of aviation. The Congress, which had shown signs of bewilderment, fastened on to these valuable pronouncements, and duly named him as their delegate to the Pan-American Conference of Aeronautics, due to be held the following year in Chile.

After another rest in Brazil he attended the Conference, held at Santiago in 1916. Fortunately he was in still better health, and he needed to be, to make head or tail of the ramblings of the latest example of the all-embracing, international type of convention. His speech before this body was much more balanced and tranquil. And he actually flew as a passenger in a Chilean military aeroplane, and crossed the Andes into Argentina.

From Chile he went on, wherever interest led him, on a tour of the South American countries. In Argentina he met two aviators who had just made their first crossing of the Andes. "For both of you, who yesterday were greeted by the condors, my greeting is insignificant." This charming sentence was balanced, shortly afterwards, by his misguided but fervent congratulations to the people of Buenos Aires for choosing— when they could have had a good airfield ten minutes journey from the capital—a site some hours away, so that they could have a better.

Thus he wandered, rudderless, from one country to another, but everywhere received with the honour and esteem that were certainly his due. The war in Europe was far away, but when the United States joined the fighting it began to come nearer, and he returned to Brazil. He spent most of the next four years there. His illness gained very slowly on him, and he was near to happiness for long periods of time. He began to pick up old interests, and built a seaplane hangar at Rio. But he did not persevere, and shortly after it was finished he presented it to the Brazilian Government.

After visiting all his old haunts, he fell in love with the peace and charm of Petrópolis, forty miles inland from Rio, and bought a piece of land on the Encanto hillside. There, to his own design, he had a villa built which he christened *A Encantada*

(The Enchanted House). He constructed an observatory for his telescopes, fitted countless gadgets, and included such devices as recesses in each step of the staircase, so that he could, if he wished, take half-steps while mounting them. This was not just playfulness, but grim necessity. Dona Eulália, a respectable local widow, was installed as housekeeper, and reported that her master was fond of taking an occasional hand in small household tasks, rose early in the morning to make his own coffee, and appeared thoroughly domesticated.

Here he received friends, took increasingly short walks, studied, kept a small sailing boat in Rio harbour (called *Tico-Tico*) and lived the classic life of retirement. For a while he was content. Here he wrote (in Portuguese) his second book; *O Que eu Vi, O Que nós Veremos (What I Saw, What we Shall See)*. And this volume shows, only too well, what lay beneath the tranquillity of these years.

It is a short, sad book, hopelessly muddled and confused. Even the date on which he won the Aéro Club Prize with *No 14 bis*, is wrongly set down. The first half is a jerky account of parts of his career, full of inaccuracies. The second is a mixture of prophecy, philosophy, and self-justification. All the perkiness, bounce, and panache, that had made his vanities so endearing, are submerged in heaviness and gloom. It is bitter and sour. We would do well to remember that it was written by a sick man, hugging a mortal illness. For his own sake, and that of his splendid memory, one must wish it were never printed. No translations were published, in French or English.

In 1918 the Brazilian Government made him a present of the house and grounds at Cabangu, where he was born. This gift pleased him, and for a time he dabbled in farming, extending the grounds, and installing a manager. Between them, however, since Santos went on living at Petrópolis while controlling Cabangu through the mails, the venture was a failure, and finally he sold everything but the original house, where his father had lived as a railway engineer. This disappointment, coupled with the death of his favourite brother, Henriques, plunged him again into melancholy, and in 1920 he began another long tour of the South Americas.

Here and there he wandered, unable to rest. From one country to another he went, accompanied now by slightly diminished attention and enthusiasm. In 1922 he suddenly booked a passage for Bordeaux on the liner *Lutetia* and reappeared in Paris, after seven years absence. He was met by friends and reporters, on the morning of the 9th of May, at the Gare d'Orsay. Old friends from the Aéro Club ran to hand him down from the carriage, and a few photographers edged up to take pictures of a man almost forgotten. The reception committee felt awkward, remembering the spy story. It was a difficult moment. But slowly he thawed, and the return was pronounced to be a reconciliation.

It was a different Paris now, and he was a different man. He did not lunch in the Bois, or dine at Maxim's. Instead he went to stay at the house of his old friend Sylvio Alvares Penteado, and he lived there throughout the summer. He was a stranger; in Paris, of all cities.

It was no good. Everything was unfamiliar. At the end of the year he went back to Rio. The Government presented him with the copy of Colin's Icarus which had been on show in Rio, and he had it re-erected over his parents' tomb. Then he started wandering again. He moved restlessly around Brazil, from town to town. The following year he was back in Paris, and surprisingly took a short-lived interest in greyhound racing, buying a dog, "*Sabreur du Diable*", which won the St. Cloud *Grand Prix*.

France, Brazil, Spain, Portugal, France. Always moving on, to meet new strangers, finding them to be only new names and different faces. He could not stop. His health was slowly deteriorating, and his horrors of guilt were coming back, as his physical condition worsened. In February, 1926, he wrote an appeal to the League of Nations, calling for a ban on the use of all flying machines for war. The League, which had enough troubles already, took no action beyond a formal reply.

During the autumn the Aéro Club, to mark the 20th anniversary of his Bagatelle flight, gave him a banquet in Paris. He was presented with a commemorative plaque, but he could barely nerve himself to make his speech of thanks.

His illness grew ever more obtrusive. At last, in the winter of 1926, he agreed to enter the Swiss sanatorium of Valmont-sur-Territet, for such treatment as was possible. In Switzerland he spent his time walking in the sanatorium grounds, or if the weather was bad, in binding books. . . . The months dragged by.

He was still there in May, 1927, when Charles Lindbergh flew the Atlantic. The Aéro Club de France wrote to him, with a last fine gesture, inviting him to preside at a gala banquet, to be given in Paris for the American airman. Santos wept when he read the letter. He was too ill to go. He wrote and refused the honour, and his hand shook so that the writing was barely legible.

Chapter 20

☆☆☆☆☆☆☆☆☆☆☆☆☆☆☆☆☆☆☆☆☆☆☆☆☆☆☆☆☆☆☆☆☆

The Gathering Darkness

Before the snows came to Valmont his condition improved. The peaceful life of the sanatorium, with all the attention that skill and money could procure, restored him at least to the appearance of health. In any case he was probably going through a recession period in his illness. Let us look at the casebook, for the last time. "The patient retains to the end a periodic characteristic cheerfulness, lack of insight, and emotional unrestraint. There are occasional delusions and hallucinations. Pain is rare."

When he left the sanatorium he rented the fine house of his old friend, the Marquis de Sorieno, in Biarritz. Here he spent the winter, so much recovered that he felt, as he had not done for many years, the magic urge, the restless longing, of the productive man with something inside him that must be born. A light came back into his sunken eyes, he reached for his pad of paper, and began again to note, calculate, and draw.

It is always tragic when the compulsion to create is still there, and the means to manifest it is gone. Poor Santos. These were to be his last researches, seeking for the poetic image of flying itself, the ultimate solution of the problem he had wrestled with so long. He was trying to find a means of giving individual flight to man, with only such apparatus as the flyer could carry on his body: the vision of Daedalus, driven by a tiny motor.

Thirty years later it would be possible. But even then not as he dreamed it, for his fumbling mind and shaking hands were attempting to fashion a mechanical bird; and his mind's eye saw his goal as a liberation of the individual, the man soaring into the sun; a picture as far removed from modern civilisation and its regulation as his machine was different from those which eventually succeeded. He put some of his ideas into a paper entitled *L'Homme Mécanique*, found, after his death, unpublished among his effects.

His new interest took him back to techniques of the Middle Ages, for he began by constructing synthetic wings built up of swan's feathers and wire. He went over the old ground, of mechanisms to produce the proper beating of the wings. But he knew it would be beyond human muscle power, and so a great part of his effort went into the design of a powerful miniature engine, light enough to be comfortably strapped to a man's back.

Some of his old friends and companions came to stay with him at Biarritz. Slowly, hesitantly, but with some of his old spirit, he would explain his ideas to them, mixing mysticism and mechanics, philosophy and physics, reality and dreams. To see the lamp of his genius flicker low was to suffer with him, yet his natural charm had not gone, and his pathetic eagerness touched his visitors to their hearts. "With my new apparatus," he would say, "the human flyer will be able to pass through the air like a bird . . . he will conquer space individually, and like a great eagle pass over the summits of the highest peaks."

The flying bird came to nothing. The various parts were never assembled. It remained a dream, and he was spared the uncouth flappings and ludicrous mishaps suffered by the other would-be inventors of the ornithopter. The little engine, however, though it weighed only 17 pounds, produced a quarter of a horse-power, and would run when carried on a frame slung from the shoulders.

Leaving the ornithopter, he decided to use the engine for another purpose. He remembered his ski-ing days, and the labour of toiling uphill. (Ski-hoists were unknown in 1900.) More sketches followed, with pieces made up by a local workshop to his design, and then he had a strange invention indeed.

The motor was mounted on the skier's back, and was furnished with a drive that produced an alternate pulling motion. The impulses were transmitted to two steel wires, which hung down behind, passed under a small pulley fixed to the heel of each boot, and were finally fastened to the back of the ski on the opposite foot.

As each wire tightened in turn, the back of the rearmost ski was pulled forward against the resistance of the foremost, the resistance being assured by wearing ordinary climbing skins on the skis. The apparatus never got beyond the prototype stage. It is said to have worked, but the chances were that a small malfunction might reduce the wearer to a rhythmically twitching bundle, and nobody seemed very anxious to test it. In the old days he would not have considered anyone testing it but himself; but now he could not take the work past the elementary stages, and this invention too was reluctantly shelved.

His reborn enthusiasms took him back to Paris, always his ideal climate for investigation. But his latest efforts affected his health once more. His remorseful and guilty nightmares returned, shouting in his head that every aeroplane crash was a death laid at his door. He became very nervous, and could not bear the slightest sound. Paris was the last place for anyone in this condition.

"The only thing to be done was to keep from him news of the flying accidents that occurred. People took him books to read, and old collections of magazines full of his achievements. He used to smile, but what he wanted was to read the newspapers. It was difficult to prevent him doing so, and every disastrous accident causing death, which he managed to find out, put him into veritable crises of despair."*

At the end of 1928 he boarded the liner *Cap Arcona*, and sailed for Rio. Undeterred by his constant comings and goings, his countrymen prepared a new welcome for him, including a special surprise and compliment. It was intended to elect him to membership of the Brazilian Academy of Letters, and the reception was therefore planned to have a part literary, part aeronautical flavour.

As the *Cap Arcona* came in sight of Rio harbour, a large seaplane, hurriedly christened *Santos-Dumont*, took off, carrying

* Martin du Gard.

the reception committee on board.* They represented a large proportion of the most celebrated professors and intellectuals of Brazil. They carried with them a message, which they intended to parachute to the ship below:

> On board the hydroplane *Santos-Dumont*, 3rd December, 1928.
>
> Flying in the hydroplane that bears your glorious name, preceding the reception prepared in your honour by the people of the capital of Brazil, we have come to welcome the great Brazilian who, by realising the conquest of the air, enhanced the fair name of our country abroad.
>
> Tobias Moscoso. Amauri de Medeiros. F. Laboriau. Frederico Oliveira Coutinho. M. Amoroso Costa. Paulo de Castro Maia.

Amid cheers and waving handkerchiefs the seaplane rose, and flying just above the wave-tops, turned to meet the liner. While the crowds watched from the shore, and in full view of Santos on the ship, it suddenly lurched one wing-tip into the water. There was an explosion of spray like a shell-burst, and when the air cleared, it was gone. All on board were killed.

This terrible disaster, when Brazilians saw the cream of their intelligentsia vanish before their horror-struck eyes, instantly changed a day of rejoicing into one of national mourning. On board the liner, now moving into its dock, Santos was prostrated. It was the very worst thing that could have happened to him. Shaking like a leaf, white-faced, and scarcely able to speak, he insisted on the cancellation of all the welcoming ceremonies. Instead he had himself put aboard a salvage boat, and went out to the scene of the accident.

For days on end, while everyone implored him to desist, he tried to help in the recovery of the bodies. When this was finished he attended the funerals of all the victims. He repeated again and again: "How many lives sacrificed for my humble self!" By the time the week-long ordeal was over he was dazed and numb, and seemed unable to decide what to do next. He shut himself up in the Copacabana Hotel for two weeks, and then journeyed to his Enchanted House at Petrópolis.

* It was a 3-engined Junkers G.24.W belonging to the *Kondor Syndikate*, a German/Brazilian combine.

But he could not stay there either. The disaster lay always behind his eyes. Within a month he was on a ship sailing to France. An Englishman who happened to be travelling with him, found him completely unapproachable, surly, and haunted by castastrophe. He arrived in Paris unheralded and alone, and hurried to the house of Antônio Prado, where he stayed for weeks, immured. He spent the next year living very quietly in Paris, trying to get over the shock.

One more pleasure was still in store. At the end of 1929 he was promoted to the highest class of the Legion of Honour, that of Grand Officer. By then he was sufficiently recovered to take real pride in this rare distinction, and to attend the small private ceremony planned for the presentation. On this occasion, now in his fifty-sixth year, he showed surprisingly few outward signs of the illness that was consuming him. His moustache and the remaining side-brushes of his hair were white, but his face was bronzed and almost unlined, and his figure was as elegant, well dressed, and as carefully groomed as in his youth. He wore a dark suit, and a high, starched collar.

Monsieur Laurent-Eynac, Minister of Air, himself placed the insignia of Grand Officer round his neck. Also present were the Brazilian Ambassador and a number of Santos's personal friends. After the accolade had been given to him, and everyone had shaken him by the hand, he nerved himself for a great effort, and began a speech of thanks. He had taken much pains in preparing it, and he delivered it slowly, in a low voice, but clearly, with warmth and modesty. His hearers were strongly moved, for they knew how much strain he was under.

The little lapel rosette of this order was the only honour that he ever displayed, for he wore it always. That, and the medal of St. Benedict, given to him thirty years before, by the Comtesse d'Eu. He made no parade of his many distinctions, which are too various to list, and even extended to the use of his face on Brazilian five-cruzeiro silver pieces and hundred-cruzeiro notes, and to the naming after him of the airport of Rio de Janeiro.

In February, 1930, he visited the Palace Hotel at St. Moritz, taking his ski-climbing device with him. He sat quietly in obscure corners, and spoke to nobody. But one other guest recognised him. Lord Brabazon, the holder of the Royal Aero

Club's pilot certificate No. 1, and then as ever a keen skier and Cresta rider, was staying in the same hotel. Delighted to see the great air pioneer, he cordially asked him to a special dinner. Brabazon also invited eight of his own friends and acquaintances, all connected with aviation either directly or indirectly. Santos accepted, but came late. While Brabazon waited, talking with his other guests, it suddenly dawned on him, to his incredulity, that none of them knew who Santos-Dumont was. Once world-famous, he was now almost forgotten. He spoke little during dinner.

"Greatly moved, and quite content, I accompany the conquest of the air by man." These earlier words of his must have mocked Santos, while he tried to live quietly in Paris. For some time he had found solace in the progress of the big dirigibles, the most spectacular, if not the truest, descendants of his pioneering craft. In May of 1930 the *Graf Zeppelin* flew from Germany to Brazil. She carried a brilliant list of fare-paying passengers, who were subjected to a modified and more refined Neptune ceremony as they crossed the Equator, in which "the ladies were sprayed lightly with Eau-de-Cologne and the gentlemen with soda-water, while each had to recite a humorous little poem". Airships seemed to have come into their own.

But later in the year came the terrible disaster to the British dirigible *R.101*. Once more Santos was prostrated; once more he beat his breast, and loaded the guilt on to his own head. He suffered a complete breakdown, and his friends arranged for him to be admitted to another sanatorium at Biarritz.

Trouble came thick and fast. At the end of 1930 Vargas seized power in Brazil, as the culmination of a turbulent decade of political violence. The news filtered through to Santos, despite his doctor's vigilance. In the spring of 1931 Antônio Prado arrived in Paris, exiled by the new administration. He sought out Santos at Biarritz, and was dismayed to find him very ill. He cabled immediately to the family in São Paulo, advising them to bring him home. Family life might ease his mind, and in any case he might not last much longer. . . .

His relatives were not unprepared for such a message. His nephew, Jorge Dumont-Villares, was sent at once to France. He arrived at Biarritz in June, took Santos out of the sanatorium, and escorted him on the long journey back to Brazil. The

schoolboy of Kelly College, now a middle-aged man, and his
palsied and broken uncle, sadly mounted the gangway of the
liner, and Santos watched the familiar shore recede. So he left
France, for the last time.

For this home-coming there was no reception at Rio. For one
thing, he was too ill, and for another, his country was still
rocking from the take-over by Vargas. Brazil had seen some
stirring times during his life-span; it was another burden on
him that his last year should be spent amidst the clamour of
renewed strife. Since Petrópolis was too far from his family he
was taken to a house on the outskirts of São Paulo, and Jorge
Dumont-Villares moved in with him. From then until the
day of his death Jorge was his inseparable companion. Doctor
Rangel Pestana, a local specialist, took charge of him medically,
and his nephew ministered to all his other needs.

What they could do they did, but this was little enough.
He had some quiet and lucid periods, when he could still
enjoy the company of old friends. He even managed short
outings, to spend a morning at the Hipica Paulista, or at the
Athletic Club. On these occasions he would sit withdrawn
from all but his intimates, for he dreaded pity, and during his
rational periods his sensitive nature would re-assert itself,
making him unbearably touchy and self-conscious.

"I do not like to visualise death," he said to an acquaintance,
"but what I fear above all is to leave nothing behind me as a
token of all my efforts."

There were increasingly frequent bad periods. His nephew
had much to contend with, and it is greatly to his credit that
he held out to the end. The humiliating aspects of the late stages
of Santos's illness, when the patient begins to lose control of bodily
functions, lacerated his fastidiousness, and plunged him into the
depths of despair. He had become more punctilious in religion
during his later years, and the dark thoughts of suicide, normal
to his disease, which now rose before his mind, had to be beaten
back by the power of his faith.

In these bad periods he was no longer responsible for his
actions, and Jorge had to watch him closely. At last what he
feared happened, and Santos made an attempt to hang himself.
His nephew was in time to stop him.

It would be cruel and impertinent to censure him. His

condition was hopeless, and increasingly burdensome, even when judged by a rational man. But in his worst moments the real Santos was no longer there, only a poor wreck who rocked his head in his hands, and cried out and pressed his palms to his ears when he heard a noise. The sound of aeroplanes particularly affected him, bringing back the twisted thoughts of the woes he had unleashed upon the world.

His last months, as if in emphasis of his contrastingly public and private life, have a flavour of dark mystery and drama. The subject is avoided in his own country, and his native biographers pass over his death with a vague sentence or two (Napoleão: "His existence came to an end." Dumont-Villares: "His eyes closed for ever.") The account which follows, therefore, results from very careful comparison of reliable and authentic, but unofficial sources.

In the spring of 1932 he grew still worse. Doctor Pestana suggested that São Paulo, fast growing, was too noisy for him, and that sea air might help him to sleep. A house was rented on the beach at Guarajá, near to the port of Santos (the name has no connection with his family), and uncle and nephew moved there. Here he spent his last months. The change seemed to do him good, and there were better times again, when he could walk slowly along the beach, and watch the children playing, and gaze over the South Atlantic, along the sea route to France. He was gentle, and calm. The days grew cooler in the Southern latitudes, and by July the children had gone, and he and his nephew were the only dark figures on the golden beach.

On the 9th of July, with little warning, Brazil burst into civil war once more. The state of São Paulo rose against Vargas. Minas Gerais joined the struggle, and fighting broke out, not only between civilians and the Vargas Government, but within the armed forces also. Surrounded by violence and hate, in the last extremes of his illness, Santos-Dumont's reason tottered precariously. He managed to draw up a manifesto addressed to the rebel states, urging them to restore order, but nothing is known of who received this letter, or what they did with it.

The fighting went on spasmodically for two weeks. The 20th of July was his 59th birthday. Then, on the morning of the 23rd, aircraft passed over Guarajá beach, on their way to bomb a rebel light cruiser near Santos. The sound of their engines reached his ears, followed by the hollow boom of distant explosions.

This was the last horror. His own countrymen were killing one another, using his own invention. All day he was silent, while Jorge watched uneasily. He sat unnaturally still, while the shadows lengthened, and the sunlight turned golden. Towards evening he excused himself, and went to the bathroom. After the shortest delay his nephew grew apprehensive, and burst into the room. This time he was too late. Santos-Dumont had used a necktie, and a bracket on the bathroom door. It was not strong, but strong enough. He weighed only fifty kilos.

The shock of his death, when it flashed round the country, acted like a douche of cold water on the combatants. Two days later a proclamation was issued by the Government:

Decree No 21668 of 25 July, 1932.

The Head of the Provisional Government of the United States of Brazil: Considering that the perpetuating of the memory of those who have deserved well of their Country is a duty which should be fulfilled both by the people and those who govern them:

Hereby decrees national mourning for three days, counting from today, the necessary communications being made to the Federal Interventors in all the States of the Union by telegram.

Rio de Janeiro, 25th July, 111th year of Independence and 44th of the Republic.

Getúlio Vargas
Francisco Campos.

The fighting stopped for two at least of the three days, while Brazil mourned her most famous son. He was known to have been desperately ill, with little time to live, and nobody had any reason to question his illness as the cause of his death.* Neither can we say, of a man in his condition, that he ended his own life. He was killed by his disease, when his hands no longer obeyed him.

His body was taken from Guarajá to São Paulo, and the Arch-

* His death certificate gave the cause as "cardiac collapse".

bishop caused it to rest in state in the crypt of the Cathedral. The fighting had begun again when they took him to Rio, to lay him beside his parents, in the Cemetery of Saint John the Baptist.

His estate was much less than expected. He had overspent his income for many years. Everything was left to his nephews, including the Enchanted House at Petrópolis. They gave it to the town, to be used as a school. The house at Cabangu went back to the Brazilian Government. Another property he had owned in Switzerland was made into a children's playground. So Santos, who left no children, left a place for some at least, in the surroundings he had called home.

What did he leave to the world? Opinion in Brazil is quite definite. He is the Father of Aviation, the engineering genius, the discoverer of the art of flying both by lighter- and by heavier-than-air machines. He is the harbinger of peaceful air commerce, the international ambassador of good will, the idealist, the visionary, the inspiration of future generations. He is a national hero, and his name is universally revered. In São Paulo a museum is devoted to his life and works.

This assessment is supported, more or less, throughout South America and in Portugal. The rest of the world is more guarded. Judgements have been passed on him which vary between support of the Brazilian view; and dismissal as a mere poseur, playboy, and dabbler in mechanics. Both extremes have distorted their cases by an over-concentration on the question of whether or not he was the first man to fly; and between the two extremes lies, too often, an area of indifference and undeserved neglect.

France had her own champion—Ader—though his promotion to this status was an afterthought hastily produced in 1908, after seeing Wilbur Wright. Before that Ader's own countrymen had themselves discounted him. The United States, which at first had ignored and scoffed at the Wrights, allowed the dust to settle and the argument to emerge, and then strenuously supported their claim. England had one or two very dubious possibilities to put forward but wisely did not try, though there remains a trace of her "pragmatical and cold" attitude towards Santos-Dumont.

Since by now most responsible people know the answer to

the argument, which became increasingly tiresome, of who was first, and since in any case the aeroplane has declined a good deal in public esteem since those early days, it is wiser to base our judgement on more general grounds. Gabriel Voisin wrote, when Santos died: "He left us, as a legacy, nothing but his name, engraved on our hearts."

He may not have meant it to sound quite like that (it is of course a translation), but a fair section of aviation opinion adopted the same outlook. Santos was admired and loved as a man, while his technical achievements tended to be under-valued. It has been pointed out that anybody who had bamboo, silk, and a little common-sense, could have constructed a soaring glider some thousands of years ago, and it has even been suggested that flying was a lost art in China, before the days of Marco Polo. Thus it is argued that the achievement of flight was not so wonderful, and should really have been done much earlier than it was.

Yet the fact remains that Santos and the Wrights, almost independently, did what the whole weight of the civilised world's technical effort could not do, and it is as a doer, an empiricist, that he should be chiefly remembered. Charles Dollfus, one of the world's foremost air historians, declares: "His technical work remains important, because we owe to him the use of new materials and devices, which have been adopted by all his successors."

His work with airships (which the Wrights never touched) had far-reaching results. He showed for the first time how a man could navigate the air, under control, going where he willed. He broke the spell which appeared to have been laid on mankind, binding them to the earth, or condemning them to drift like leaves at the mercy of the winds, a spell so strong that it seemed almost impious to dream of riding into the sky and mastering it. And in the end the "Santos-Dumont" type of airship proved its worth. The great dirigibles were founded on a false concept, and although they had their day they ended in spectacular disasters, but the small handy semi-rigids had a long and useful life, and could be applied to some uses today.

When he turned to the aeroplane it was the same story. He opened the door in Europe, and the crowds streamed through. It is undeniable that he did not contribute very much to the science of aeronautics. He was too unsystematic. But with the *Demoiselle* he built the world's first light aeroplane, and one of the safest ever made. Nobody was ever killed in a *Demoiselle*. In it too, he exemplified his other great contribution, the lessons of lightness and simplicity, that all engineers can never take sufficiently to heart. With this simplicity of conception went a directness of action. In a world over-full of committees, more Santos-Dumonts are needed, people who will get on and do something, even if it is wrong, rather than founder in endless deliberations and debates. *No 14 bis* may have attracted some unkind remarks. Nothing can detract from her glory.

In the various inventions that formed his side-interests he was less fortunate. But sometimes he made a useful contribution, if only by exasperating others into finding the answer. He was an erratic designer, but a beautiful craftsman. Georges Goursat would often watch him in his workshop, while he filed or hammered some small component, with exquisite skill and exactness. This gift for working with his hands allowed him to enter the world of his mechanics, while his wealth and social position helped to make activities respectable which were previously considered to be the province of dangerous lunatics.

When, in later years, he turned to the broader aspects of aviation—work of the Pan-American Aeronautical Federation type—he was a fish out of water, too practical on the one hand, and too visionary on the other. But he was ill, and tired. He had only his great reputation to sustain him. And it is undeniable, whether or not he was responsible, that France and South America combined at an early stage, to found one of the most avant-guard airline systems in the world.

With so much to claim, and justly, it is sad that he has been unduly neglected and forgotten, mostly because his partisans demand not only his tremendous share, but everything. His life's work was inspired by noble ideals, only occasionally modified by the normal human frailties and absurdities. Towards the end of his life, during an argument, one of the company was provoked into rudely demanding, "What have you produced that another could not have done in your place?"

Santos mildly replied: "I did what I could. I was not always successful. I made mistakes. But I persevered, and it is to aviation that I owe the happiness of my life."

No answer is more typical of him. And no disputing of achievements or weighing of values can place anything to his memory, greater than his own character. His greatest richness was himself. By his very lack of the sounder engineering virtues he made invention a joyous thing. The plodding march of great teams of researchers, with all their many achievements, cannot lift the heart like the hop and skip forward of a Santos-Dumont.

Everybody who met him formed a sort of protective affection for little Santos, the lion-hearted. "His courtesy was proverbial," said Voisin. "As for his courage, one would have to see him in his little wickerwork car, beside an engine with an open exhaust belching flames under a primitive hydrogen balloon."

This was the essence of him. He was a fine example of that inquisitive, cheerful, prying, optimistic, indomitable little race of bipeds, who may ferret and fumble their way into the unknown until they blow their own species out of existence, but whom no God with an ounce of humour could utterly condemn. Alberto Santos-Dumont enriched the world he moved in, more perhaps by being himself, than by the feats that made him famous. His prim, kind, fastidious nature, his strangely pernickety ways, made an odd contrast with his highly dangerous calling. He was a perfect ornament to the City of Light, in its greatest days.

Like the capital itself, he was dynamic, vain, and charming. They were made for each other, and when he could no longer live there his life had already ended. Just as he needed Paris, so she has never been the same since he has gone. She is meant to have gaily-coloured balloons overhead, drifting across her wide sky, and the slim golden-yellow shapes of his airships, trailing on a long red banner,

Por ceos nunca d'antes navegados!

BIBLIOGRAPHY

Dans l'Air, A. Santos-Dumont, Paris, 1904.
Os Meus Balões, Biblioteca de Divulgaçao **Aeronáutica.** Translation
of *Dans l'Air.*
My Airships, London, 1904. Translation of *Dans l'Air.*
O Que eu Vi, O Que nós Veremos, A. Santos-Dumont, São Paulo.
Santos-Dumont and the Conquest of the Air, A. **Napoleão,** English
version by d'Oliviera, 2 vols., Ministry of State for Foreign
Affairs of Brazil.
Quem deu Asas ao Homen, Henrique Dumont-Villares, Empressa
Gráfica da Revista dos Tribunais Ltd.
Vida de Santos-Dumont, **Ofélia** and Narbel Fontes, Editora A.
Noite.
Alberto Santos-Dumont, Oscar **Fernándes** Brital, Instituto Argentino-
Brasileño.
The Aeroplane: An Historical Survey, C. H. Gibbs-Smith, London,
Her Majesty's Stationery Office, 1960.
Histoire de l'Aéronautique, Dollfuss and Bouché, Paris, Société
Nationale des Enterprises de Presse, 1942.
Late Nineteenth Century (Vol. 5 of *A History of Technology*), ed. by
Singer, Holmyard, Hall, and Williams, London and New York,
Oxford University Press, 1958.
A History of Flying, C. H. Gibbs-Smith, London, B. T. Batsford,
Ltd., 1953; New York, Frederick A. Praeger, Inc., 1954.
The Development of Modern France, D. W. Brogan, London, Hamish
Hamilton, Ltd., 1940; *France under the Republic: The Develop-
ment of Modern France,* New York, Harper & Brothers, 1940.
The Wright Brothers, F. C. Kelly, New York, Harcourt, Brace &
World, Inc., 1943; London, George G. Harrap & Company,
Ltd., 1944.
*Andrée's Story: The Complete Record of His Polar Flight, 1897, from
the Diaries and Journals of S. A. Andrée, Nils Strindberq, and K.
Fraenkel Found on White Island in the Summer of 1930,* translated
from the Swedish by Edward Adams-Ray, New York, Viking

Press, Inc., 1930; *The Andrée Diaries,* London, John Lane, The Bodley Head, Ltd., 1931.

Der Vogelflug als Grundlage der Fliegerkunst, Otto Lilienthal, Berlin; *Birdflight as the Basis of Aviation,* compiled from the results of numerous experiments made by O. and G. Lilienthal, translated from the 2nd edition by A. W. Isenthal, London, Longmans, Green & Company, 1911.

Claude Grahame-White, Graham Wallace, New York and London, G. P. Putnam's Sons, 1960.

Paris Fin de Siècle, Jean Roman, Encyclopédie Essentielle.

"Santos-Dumont, Vainqueur et Repentant," Martin du Gard (article in *Le Petit Journal*).

My Zeppelins, Hugo Eckener, translated by Douglas Robinson, New York and London, G. P. Putnam's Sons, 1958.

Santos-Dumont, Maître d'Action, Col. Pierre Paquier, Editions Conquistador.

L'Homme a Conquis le Ciel, Willy Coppens de Houthulst, Hachette.

Mes 10,000 Cerfs-Volants, Gabriel Voisin, La Table Ronde.

APPENDIX

AERIAL VEHICLES DESIGNED BY A. SANTOS-DUMONT

Year	Name	Particulars	Remarks
1898	Brazil	Spherical free balloon, hydrogen filled, 113 cubic metres.	Directional control by rudder, longitudinal by moving ballast weights. Compensating airpump. Engine and propeller mounted on passenger basket.
1898	Santos-Dumont No 1	Elongated envelope non-rigid airship, 186 cubic metres of hydrogen. Petrol engine, 3½ h.p., designed by Santos-Dumont from de Dion parts. Length 25 metres, greatest diameter 3·5 metres.	
1898	No 2	Non-rigid airship, 200 cubic metres of hydrogen. Engine and many fittings from No 1.	Same controls. Compensating airpumps with internal ballonet. Similar engine mounting.
1899	No 3	Semi-rigid airship, 500 cubic metres of coal-gas. Length 20 metres, greatest diameter 7·5 metres. Engine and many fittings from No 2.	Same controls. No airpump or ballonet, rigidity maintained by shape and pole stiffener. "Semi-rigid", here and below, signifies only just stiffer than non-rigid.
1900	No 4	Semi-rigid airship, 420 cubic metres of hydrogen. Length 29 metres, greatest diameter 5·2 metres. New engine, designed by Santos-Dumont, on same lines as that fitted to No 3.	Same controls, plus water ballast. Airpumps and ballonet. Engine, tanks and pilot position mounted on longitudinal pole slung below envelope.
1901	No 5	Semi-rigid airship, 550 cubic metres of hydrogen. Length 34 metres, greatest diameter 5·2 metres. Girder keel slung	Same controls. Structure braced with piano wire.

Year	Name	Particulars	Remarks
		below envelope, carrying engine, control basket, tanks, etc. Buchet petrol engine, 15 h.p., air-cooled, based on Daimler-Benz design.	
1901	No 6	Semi-rigid airship, 622 cubic metres of hydrogen. Length 33 metres, greatest diameter 6 metres. Girder keel. Buchet/Santos-Dumont water-cooled petrol engine, 20 h.p. Single propeller 4 metres diameter.	Deutsch Prize winner. Same controls and general arrangement as No 5.
1902–1904	No 7	Semi-rigid airship, 1257 cubic metres of hydrogen, at high pressure. Length 40 metres, greatest diameter 7 metres. Clement engine, water-cooled, 60 h.p.	The Racer. Little used, and never raced. Two propellers (front and rear) driven from single engine.
—	No 8	Not allocated to any design.	Superstitious dislike of the number.
1903	No 9	Semi-rigid airship, 220 cubic metres of hydrogen. Length 11 metres, greatest diameter 3·5 metres. Clement engine, air-cooled, 3½ h.p.	Baladeuse.
1904	No 10	Semi-rigid airship, 2010 cubic metres of hydrogen. Length 42 metres, greatest diameter 9·2 metres. Girder keel, controls and engine interchangeable with No 7.	Omnibus. Designed for 10 passengers. Test flights only.
1905	No 11	Monoplane heavier-than-air design project. Wing area 22 square metres. Designed first as a glider, later re-designed as twin propeller power aircraft.	Glider completed, and given short tests towed behind motor-boat. Never developed for power.
1905–1906	No 12	Helicopter with double set of rotors.	Built to "mock-up" stage, but no

Date	No.	Description	Remarks
1905	*No 13*	Semi-rigid airship, 1902 cubic metres combined hydrogen and hot air. Hot air generated by special plant, as replacement for expended hydrogen.	suitable engine available. Therefore no attempt to fly it.
1905	*No 14*	Semi-rigid airship, 136 cubic metres of hydrogen. Clement engine, 3½ h.p.	Completed except for engine. Static tested, but not flown.
1905–1906	*No 14 bis*	Biplane canard pusher. Wing area approx. 42 square metres. Wingspan 10·8 metres, length 13·1 metres. Construction, fabric on pine framework. Levavasseur/Antoinette petrol engine, 50 h.p.	Designed as test vehicle for lifting heavier-than-air craft. Used in this capacity, and as simple airship. Control by forward box-kite cell. Ailerons fitted later.
1906–1907	*No 15*	Tractor biplane, plywood construction. Antoinette engine 100 h.p.	Crashed before becoming airborne on first test, and never rebuilt.
1907	*No 16*	Semi-rigid airship, 99 cubic metres of hydrogen with wings fitted to keel girder, to enhance the envelope lift. Antoinette engine, 50 h.p.	Designed as a combination lighter/heavier-than-air craft. Destroyed on the ground before first flight.
1907	*No 17*	Tractor biplane design study, development of *No 15*.	Designed only, not built.
1907	*No 18*	Wingless float hydroplane Antoinette engine, 100 h.p.	Tested on the water. Included here because it was probably intended to be fitted with wings later. Not followed through.
1907	*No 19*	Tractor monoplane, wing area 10·2 square metres. Wing-	Flew short hops, but badly damaged

Year	Name	Particulars	Remarks
		span 5½ metres. Length 8 metres. Construction bamboo and treated silk. Dutheil-Chalmers engine, modified by Santos-Dumont, 35 h.p. Propeller belt-driven from engine, which was mounted low.	during early testing. Prototype of *Demoiselle*.
1908	No 20	*No 19* modified (principally by replacement of single spar fuselage by bamboo girder skeleton). Same wing area. Same engine as *No 19*, now mounted high, driving propeller, 1 metre diameter, direct.	The *Demoiselle*. Controls included rudder and elevators, and lateral control by wing-warping.
1909	No 21	*Demoiselle* with Antoinette or Darracq engine.	Otherwise only minor modifications.
1909	No 22	*Demoiselle* with Bayard water-cooled engine. Design strengthened.	Claimed max. speed of 70 m.p.h.

Finally:

I am indebted to Mr. L. A. Speed, of the Ministry of Aviation Research and Development Establishment, Cardington, for the following outline figures for the design of a modern two-seater airship.

Suggested capacity of envelope, using hydrogen	..	20,000 cubic feet (giving a lift of 1300 lbs.)
Weight of envelope, stabilisers, rigging	.. ..	550 lbs.
Engine, mounting and propeller	.. .. ..	200 lbs.
Five gallons of petrol in fabric tank	.. ..	50 lbs.
Passenger car	.. ..	100 lbs.
Two passengers	.. ..	300 lbs.
Total Weight	.. ..	1200 lbs., against lift of 1300 lbs.

These figures produce approximate dimensions of 75 feet length and 24 feet greatest diameter.

An engine of 15 h.p. would give a speed of roughly 30 m.p.h.

The cost is conjectural: the unknown figure being the envelope. The rest of the craft might be improvised for about £300.

INDEX